I0890415

The Modern Androgyne Imagination

The Modern Androgyne Imagination

A Failed Sublime

Lisa Rado

University Press of Virginia • *Charlottesville and London*

The University Press of Virginia
© 2000 by the Rector and Visitors of the University of Virginia
All rights reserved
Printed in the United States of America

First published in 2000

∞ The paper used in this publication meets the minimum requirements of the American National Standard for Information Sciences—Permanence of Paper for Printed Library Materials, ANSI Z39.48-1984.

Library of Congress Cataloging-in-Publication Data

Rado, Lisa.
The modern androgyne imagination : a failed sublime / Lisa Rado.
p. cm.
Includes bibliographical references and index.
ISBN 0-8139-1979-7 (alk. paper) — ISBN 0-8139-1980-0 (pbk. : alk. paper)
1. English fiction—20th century—History and criticism. 2. Androgyny (Psychology) in literature. 3. H. D. (Hilda Doolittle), 1886–1961—Criticism and interpretation. 4. Faulkner, William, 1897–1962—Criticism and interpretation. 5. Woolf, Virginia, 1882–1941—Criticism and interpretation. 6. Joyce, James, 1882–1941—Criticism and interpretation. 7. American literature—20th century—History and criticism. 8. Gender identity in literature. 9. Sublime, The, in literature. 10. Modernism (Literature) I. Title.

PR888.A52 R33 2000
823'.9109353—dc21

00-028103

In memory of my mother,

Leanore Levy Rado,

whose love will forever be my inspiration

Contents

Acknowledgments

THE FOLLOWING PROFESSORS at the University of Michigan deserve special thanks for their help in creating the first version of this book: Patsy Yaeger, for her unflinching expectations and encouragement; Ralph Williams, for his warmhearted support and advice; and John Whittier-Ferguson, for his extremely rigorous and useful commentary. In addition, I would like to acknowledge Professor William Cain, who first gave me the opportunity to edit two books in his Wellesley series and thus enter fully into the scholarly community; Professor Cassandra Laity, whose enthusiasm and support for this project at the end of its composition helped significantly to bring it into print; and humanities editor Cathie Brettschneider at the University Press of Virginia for her years-long commitment to the book. There is a larger community of scholars I would also like to recognize, whose groundbreaking work in the field of modernism and gender studies has been pivotal in inspiring and stimulating my thinking and research; among these critics, I include Shari Benstock, Marianne DeKoven, Rachel Blau DuPlessis, Rita Felski, Susan Stanford Friedman, Christine Froula, Sandra Gilbert, Susan Gubar, Suzette Henke, Carla Kaplan, Jane Marcus, Margot Norris, Bonnie Kime Scott, and Susan Squier, to name only a few. The professional support and encouragement many of these individuals have offered me over the past decade is something for which I am profoundly grateful.

As important to the realization of a project this size as any professional connections are the personal ones. I would also like to remember all my friends and family who have encouraged, supported, and sustained me over the years, and, most especially, my husband, Eric Fodor, for helping to make each day the kind in which anything is possible.

An earlier version of chapter 2 appeared, in different form, as "'Hypsos' or 'Spadia'?: Rethinking Androgyny in Ulysses with Help from Sacher-Masoch" in *Twentieth-Century Literature* 42, no. 2 (summer 1996): 193–207, and is reprinted here with permission. An earlier version of chapter 4 appeared, in different form, as "'A Perversion That Builds Chartres and Invents Lear Is a Pretty Good Thing': *Mosquitoes* and Faulkner's Androgynous Imagination" in *Faulkner Journal* 9, no. 1 (spring 1995): 23–42; the article is reprinted with permission of the *Faulkner Journal.* An earlier version of chapter 5 appeared, in different form, as "Would the Real Virginia Woolf Please Stand Up: Feminist Criticism, the Androgyny Debates, and *Orlando*" in *Women's Studies: An Interdisciplinary Journal* 26, no. 2 (spring 1997): 147–69, and is reprinted here with permission.

The Modern Androgyne Imagination

1

Modernism, Androgyny, and the Sublime

Toward a Cultural Theory of the Imagination

The "imagination" is one of those troubling ontological terms, like "being," "mind," and "soul," that are alternately infuriating and exhilarating in their imprecision. Discredited by modern philosophers, such as Ludwig Wittgenstein and Richard Rorty, who have argued that such seemingly transcendental categories are actually the product of complex, culturally defined language games (Wittgenstein 11e; Rorty 22), the idea of a so-called creative mind or genius is now being met with zealous distrust. In today's theoretical circles, even the concept of an autonomous subject—upon which the existence of a subjective imagination depends—has been branded essentialist and oppressive by feminist critics such as Judith Butler, inherently racist and patronizing by postcolonialist critics such as Chinua Achebe, and ultimately irretrievable and therefore meaningless by deconstructionists such as Jacques Derrida.[1] Following the lead of theorist Roland Barthes, who in 1968 asserted the nonexistence of a "being which precedes or exceeds his writing" (1132), scholars have supplanted the word "imagination" with more complex loci of artistic creativity, including, for example, the Kristevan "semiotic," and Fishian "interpretive community."

It is thus a risky business to talk about "the imagination" these days; it has become something from which many literary critics—even if they secretly envision one—will go to great lengths to dissociate themselves. One has a sense that merely talking about the imagination is tantamount to admitting to believing in ghosts. Yet rather than discarding the concept as an impossibly romantic, overly sentimental, quasi-religious mystery, I would like to consider the various ways in which authors have represented the process of poetic production as strategies that have enabled them, at various historical moments, to overcome or at least to assuage cultural crises of authority and inspiration. The ways in which writers have portrayed the source of their inspiration can serve in part as a reflection of literary and cultural history. One thinks, for example, of Homer and his Muses, Dante Alighieri and his Beatrice, Percy Bysshe Shelley and his veiled maidens; each author, to reword a phrase of Richard Poirier, posits a "being or self elsewhere" that inspires and authorizes his work.

Of course, we cannot "find" these "selves elsewhere" if we look for them on a map. Like the sexual body whose image, cultural critics argue, reflects "our needs in speaking about it" (Laqueur 115), the imagination and its processes assume forms that reflect particular cultural anxieties and demands.[2] Central to my argument is the premise that the greatest of these imperatives is not so much the artist's need to be inspired as to be empowered and authorized by the culture within which he or she creates. It is no accident, for example, that Homer's Muses, Dante's Beatrice, and Shelley's maidens implicitly link the writers with Zeus, the Judeo-Christian God, and Nature, all loci of ultimate authority for classical, medieval, and romantic cultures, respectively. By figuring the source of their inspiration, however unconsciously, in such a way as to recall such powerful and familiar social and spiritual icons, these writers thereby ensure for themselves a position of cultural prominence, as well as the receptive (if not always embracing) audience that comes with it.

Briefly recalling the Western literary tradition, I would like to contextualize the assumptions about authorship that the moderns inherited and ultimately outgrew. Up until approximately the eighteenth century, most male poets represent their songs as—in varying degrees—transcriptions of divine utterance, and thus implicitly sanctioned formulations of spiritual truth. Interestingly, however, the voice of the godhead often speaks not through the poet's lips but through those of an imagined female entity with whom he engages in some sort of psychosexual relation. The earliest representations of these heavenly agents are, of course, the Greek Muses; according to Hesiod, these daughters of Zeus and Memory "breathed into [the poet] wondrous voice," dictating to him "the famous deeds of men of old, and of the blessed gods who dwell in Olympus" (4, 6). Such depictions not only afford considerable authenticity to the poet's narrative, they also underscore the poet's heroic manliness and virility by showing him as the one whom such divine consorts have chosen above all other men to open their lips. Although Homer tells us that he "whom the Muse had loved greatly" was given "both good and evil," in that his "sweet singing art" came at the price of his mortal sight, his Phaiakian singer alone among men has the power to render mighty hero Odysseus "shamed for tears running down his face" (*Odyssey* 8.63, 64, 86). Hesiod characterizes his gifts in even more direct terms; the Muses offer him a "staff, a handsome one" at the same time that "they [teach him] fine singing" (4, 2). Even beyond its symbolic significance as speaker-designate, the phallic staff suggests that the Muses bequeath to the poet heightened sexual powers as well.

This latter representation of the poet is most dramatically illustrated by Plato in "Ion." Describing the process of poetic production, he explains:

> the Muse first of all inspires men herself; and from these inspired persons a chain of other persons is suspended, who take the inspiration. For all good poets, epic as well as lyric, compose their beautiful poems not by art, but because they are inspired and possessed. And as the Korybantian revelers when they dance are not in their right mind, so the lyric poets are not in their right mind when they are composing their beautiful strains: but when falling under the power of music and meter they are inspired and possessed; like Bacchic maidens who draw milk and honey from the rivers when they are under the influence of Dionysus but not when they are in their right mind. And the soul of the lyric poet does the same, as they themselves say; for they tell us that they

> bring songs from honeyed fountains, culling them out of the gardens and dells of the Muses; they, like the bees, winging their way from flower to flower. And this is true. For the poet is a light and winged and holy thing, and there is no invention in him until he has been inspired and is out of his senses, and reason is no longer in him. (14)

Like Hesiod and Homer, Plato envisions authorship as a product not of individual agency or talent ("art") but of a kind of psychosexual possession. Again, inspiration is figured as external; that Plato repeats the word "possessed" continually here and in other texts when referring to poets suggests that they are literally inhabited by spiritual presence(s).[3] Anything but chaste, however, Plato's Muses seduce the poet and the poet's audience into an orgiastic departure from reality through their Dionysian mysteries. Deprived of human reason, the poet becomes a kind of flying phallus, "winging" his way from Muse to honey-sweet Muse, gathering from her inner folds the music for his song; in this sense, he thus possesses her as much as he is possessed by her. Despite this evidence of human agency, to create poetry—as Plato describes it—is to be literally out of one's mind. Although "holy," the singer has sacrificed his mortal consciousness and abandoned his human reason; simply put, he (temporarily) *is no longer himself.* No wonder Plato will decide, albeit with regret, to banish such individuals from his Republic.[4] Nevertheless, what is most important to recognize, for the purposes of this study, is the absolute insistence on the minimal role the individual consciousness assumes in poetic composition.

The Greek's representation of the imagination is thus essentially that of divine inspiration. Although Aristotle emphasizes the significance of specific principles of aesthetic craft, he persists in representing the poet as at least figuratively possessed by the female emissary of a male god.[5] Thus, rather than creator, the Greek poet is *aoidos,* singer or spiritual medium whose voice is not his own, whose verses bear evidence of Zeus's power and the Muses' love. This representation of literary creativity continues, at least as a convention, through the classical period.[6] With the rise of Christianity, the figure of the muse changes somewhat, but only in relation to her "father"—

now figured as the Judeo-Christian God. Although Boethius's incarnation of Philosophy (interestingly also figured as female) banishes them as untrustworthy, Dante—in his Christian epic *The Divine Comedy*—invokes the "holy Muses" (*Purgatorio)* no fewer than five times. When, in *Paradiso*, he does abandon them because of their ineffectiveness "in singing the holy smile" (*Paradiso* 23), he merely replaces them with a superior model. Temporarily blinded by the light of heaven, this poet gets his new sight—and insight—from "the happy light that is within" Beatrice's eyes (*Purgatorio* 409). Likewise, although John Milton will invoke the muse Urania, he will insist it is

> The meaning, not the name I call: for thou
> Nor the Muses nine, nor on the top
> Of old Olympus dwell'st, but heavenly born,
> Before the hills appeared, or fountain flowed,
> Thou with eternal Wisdom did converse.
>
> (7.5–9)

Although referring to the Holy Spirit, Milton nevertheless persists in retaining "the meaning" of the muse as inspirational source; consistent with his Western literary tradition, he locates the source of his verses not in his own consciousness but in God's as related once again through a figurative—but significantly female—emissary. While not nearly so explicit as Plato's depiction of the poet as pollen-seeking bee, Milton's explanation of his creative process retains the psychosexual dynamic of male poet–female muse even as it equivocates over "meaning" and "name."

During the eighteenth century and with the onset of the Industrial Revolution, changes in the ways in which scientists and philosophers construed the universe gave rise to a new vocabulary for describing a nevertheless similar dynamic. As M. H. Abrams points out, "the sensationalist theory of mind, with its reliance on the mechanical motions and combinations of conscious, mirror-like images, afforded no place either for the mysterious facts or the supernatural theory of inspiration"(190). Indeed, we do see in writers such as Alexander Pope, Joseph Addison, Samuel Johnson, and Edmund Burke various attempts to renegotiate inherited models of creativity in light of their more mechanized worldview. While Pope—in his pivotal "Essay on

Criticism"—insists that both poets and critics "must alike from Heaven derive their light" (l. 13), he represents the divine as the "one clear, unchanged, and universal light" (l. 71) of nature. Furthermore, "imagination," as understood by the eighteenth-century poets, involves an inspired imitation of divine creation as portrayed in the visible world. Burke explains, "besides the ideas . . . which are presented by the sense; the mind of man possesses a sort of creative power of its own; either in representing at pleasure the images of things in the order and manner in which they were received by the senses, or in combining those images in a new manner, and according to a different order. This power is called Imagination. . . . But it must be observed, that this power of the imagination is incapable of producing anything absolutely new" (16). Likewise, Addison depicts the poetic method as one including the pleasure of "mending and perfecting nature" (287), not of re-creating it.

Yet despite the simplicity of these descriptions, many of these writers struggle with just what their relationship with nature entails. Part of their problem can be traced to the transformation of transcendental categories toward the deistic models of the Enlightenment. By insisting that poets "first follow Nature" (l. 68), Pope—and his contemporaries—commit themselves to submitting to a historically sexualized and feminized realm.[7] Unlike their literary predecessors, whose female muses speak for an unequivocally male god, these eighteenth-century writers have more difficulty recapitulating the psychosexual dynamic we have seen to have characterized a major line of poetic production in the past. Indeed, negotiating his relationship with the muse becomes the writer's full-time job, as Pope explains:

> 'Tis more to guide than spur the Muse's steed;
> Restrain his fury, than provoke his speed;
> The winged courser, like a generous horse,
> Shows most true mettle when you check his course.
>
> (ll. 84–87)

Rather than being "possessed" by the muse, this poet claims he must "guide" or control her; rather than lose himself in her honeyed lips, he must "check" his desires. As distinctions between God, Nature, and Muse begin to blur, Pope consciously strives to avoid being feminized by his vocation. Whether Pope actually believed in the reality of dream maidens on horseback, he nevertheless insists on being inspired by a "Nature methodized" (l. 89) by the powerful steady hands of an experienced male poet—in this case, himself. Going still further, Samuel Johnson chooses to veil his eyes altogether to the muses' most seductive forms, insisting that "it is necessary to distinguish those parts of nature which are most proper for imitation" (2334)—and those, presumably, which are not. As for Burke, his theories of the sublime and the beautiful involve—as several scholars have noted—a complex attempt at inhibiting the threat of incorporation and loss of control that for him certain aspects of nature, and specifically the female body, represent.[8]

With the advent of the French Revolution and the concomitant valuation of the "feminine" qualities of feeling and emotionalism, conceptions of the imagination only become more complicated, particularly as women readers and writers establish themselves more firmly on the literary scene. For the first time, some women begin to challenge male models of poetic production, replacing the seductive muses with more sisterly helpmates, as we see in Anna Barbauld's invocation at the beginning of her poem "Washing Day"

> The Muses are turned gossips; they have lost
> The buskined step, and clear high-sounding phrase,
> Language of gods. Come, then, domestic Muse,
> In slip-shod measure loosely prattling on. . . .
>
> (ll. 1–4)

Anything but otherworldly maids, Barbauld's muses are earthy housewives helping to translate womanly conversation and domestic rites into song. Likewise, in Elizabeth Moody's ironic poem "The Housewife; or, the Muse Learning to Ride the Great Horse Heroic," the narrator charges her muse to "Attend her flight through regions sacred / To domestic use" (ll. 12–13), reminding her that she "has not disdained to sing, in days / Of yore, of culinary arts" (l. 50). Using as examples Milton's description of Eve's repast for Gabriel and Homer's rendition of Agamemnon roasting his warriors' dinner, Moody goes beyond Barbauld to posit the existence of a more "feminine" poetic precedent.[9]

In response to challenges to male literary traditions from women writers like these as well as a newly bourgeois, increasingly female readership, male romantic poets begin to do more than appropriate the feminine domain of nature; they additionally usurp the realm of sensibility to reestablish their artistic prerogative. As feminist critic Anne K. Mellor explains, "by taking on the feminine virtues of compassion, mercy gentleness and sympathy, the male Romantic poets could speak with ultimate moral as well as intellectual authority" in what had become the Age of Feeling (*Feminism* 23–24; see also A. Richardson 15, 13). They accomplish this task by figuring poetic production, now identified as centering in the poet's imagination, as an erotically charged interaction between a specifically male artist, the "romance quester" (Ross, "Troping" 34), and his vision of a female muse whom he seeks to dominate or repossess in order to ensure that creativity remains a masculine domain.

While this strategy sounds familiar, there are important differences between it and its predecessors. Like their literary forefathers, the male romantics struggled with the conflation of Nature, God, and Muse; however, they did so without the saving solution of "masculine" rationalism that writers such as Pope and Johnson used to prevent the collapse of the empowering psychosexual dyad of male self and female Other. For the romantics, women represent not only "the fireside muses whose sympathy the imagination requires, but they also signify the contamination of the marketplace" (Ellison 162), as well as the loss of a historically masculine aesthetic order. Faced with this paradox, the male romantic poets locate their muses not in heaven or nature per se but rather in specific female types—the Mother, Sister, Muse, Beloved, Femme Fatale—whose energies they appropriate and whose identities they ultimately—if successful—make disappear.[10] In poems such as William Wordsworth's "Tintern Abbey," Shelley's "Epipsychidion," and John Keats's "La Belle Dame sans Merci," the poet envisions a female presence who figures as "the psychic embodiment of all those qualities the hero needs to fictionally complete himself" (Hoeveler 11). Whether Sister Dorothy, whose voice recalls "the language of [the poet's] former heart" (l. 117); Lover Emily, whose "Spirit was the harmony of truth" (l. 216); or the Ruthless Belle Dame, whose most seductive feature is her "fairy's song" (l. 20); each female holds the key to making a certain kind of music. How to possess her melody without being possessed himself is, however, often difficult to negotiate; Shelley, for instance, anticipates the poet's imminent "annihilation" (l. 587), while Keats's knight has already failed in his attempt, left "alone and palely loitering" (l. 2) in hopes of his lady's return.

Much has been written about what Diane Hoeveler calls this "romantic androgyny."[11] Critics agree that in their fixation with mother, sister, and lover muses these male poets seek "to reclaim 'feminine' qualities through incorporating something of these same figures" (A. Richardson 15); in other words, their "androgyny" involves a desire to appropriate certain gendered characteristics, but it does not extend to a wish to erase gender boundaries altogether. While poems such as Blake's "Jerusalem," Coleridge's "Kubla Khan," and Shelley's "Prometheus Unbound" do gesture toward a more transgressive androgynous union encompassing the spiritual merging of male and female characters or energies, in all these works the male presence succeeds in engulfing (and effectively silencing) the female voice.[12] Thus the male romantic poet pursues the empowerment and authorization that the feminine realms of nature and sensibility represent, but he also attempts (not always successfully) to externalize his muses, all the while insisting on his authorial independence; as Keats asserts in "Ode to Psyche," "I see, and sing, by my own eyes inspired" (l. 43). While it certainly has other causes (for instance, the increasing secularization and democratization of culture as well as the development of a mass market for literature), the romantic concept of the imagination—referring to that singular, subjective aspect of mind, apart from God, society, and the common man—that takes divine creation and "dissolves, diffuses, dissipates, in order to re-create" (Coleridge 263)—reflects a new defensiveness about the uniqueness of authorship and the autonomy of the (male) artist in the creative process.[13]

What happens to the poet's increasingly fragile accommodation with the muse, however, when even the most conventional assumptions about the hierarchical, binary relation between the sexes become destabilized, challenged by changing mores, medical science, and a fresh generation of women writers for whom seductive or even "domestic" muses offer little in the way of authorization or empowerment? Starting in the late nineteenth century, there is a universal concurrence among intellectuals that the relations between and even the nature of the sexes has changed forever. As the well-known British sex theorist Edward Carpenter remarks in 1907 in *The Intermediate Sex*:

> In late years (and since the arrival of the New Woman amongst us) many things in the relation of men and women to each other have altered, or at any rate become clearer. The growing sense of equality in habits and customs—university studies, art, music, politics, the bicycle, etc—all these things have brought about a *rapprochement* between the sexes. If the modern woman is a little more masculine in some ways than her predecessor, the modern man (it is to be hoped), while by no means effeminate, is a little more sensitive in temperament and artistic in feeling than the original John Bull. (143)

There are innumerable reasons for this growing sense of sexual indeterminacy, among them the suffrage movement, the new science of anthropology and its discovery of primitive matriarchy, and the effects of the Industrial Revolution and the First World War—specifically the entrance of rising numbers of women in traditionally male professions.[14] What particularly interests me, however, is that faced with a new sexual landscape of increasingly "feminine" men and "masculine" women, a number of male, predominantly German and British sexual scientists (sexologists) respond by attempting to redefine sexual categories. Their efforts, as we shall see, have far reaching cultural effects upon early-twentieth-century British and American writers, prompting many male authors to redefine romantic models of imagination and their female counterparts to use this moment of gender confusion to authorize their creativity in a transgressively innovative way. Such a seemingly radical—even impossible—strategy of revising these basic human categories is not so inconceivable if we remember, as Judith Butler argues, that gender has never, in practice, been "a noun"; rather, it has always been "performative—that is, constituting the identity it is purported to be" (25). As she explains, it is "the institution of a compulsory and naturalized heterosexuality [that] requires and regulates gender as a binary relation in which the masculine term is differentiated from a feminine term" (22–23). But what happens when such a powerful institution becomes suddenly so open to question, as it did in the late nineteenth century?[15]

Unable to fit an increasingly androgynous population into what Thomas Laqueur calls the "two-sex" (male-female) model of the body, modern sex theorists proposed what I will call a "three-sex" model of sexual categories consisting of men, women, and a third, or "intermediate," sex, initially comprising homosexuals but soon becoming a more inclusive category. While at first this new division allowed white men, threatened by the blurring of gender roles, to retain their sense of superiority over all things feminine by associating the potentially subversive androgynes (male or female) with the genetically degenerate, it soon became more and more difficult to preserve the old hierarchy between the sexes on biological grounds. For male modernist artists, schooled—as we have seen—to draw their inspiration from imaginative tropes based on a binary opposition between male artist and female muse-object, this artistic self-preservation became virtually impossible. It is no coincidence that in D. H. Lawrence's *Women in Love*, Ursula Brangwen exposes Birkin's penchant for real-life muses such as Hermione as just a thinly masked sexual fantasy: "Go to your spiritual brides—but don't come to me as well, because I'm not having any, thank you. You're not satisfied, are you? Your spiritual brides can't give you what you want, they aren't common and fleshly enough for you, aren't they? So you come to me, and keep them in the background! You will marry me for daily use. But you'll keep yourself well provided with spiritual brides in the background. I know your dirty little game" (388). Anything but secure in his intellectual and creative abilities, Birkin finds himself lost in a modern "spiritual mess" (390), terrified of any "horrible fusion" (391) with the opposite sex, refusing to merge with anything other than an ephemeral image. Like James Joyce and William Faulkner, however, Lawrence is ultimately unable to recapture his confidence in old models of poetic production.

Yet if for men the transformations of the modern sexual landscape throw into crisis their sense of artistic authority and inspiration, for women they raise with fresh urgency the need to find such a sense to begin with. The reconstructions of traditional gender categories offered new opportunities, but at the same time several lasting obstacles to artistic self-definition remained. As novelist Dorothy Richardson writes in an article for *Vanity Fair* in 1925:

> It is not only that there exists for the woman no equivalent for the devoted wife or mistress. There is also no equivalent for the most neglectful char known to man. For the service given by women to women is as different from that given by women to men as chalk from cheese. If hostile, it will specialize in manufacturing difficulties. If friendly, it will demand unfaltering response. For it knows that living sympathy is there. And in either case service is given on the assumption that the woman at work is in the plot for providing life's daily necessities. And even vicarious expansion towards a multitude of details, though it may bring wisdom, is fatal to sustained creative effort. (Scott 422–23)

Like Virginia Woolf, in *A Room of One's Own*, Richardson points to the real threats that patriarchy still holds for the modern intellectual woman. How is she to define herself as an artist in the face of the continued social pressure to be wife, mother, and muse?

Faced with these challenges to existing ideas about gender and authorship, many modernist writers of both sexes became increasingly attracted to a culturally specific notion of a third-sexed, or androgyne, imagination—and here I use the term "androgyne" instead of androgynous to indicate the almost hermaphroditic nature of the concept of androgyny in modernist usage—that reflected and capitalized upon the changes in the modern sexual landscape. A number of male authors envision the imagination as a partly "female" entity that has the ability to engender living words; they actually represent their creative minds as if they are characterized by a balance of sexually charged energies, fueling their artistic impulses with oppositional tensions. Unlike the romantics—who we have seen gesture toward an androgyny involving the incorporation of feminine qualities such as sensibility into a singularly male consciousness—the moderns go further to represent the imagination as a part of the subjective mind that is biologically both male and female; while Joyce experiments with the idea of the artist as the "new womanly man," Faulkner replaces the muse with the hermaphrodite. In a similar fashion, female modernists construct a model of creativity in which their imaginations are partly "male"; these writers represent inspiration not as the incorporation of "masculine" qualities but rather as generated by the precarious coexistence of a female consciousness and a masculine other-self that goes beyond mere pseudonym: while H. D. personifies her creative "overmind" as the androgyne Ray Bart, Woolf invents and identifies with her ageless androgyne, Orlando. Although they select these tropes for disparate reasons, modernist literary men and women share the desire to embody the newly perceived strengths of both sexes and to transcend sexual and artistic limitation altogether.

While the exact sources of any artistic impulse are difficult to ascertain, the fact that so many modernists figure their creative minds as third-sexed makes a cultural connection especially plausible in this case. We must keep in mind that the discourse about androgyny to which these artists responded with their various models of the creative process was vastly different than it has been of late. For the past twenty-five years, feminist critics have debated the degree to which the fusion of so-called masculine and feminine characteristics has an emancipatory potential. Those discussions, as well as the corresponding flood of interest in so-called androgynous artists such as Woolf and Joyce, ultimately call into question this sexual stance as a politically viable option for both women and men.[16] Yet for the moderns, androgyny signified a biological condition not predominantly of appearance or sexual preference but of the blood. For many, it was the interaction of male and female "plasms" within the mind or brain that determined to which of the three (or more) sexes a person belonged. To understand why androgyny becomes such a pervasive artistic trope in the first few decades of the twentieth century, we must first get a sense of the specific cultural models that inspire it. A brief look at the leading theories about the "intermediate" sex at the turn of the twentieth century will demonstrate the degree to which the idea of a third-sexed imagination offered a solution to male modernists searching for a means to restore their artistic prerogative while it provided female modernists with a way to transform their position from aesthetic objects to active creators.

Sustained explorations of human sexuality date back well before

Plato's *Symposium* and Vatsyayana's *Kamasutra.* Yet the modern science of sexology, with its reliance on the individual case study as well as the discourses of biology, anthropology, and—later—psychoanalysis, has been in existence only since the end of the nineteenth century. Scholars have traced the emergence of the field to late-Victorian concern about individual and racial hygiene (spurred by the plethora of venereal disease in metropolitan centers such as London as well as the population debate and concomitant obsession with eugenics and "racial" improvement) alongside a more liberal desire to improve relationships between the sexes and transform the discussion of sexuality from the realm of the sinful to one of central value and importance in human life.[17] For these initially controversial theoreticians and physicians, so-called sexual perversions are reread as treatable medical conditions, natural anomalies, or simply facets of normality. Interested in categorizing and classifying a range of sexual behaviors and expressions, including heterosexual desire, homoeroticism, autoeroticism, fetishism, sadomasochism, and frigidity, the early sexologists drew heavily from contemporary ethnographic data about so-called primitive (indigenous) people's sexual behavior as well as individual narrative interviews with Western men and women. They also theorized about the affective characteristics of ovum and sperm, and even in some cases—as we shall see—hypothesized the existence of gendered cells in the body.[18] Widely perceived as radical at the time, sexology's methods and conclusions have recently come under fire by some feminist scholars, who argue that these theorists' masculinist, heterosexist bias served, rather than challenged, the status quo.[19] However, while some of their conclusions could no doubt be labeled reactionary, the open discussion their research promoted proved tremendously exciting and liberating to many of their contemporaries who appropriated its discourses to serve their own agendas.[20] Such borrowings were made all the easier given the remarkable absence of a "monolithic, coherent and unified" (Bland and Doan, *Sexology Uncensored* 4) position on any sexual issue among these theorists. Of all the issues they considered, the basic nature of sexual categories remains one of the most controversial and dynamic subjects of their debates; the characterization of individuals who seem to transgress gender norms continues to be of particular interest.

Of the earliest modern sexual scientists, the most well-known and influential was Richard von Krafft-Ebing, a German who characterizes sexual "inversion" (the common term for homosexuality at the time), in his seminal 1892 volume *Psychopathia Sexualis*, as a "functional sign of degeneration" (187). Yet interestingly, he and others identify homosexuals (and their so-called pathology) not so much by their practice of same-sex attachments as by a kind of psychic androgyny (hence the term "inversion"): the men are "females in feeling; in women, males" (Krafft-Ebing 279). Such characteristics are here considered anything but appealing; while the males of this class are described as effeminate, impotent, and weak, females are regarded as unattractively masculine and oversexed. Moreover, there was general agreement among Krafft-Ebing and his followers that in addition to their psychic androgyny, these individuals possess anatomical deformities of their sex organs, which, while not quite hermaphroditic, "approach the opposite sex anthropologically" (Krafft-Ebing 304). The psychic and physical androgyny of this other category of human beings is thus considered to be freakish and abnormal; citing innumerable case studies, Krafft-Ebing and his followers lump these so-called sexual inverts in the same category as pedophilics, masochists, and other sexual deviants.[21]

That one of the first two volumes of Havelock Ellis's seven-volume magnum opus, *Studies in the Psychology of Sex*, is titled *Sexual Inversion* reflects the centrality of interest in theorizing gender categories at the time. For Ellis, Britain's most prominent sex theorist and reformer at the turn of the century, the term "invert" essentially refers to homosexuals; again, however, as Jay Prosser argues, what Ellis and others overall seek " to describe through gender inversion was not homosexuality [as defined by sexual practice] but differing degrees of *gender* inversion . . . of which homosexuality was only one aspect" (117). Ellis defines inversion as the "psychical manifestation of special characters of the recessive sex" (80), not primarily as same-sex sexual attachment. Although Ellis believed the existence of basic biological sex differences and tried to play down the myth of male homosexual effeminacy, his writings still perpetuate the idea of androgynous female inverts, "whose masculine qualities render it comparatively easy for them to adopt masculine avocations" (196). His discussions of inversion, while stopping short of characterizing the phenomenon as proof of a new gender category, nevertheless call attention to the special qualities of inverts as a type which is for him, if an anomaly, at least not a pathological one. Thus if, as Jeffrey Weeks explains, Krafft-Ebing's histories are "biased towards sickness, so Ellis's [are] biased towards 'normality'" (*Coming Out* 64). Indeed Ellis's tone is one of admiration when he relates that 56 percent of his subjects "possess artistic aptitudes of varying degree" (294), and spends over thirty pages detailing numerous intellectually and artistically accomplished inverts through history, among them Saphho, Christopher Marlowe, Michaelangelo, Walt Whitman, and Oscar Wilde. Soon after the publication of *Sexual Inversion*, however, British courts, which had in 1885 criminalized homosexuality in men, labeled the text, which Ellis wrote for a much wider audience than Krafft-Ebing's specialist volume, "lewd, wicked, tawdry, scandalous, and obscene" (Weeks, *Coming Out* 47). Although neither Ellis nor the book were ever officially put on trial (the above remarks are from a case against a reader of the book), Ellis was so affronted and discouraged by this official response to his book that he published the rest of the volumes of his *Studies* in America and, while he would continue to argue against discrimination, remained equivocal about sanctioning homosexual practice.[22]

Although Krafft-Ebing and his cohorts paint an unflattering picture of this new "intermediate" sex and Ellis struggled to update it, other—primarily homosexual—theorists hailed such individuals as uniquely gifted and socially beneficial. Following the lead of K. H. Ulrichs, whose 1868 treatise, *Memnon: Die Geschlechtsnatur des Mannliebenden Urnings, Eine Naturwissenschafliche Darstellung*, first advances the cause of homosexuals (whom he calls Uranians), Edward Carpenter (in his 1907 volume *The Intermediate Sex*) and John Addington Symonds (in his 1896 *A Problem in Modern Ethics*) defend such individuals even more vigorously than Ellis against the degeneracy theories. What is particularly interesting here is that once again it is not so much the characteristic of same-sex attraction that these writers emphasize as it is the androgynous nature of homosexuals. Popularizing the "trapped-soul theory"—an explanation of sexual inversion as a phenomenon in which an individual's mind is a different "sex" than his/her body—Carpenter and Symonds use it to depict a favorable picture of Uranians: men, who "while possessing thoroughly masculine powers of mind and body, [combine] with them the tenderer and more emotional soul-nature of the woman" (Carpenter 152), and women who possess the more aggressive, intellectual soul-nature of man. Rather than a sign of hereditary degeneration, this psychic hermaphroditism is read as a sign of superior abilities. If, as we saw previously, Ellis believed that female inverts' masculine nature "render[s] it comparatively easy for them to adopt masculine avocations" (196), Carpenter insists that Uranian men possess an "instinctive artistic nature" owing to "the swift and constant interaction between [his brain's] masculine and feminine elements" (Carpenter 155, 192) and reminds us that even Ellis and Krafft-Ebing note that the majority of "inverted" men in their case studies are in some way artistic. Furthermore, Carpenter's second book, *Intermediate Types among Primitive Folk* (1911/1919) follows the lead of Edward A. Westermarck's, *The Origin and Development of Moral Ideas* (1906), in approaching this issue anthropologically; both theorists invoke positive historical precedent to argue that in indigenous societies "effeminate men are frequently believed to be versed in magic; their abnormalities readily suggest that they are endowed with supernatural power" (123). Bestowed with superior wisdom, creativity, and visionary strength, Uranians are, according to this second school of thought, thus anything but freaks. Rather, they become the first incarnation of the utopian modernist avant-garde; as Carpenter suggests in 1907, they "may be destined to form the advance guard of that great movement which will one day transform the common life by substituting the bond of personal affection and compassion for the monetary, legal and other external ties which now control and confine society" (196).

While Krafft-Ebing and his colleagues considered sexual inverts to be essentially degenerates, and Carpenter (and to a certain degree Ellis) asserted their transcendent power, a third group of theorists—headed by Sigmund Freud and Otto Weininger—emerged in the first decade of the twentieth century and complicated the debate by expanding the category of the "third sex," completely divorcing it from sexual practice. Although Ellis resisted the full implications of this claim, he articulates the common assumption among this group that in general, "each sex is latent in the other, and each, as it contains the characters of both sexes . . . is latently hermaphrodite" (79–80); virtually all the sexologists drew from the findings of evolutionist biologists, especially the influential Americans G. Frank Lydston and J. G. Kiernan, who argued in the 1890s that the ancestors of the vertebrates were hermaphrodites.[23] Pointing out that "a certain degree of anatomical hermaphroditism occurs normally," Freud hypothesized that "an originally bisexual physical disposition has, in the course of evolution, become modified into a unisexual one, leaving behind only a few traces of the sex that has become atrophied" (*Three Essays 19*, 19–20). Discounting the trapped-soul theory and the connection between anatomic and psychic hermaphroditism, Freud diverges from Ellis and others when he postulates a universal childhood bisexuality as "the original basis from which . . . both the normal and the inverted types develop" (*Three Essays* 23). Yet perhaps Freud's most revolutionary argument is that even as adults "the proportions in which the masculine and feminine mingle in the individual are subject to quite extraordinary variations" ("Psychology of Women" 155). Instead of being an absolute and knowable category, "what constitutes masculinity or femininity is an unknown element which is beyond the power of anatomy to grasp" (156).

Vienna-born Otto Weininger, in his 1906 volume *Sex and Character*, went even further than Freud to argue that in humans "sexual differentiation . . . is never complete" (5).[24] Instead of two or even three pure and inviolate sexes, "there exist all sorts of intermediate conditions between male and female" (Weininger 7). Believing that each cell in the human body possesses varying amounts of Arrhenoplasm (male plasm) and Thelyplasm (female plasm), Weininger asserts that there are no such beings as "man" and "woman" but only the "male condition" and the "female condition" (8). However, lest this radical redefinition of the sexes threaten the hierarchical relation between them, he makes it clear that the degree to which an individual possesses Thelyplasm reveals the degree to which she or he becomes a "symbol of nothing" (297). Underlying Weininger's theory of universal androgyny, then, is a not-so-hidden fear of a castrating, even annihilating feminization. In his final chapter, he argues that male Jews—whom he describes as overly effeminate—are the perfect example of what he considers a horrifying and despicable emasculation. That the young Weininger (he was only twenty-three when he published the book) took his own life merely four months after its publication served to heighten his influence; *Sex and Character* immediately went into a second printing (going through fourteen editions by 1914) and became a best-seller in Austria and Germany, while the 1906 English edition was still being reprinted in the 1920s.

The differences between the three versions of the "intermediate sex" essentially arise from the three theories about androgyny that inform them. For the Krafft-Ebing school, androgyny is a psychic and physical anomaly that characterizes an individual with homosexual and deviant tendencies. For Carpenter and his colleagues (and, to a lesser extent, Ellis), it is a primarily psychic condition also characterizing a third, predominantly homosexual, sex, but with particularly transcendent (mainly artistic) abilities. Finally, for Freud and Weininger, androgyny (divorced from sexual orientation) becomes a universal physical condition that explodes the notion of any pure sexual or gender categories. All three theories of androgyny and the sexual body spread quickly through academic and nonacademic circles. In Britain and America, the works of Carpenter and Ellis as well as translations from the German appeared in popular presses and provoked extensive commentaries in the pages of early avant-garde and feminist journals as well as the "creative interpretation and appropriation" (Greenway 36) of their ideas. Since no one theoretical school enjoyed universal acknowledgement, the various discourses about the body had the effect of destroying the notion of two stable hierarchical sexes without leaving anything definite in its place.

For the modernist artist, imagining his or her imagination as third-sexed—as opposed to merging it with a visionary muse—thus means risking exposure to a number of positive and negative associations. Incorporating the motif of the intermediate sex into one's conception of the creative process offers the potential for a radical enhancement of artistic authority and power in a world in which traditional methods—including the poet's engagement with the muse—have been upset by the breakdown of the binary male/female hierarchy (because of the introduction of new sexual categories). As we have seen, a majority of sex theorists made the connection between psychic androgyny and artistic ability. Thought to possess heightened creative powers because of the interaction of "male" and "female" elements within their brains, members—even partial members—of this new "third sex" would appear to escape the gendered crises of authority and inspiration afflicting literary men and women. Yet while gendering one's imagination as part of this new sexual category would seem to promise a release from some of the blockages plaguing the modern artist, it was nevertheless a risky solution to adopt. The association of androgyny with homosexuality and sexual degeneracy remained a troubling legacy for many, predominantly heterosexual, male writers such as Joyce and Faulkner who feared the possibility of being "feminized," and women writers, particularly H. D. and Woolf, who believed this further repression of their female identities would turn them into "freaks." The trials of Oscar Wilde and Radclyffe Hall—and the public backlash against homosexuality in all its incarnations—were vividly etched in the memories of most modernist writers, both gay and straight.[26] In the face of these sexual threats, some modernists, among them D. H. Lawrence, at least publicly rejected the concept of a third sex—and an androgyne imagination—altogether. Proclaiming in 1923 that "every single living cell is either male or female, and will remain either male or female as long as life lasts," Lawrence finds himself unable even to contemplate any kind of sexual mind-merge and dismisses "the talk about a third sex," calling it "the hermaphrodite fallacy" (*Fantasia* 96, 96, 100).[27]

Modernist versions of an androgyne imagination are thus responses to literary and psychic blockage consisting of appropriative strategies involving both risk and fear. While on the one hand it promises the possibility of virtually unlimited empowerment and inspiration, on the other hand, the model of an androgyne imagination at the same time threatens to annihilate the self from which it has been generated. Caught in the middle of an amorphous, constantly shifting debate over the nature of the sexual body, modernist writers reach for a solution to their creative impasse that they simultaneously know has the potential to disable them both artistically and sexually.

Ultimately the perilous strategy of incorporating a construction of the opposite sex within the creative self or mind involves a level of anxiety and crisis that recalls nothing less than the powerful and terrifying experience of the sublime. Indeed, many modernist authors make the connection between their reconstruction of the imagination and the moment of sublime identification. Although they do not all use the literary term, they consistently employ the sublime vocabulary of confrontation and introjection, empowerment and transport. This idea of the sublime as both an effect and a strategy rooted in a specifically psychosexual dynamic is not new. A number of contemporary psychoanalytic critics describe the experience as a willed (if temporary) solution to cultural and aesthetic blockage that "seems to offer to the poet the truly primary power of the god" (Weiskel 164). However, unlike the culturally specific model I have just outlined, critics such as Weiskel and Neil Hertz construct a universal paradigm for the sublime based on the resolution of the Oedipus complex. According to this school, the sublime is always initiated by the contemplation of an external, "excessive object [that] excites a wish to be inundated, which yields an anxiety of incorporation; this anxiety is met by a reaction formation against the wish which precipitates a recapitulation of the Oedipus complex; this in turn yields a feeling of guilt (superego anxiety) and is resolved through identification (introjection)" (Weiskel 105). Simply put, the transport of the sublime corresponds to the empowerment gained by the male (artist) who has successfully negotiated the oedipal struggle; it is the experience of the boy confronting the all-powerful Father, repressing that threat, and experiencing the influx of power corresponding to his triumphant identification with him. More recently, feminist critics such as Anne K. Mellor and Patricia Yaeger note the degree to which these theories render the sublime solely "an experience of masculine empowerment" (Mellor, *Romanticism and Gender* 85) and have proposed the possibility of a "'pre-oedipal' sublime" (Yaeger 204) based on Hertz's observation that the experience is an "oedipal confrontation that masks an oral, primordial desire to merge with (rather than to possess) the mother" (Yaeger 204). However, while both these psychoanalytic models do capture the psychosexual nature of sublime, they underestimate the degree to which it serves to fulfill specific cultural needs. As Rob Wilson asserts, "to oedipalize the sublime . . . is to dehistoricize its implied workings" (12). The fact remains that since the eighteenth century, when Longinus's theory became popularized, the sublime has been defined and redefined countless times. As Samuel Monk reminds us, "the course of the sublime never did run smooth, since at any moment a writer might seek to deny validity to all that had been written and thought on the subject, and to revert to older ideas and tastes" (134).

What is particularly enlightening about the heightened states of consciousness toward which Joyce, H. D., Faulkner, and Woolf gesture are the ways in which they fall apart, when what promised to be a supreme experience of empowerment dissolves into feelings of despair, panic, collapse, and engulfment. Why their attempts fail is a topic I will discuss more thoroughly later. Much of it has to do with the difficulty with which many of these writers are able to assimilate the more problematic cultural associations of androgyny (such as its link with sexual degeneracy) within their consciousnesses. Yet, as I explain more fully in the concluding chapter, at the root of their difficulties is an enhanced awareness of a problem within the theory of the sublime: its assumption of a unique and unassailable subjectivity. As feminist critic Frances Ferguson argues, "the sublime seems designed to stage the illusion of control and thus the illusion that one can have a self, if only temporarily. The self, always wanting to be the self, gets to remedy its own sense of deficiency in setting a limit between the finite and the infinite" (86). Faced with the possibility of disappearing in the mass, the artist looks to the sublime as "an area in which an isolated self can achieve a heroism of subjectivity" (Ferguson 38).[28] For modern writers terrified of losing their artistic authority within the facelessness and genderlessness of twentieth-century mass culture, the chance of recovering a sense of individual empowerment through the transport of an androgynous sublime was one worth taking. Yet without a stable sense even of the androgyne imagination they were trying to represent (because of the constantly shifting cultural definitions of sexual categories), their project was doomed to failure and these writers knew it. As Wilson notes, "the modernist sublime had hollowed out into a compound of hyperbole and irony, rhetoric hedged by self-mockery, as the sublime comes to refer less to superlative revelation than to the circumstances in which such a revelation might have taken place" (45). Despite their self-consciousness, many modernists nevertheless could not rid themselves of the nostalgic hope that such empowerment was indeed possible if they could only try hard enough to make those precious "circumstances" come together. Even their efforts to achieve it function to provide them with the creative energy and purpose they feel they lack.

It would be impossible in a study of this size to discuss these dynamics in the works of all the writers who attempt to engage them. In the interests of space and clarity, I have had to omit a number of authors from extended treatment. For a moment, however, I would like briefly to recall Wallace Steven's representation of his imagination as androgynous "Sister and solace, brother and delight" (219); Ezra Pound's efforts in "Ortus" to create or construct a feminine element within his creative mind; Lawrence's early experiments with androgyny in *The Rainbow;* Sherwood Anderson's psychically pregnant male narrator of *Winesburg, Ohio;* Ernest Hemingway's "quarrel with androgyny" (Spilka 225) in works such as *A Farewell to Arms* and *The Garden of Eden;* and Anais Nin's determination to destroy the imprisoning muse-model by helping men "create another womb" while insisting that women find themselves a male "fecundator" (Nin 184, 234).[29]

Even more than these other writers, however, James Joyce, H. D., William Faulkner, and Virginia Woolf made the artist's need for an empowering, sublime confrontation with an androgyne imagination a primary theme and focus of their works. Joyce—who, of all these writers, perhaps comes closest to recognizing the ironic implications of the modern nostalgia for the sublime, a yearning he ultimately labels masochistic—nevertheless exposes as all too real the crisis of the male artist forced to confront the inadequacy of inherited imaginative representations in the face of new cultural realities. Although Joyce flirts with the possibilities of an androgyne imagination, he recognizes the degree to which its empowering potential would be thwarted by patriarchal prejudice and forever changing cultural assumptions about gender. H. D.'s lifelong struggle to accept and understand her bisexuality and to transform early feelings of alienation (from her role as daughter, wife, mother, and especially as woman artist) into triumphant artistic power through the androgynous tropes of the overmind, Ray Bart, and the transsexual Ka involves a tremendous amount of pain. Constantly threatening to subsume her fragile female ego, her imagination becomes as much a handicap to be suffered through as a solution to her authorial crisis. For Faulkner, the autoerotic overtones of his version of the androgyne imagination are always on the verge of turning his mind into a site for a kind of "psychic incest"; his fears of sexual transgression manifest themselves in guilty fantasies of physical incest, terrible nightmares involving the female body and more specifically of being "feminized," and insistent anxieties about homoeroticism. Woolf, who constructs her version of an androgyne imagination in response not only to a crisis of audience and authorship but to an underlying fear of and discomfort with her own body, fantasizes about sublime empowerment in novels such as *Orlando* where it is nearly always complicated by guilt over the repression that precedes her imaginative transport. Even more than H. D., Woolf is continually faced with the threat of psychic dissolution through the terrifying loss of boundaries that her androgynous model necessitates.

I will present two men, two women, two Britons, and two Americans each writing in different local circumstances but each responding to an inescapable sense of historical and cultural change. While their versions of an androgyne imagination are all unique, each model is intricately bound up with anxieties about how to generate inspiration and art. That their efforts resemble a struggle for the sublime experience and betray an intense crisis of empowerment and authority suggests the intensity of their unease, the desperation of their methods. Although designed to generate inspiration and empowerment, their androgynous imaginative models ultimately end up falling apart. But that these methods fail suggests not so much that modernists were prisoners of a divisive and brutal sex war (as Gilbert and Gubar have suggested in *No Man's Land*) as that by the late 1930s the idea of an unassailable, individual creative mind was no longer one that could be defended or used. By the time Djuna Barnes writes *Nightwood* in 1937, such faith in the possibilities of the imagination no longer seems justifiable or necessary. This novel's androgynous writer-hero, Matthew O'Connor, is essentially a tormented transvestite, a self-proclaimed "charlatan" (Barnes 96) who will do and say anything to get an audience. Yet his voluminous and voluptuous discourse is doomed to remain unheard. For his tragedy is not only to remain a sexual misfit, but to experience firsthand the "death of the author" in a deafened world that has long since ceased to care; as O'Connor laments, "it's all over, everything's over, and nobody knows it but me" (166). Of course, the world of life and art is not quite so desolate for the prolific authors to whom we shall now turn. All of them continue to go on living and writing well after their experiments with an androgynous imagination fail. What they cannot ignore, however, is the culturally pervasive loss of faith in a uniquely individual creative mind or process. Like Matthew O'Connor, they must confront an increasingly mechanical world driven by so many interconnected forces that any traditional idea of a subjective "imagination" becomes immediately irrelevant.

2

"From the Sublime to the Ridiculous Is But a Step"

Androgyny and Masochism in Joyce

> His love-verses gave him pleasure: he wrote them at long intervals and when he wrote it was always a mature and reasoned emotion which urged him. But in his expressions of love he found himself compelled to use what he called a feudal terminology and as he could not use it with the same faith and purpose as animated the feudal poets themselves he was compelled to express his love a little ironically.
>
> —*Stephen Hero,* James Joyce

FOR JAMES JOYCE's modern male artist, romantic tropes no longer work the way they used to. Struggling to express a new idea in outworn modes of discourse, Stephen Dedalus finds himself face to face with a crisis not only of creative expression but of patriarchal authority. How is he to succeed at capturing the attention and admiration of a contemporary reading audience by using poetic conventions that he regards as antiquated and anachronistic? Despite the protests of his classmate Cranly, who claims that "the civil life affected in no way the individual life, and that it was possible for men to preserve ancient superstitions and prejudices in the midst of a machinery of modernity" (*Stephen Hero* 174), Stephen recognizes that "though humanity may not change beyond recognition during the short eras known as the ages of man yet these ages are the preys of different ideas in accordance with which every activity, even the least, which they engender is conceived and directed" (*Stephen Hero* 174). Simply put, transformations in history lead to transformations in culture. That so-called feudal discourse no longer inspires Stephen with faith and confidence in his authority as a writer implies that the patriarchal power structure—presumably one of Cranly's immutable ancient prejudices—that informs romantic literary figures is in crisis.

The fact that Joyce situates Stephen's artistic blockage in the specific context of love poetry—a genre traditionally aglow with the fire of the male poet's desire to possess the female object, whether she be maiden or muse—suggests that the primary impetus behind this disruptive failure of the male poetic imagination is the changing relations between the sexes. Indeed, after several decades of intensified scientific and philosophical inquiry into the biological and sociological nature of gender, the modern sexual landscape is anything but familiar. The Stephen of Joyce's *Stephen Hero* is highly conscious of the increasing permeability of gender categories: he participates in intellectual discussion groups both men and women attend; he hears of female authors of sexually ambiguous novels such as *The Female Fellow;* and he observes university presidents who speak with "slow hermaphroditic gesture[s]" (*Stephen Hero* 98). Rather than being liberating, however, this conflict between old and new sexual ideologies causes him a considerable amount of confusion. On the one hand recognizing and at least attempting to refute the painful legacy of patriarchy, Stephen laments that "A woman's body is a corporal asset of the State: if she traffic with it she must sell it either as a harlot or as a married woman or as a working celibate or as a mistress. But a woman is (incidentally) a human being: and a human being's love and freedom is not a spiritual asset of the State" (*Stephen Hero* 202). He gives his overworked mother Henrik Ibsen's plays to read and determines to renounce the misogynist and patriarchal father whose beliefs and actions "he now regarded . . . as the most deadly part of a tyranny, internal and external" (*Stephen Hero* 209).[1] Yet at the same time, Stephen enjoys ridiculing "with agile bullets" the theories of his feminist friend McCann and has the reputation among the ladies of being a "woman-hater" (*Stephen Hero* 49, 153). When one of them refuses to be his mistress, he ends "by anathemising [*sic*] Emma as the most deceptive and cowardly of marsupials" (*Stephen Hero* 210). We must always guard against conflating Joyce with his characters; the voice of the narrator ironizes Stephen's misogyny by insinuating that Emma's spiritual faith "really implied a more genuine emancipation than his [Stephen's] own" (*Stephen Hero* 210). Nevertheless, we cannot ignore the persistent references in Joyce's fiction to the changing politics of gender and the increasing breakdown of sexual norms in modern culture. In other words, while Joyce often problematizes Stephen's (and Bloom's) reactions and responses, he nevertheless continues to underscore the sexual and artistic crisis that precipitates them: the fact that as old sexual hierarchies continue to become destabilized, tropes for the imaginative process rooted in patriarchal structures suddenly lose their affective power.

In the following pages I will examine Joyce's repeated (and often failed) attempts to understand and ultimately to transcend this gendered crisis of authority and will focus my inquiry primarily on *A Portrait of the Artist as a Young Man* and *Ulysses*. In his efforts to reestablish his artistic prerogative, preserve a "space of his own" in literary discourse, this modernist author attempts to create new and empowering tropes for his imagination that would engage the emergent assertion of empowering gender indeterminacy while at the same time maintain his confidence in his masculinity. Yet despite the fact that his artist hero, Stephen Dedalus, employs a variation of the birth metaphor to describe and reinvigorate his creativity, and Leopold Bloom at times attempts to incarnate himself as an androgynous artist and "new womanly man," neither character succeeds in his endeavors; ultimately both succumb to anxieties about feminization, homoeroticism, and sexual taboo that are inspired by a society still reluctant to accept changing gender roles. Nevertheless, Joyce uses the occasion of Bloom's and Stephen's failures to expose their efforts at artistic authorization as little more than absurd, ultimately masochistic exercises in futility. Rather than citing the androgynous tropes as the culprits, he self-consciously chooses to place the blame for Stephen's and Bloom's humiliating defeats upon the patriarchal assumptions and prejudices within which his culture is still trapped.

Joyce's lifelong interest in androgyny—in particular in the works of turn-of-the-century sex theorists such as Richard von Krafft-Ebing and Otto Weinginger, who hypothesized the existence of third-sexed bodies—has been well documented.[2] The most comprehensive of such studies, Richard Brown's *James Joyce and Sexuality*, traces the specific cultural sources of Joyce's interest in topics such as onanism, androgyny, the third sex, masochism, matriarchy, and sexual difference. Pointing out that Joyce, who was several times a student of medicine, was familiar with the most current explorations in sexology, Brown also demonstrates Joyce's interest in the work of Havelock Ellis (Brown 83) and others—including Ernest Crawley, J. J. Bachofen, Desroix, Kardec, Guglielmo Ferrero, Edward Carpenter, and Mathilde and Mathias Vaerting—who theorized about sex and gender. Common to all their works is a recognition that much of what had been designated as gendered, such as character qualities, social and political roles, and potentially even sexual identity, was to a large extent socially constructed, and thus malleable.

However, while Brown and critics like him have identified the sources of and influences on Joyce's obsessions with divergent sexualities, they have not gone far enough in describing the crisis these ideas precipitated for his art. Locating moments of androgynous consciousness in Joyce is not difficult, but explaining their aesthetic significance has consistently challenged scholars. Many have noted that in general Joyce's aesthetics are connected to his interest in sexuality and particularly to the idea of androgyny. Until recently, critical debate on these questions has centered for the most part on whether Joyce's ideas about art and the imagination are or are not misogynistic and reactionary. To the question, "what is their function?" critics have tried to ascertain the degree to which these androgynous images represent either a violent appropriation of "feminine" metaphors of procreation or a liberalizing social gesture.[3]

As scholarly trends have shifted to more historically based approaches, feminist critics, including Margot Norris and Christine Froula, have convincingly argued that part of Joyce's interest in incorporating the feminine into his androgynous self-portraits derived from a patriarchal "law of gender" (Froula, *Modernism's Body* 12) that forced him personally and politically to disavow or repress his female-identified characteristics and attachment to his mother. I build on these groundbreaking studies to suggest that Joyce represents a crisis not only of gender identity but of artistic authority. I want to pursue the question of how the addition of new sexual categories functioned, along with the entrance of women into the world of arts and letters, to render his inherited model of artistic production obsolete by destabilizing the once normative relation between male artist-subject and female muse-object. This specifically aesthetic consequence of a regendered landscape manifests itself from the beginning of Joyce's career, when, in *Stephen Hero*, a young, ambitious Stephen shows his brother his poems, and "Maurice asked who the woman was. Stephen looked a little vaguely before him before answering and in the end had to answer that he didn't know who she was" (*Stephen Hero* 36). Rather than a source of transcendent inspiration, the romantic muse has been reduced to an outworn, ultimately meaningless trope—Stephen's dream maidens bear little resemblance either to the real-life struggles and aspirations of modern Dublin women such as the enterprising Emma Clery or the repressed May Dedalus.

Breaking old habits is not so easy, however. In his first novels, Joyce takes pains to show how even this somewhat rebellious modern artist, who embraces Lord Byron over Alfred Tennyson, is still brainwashed into employing traditional literary conventions. Schooled in a male literary canon, and in an all-male institution that reinforces Victorian attitudes about male and female roles, Stephen Dedalus is taught that the female's relation to art is to serve as the (male) poet's object of inspiration; when he thinks about writing a poem, for instance, he titles it "To E.C.," "for he had seen similar titles in the collected poems of Lord Byron" (*Portrait* 70). Yet rather than guiding him to privileged spiritual truths, Stephen's dream maidens merely reflect his repressed sexual fantasies; realizing this fact leads him almost immediately to doubt his authenticity and ability as an artist.

During his first attempts to write poetry, Stephen invokes his romantic muse, his own "Mercedes," to stimulate his imagination to what at first he believes are transcendent heights:

> [H]e was different from the others. He did not want to play. He wanted to meet in the real world the unsubstantial image which his soul so constantly beheld. He did not know where to seek it or how: but a premonition which led him on told him that this image would, without any overt act of his, encounter him. They would meet quietly as if they had known each other and had made their tryst, perhaps at one of the gates or in some secret place. They would be alone, surrounded by darkness and silence: and in that moment of supreme tenderness he would be transfigured. Weakness and timidity and inexperience would fall from him in that magic moment. (*Portrait* 65)

Masquerading as a divine visitation, this reverie is soon exposed as little more than a sex dream. Only a few pages earlier, Stephen connects "another Mercedes"—his real-life sweetheart, Emma Clery—with his celestial dream maiden. Frightened by the fact that "as he brooded upon her image, a strange unrest crept into his blood" (*Portrait* 63, 64), he sublimates his sexual passions into his art, turning it into "aesthetic compensation for frustrated erotic desire" (Henke, "Stephen Dedalus" 89). Tellingly, the verses that "Mercedes" inspires repress the transfiguration that he both desires and fears: "nor did he and she appear vividly. The verses told only of night and the balmy breeze and the maiden lustre of the moon" (*Portrait* 70). That the writing of the poem concludes with Stephen's visit to a prostitute adds an ironic twist to the high style of his verses; exposing his work as a failed attempt at sexual sublimation, Joyce calls into question both the stature and authority of this self-inflated male poet.[4]

Yet immediately after Stephen completes his conventional, romantic seduction poems, "he went into his mother's bedroom and gazed at his face for a long time in the mirror of her dressingtable" (*Portrait* 71). This is an odd detail, and a critical one. The romantic muse-convention requires the (male) artist to pose as a poet-lover. Yet the act of looking in his mother's mirror suggests that for

Stephen, the artistic process involves some kind of identification with the mother, or at least the female creative potential that the mother represents. Recently, both Suzette A. Henke and Jane Lillienfield have offered that Stephen exhibits unresolved and ambivalent preoedipal desire for the maternal figure and have identified the confused incestuous desires that underlie the novel.[5] I would argue, however, that these desires are not only the result of arrested oedipal development, or—as Froula has proposed—of a repressed wish to recapture those feminine characteristics denied by the Law of the Father. The fact that Joyce connects them with Stephen's artistic efforts implies that Stephen's ambivalent, troubled wish is not so much to possess the mother sexually, or even to recover the so-called feminine side of his psyche, but to possess her (pro)creative powers. It is no coincidence that Stephen attempts to incorporate his mother's mirror image within his own immediately after an extended effort at artistic creation. The fact that this scene is quickly dropped and repressed suggests that it generates concerns about sexual identity and transgression which Stephen cannot face. Nevertheless, as we shall see, these feelings and associations never completely disappear.

In the oft-cited bird-girl passage, we can see further proof of Stephen's ambivalence about incorporating a construction of the female within his imaginative framework. While some critics have read this scene as another example of Stephen's habit of "romantic sublimation" (Henke, "Stephen Dedalus" 96)—his conflation of sexual arousal with poetic inspiration—Stephen's response to the young woman on the beach also indicates to me the kind of imaginative merging we saw happen at his mother's dressing table. This moment occurs just after Stephen has invoked the bird-man/father, Daedalus "flying sunward above the sea"; identifying with him, "the body he knew was purified in a breath . . . and made radiant" (*Portrait* 169). Yet Stephen's ecstasy soon leads him away from the father's airy heavens, his imperishable purity, and toward the sea that lies seductively and dangerously beneath him. His vision of the bird-girl parallels that of the bird-man/father he has recently invoked; however, this "seabird" has her own medium, preferring the watery engulfment of the "midstream" (*Portrait* 171) to the empty spaces of the sky. While the meeting starts out much like Stephen's other sex fantasies, his dream about her suggests that it has a larger significance for him; in it, he senses "his soul was swooning into some new world, fantastic, dim, uncertain as under sea" (*Portrait* 172). That world, represented by the vast ocean and an opening flower that "spread in endless succession to itself" (*Portrait* 172), suggests the female body, in particular the female sex organs. I would argue that Stephen's dream reveals a deep-seated but repressed wish to incorporate the power and beauty of the female within himself, to merge the masculine—that "vast indifferent dome and the calm processes of the heavenly bodies"—with the feminine—"the earth that had borne him"—into an androgynous, creative whole (*Portrait* 172). Again, it is no coincidence that it is almost immediately after this experience that he attempts his most extensive literary effort of the novel: the villanelle.

For years, critics have debated the relative merits of what is in fact Joyce's adolescent poem.[6] Like Charles Rossman, I read the work as "an outraged cry of protest against the flesh in which the poet laments the inherent shame of woman's sexuality and manages to sublimate his own" (281). Composed in a mood of sexual jealousy after convincing himself that his beloved Emma has been flirting with a priest, Stephen's villanelle transforms his errant lover into an evil temptress, and in doing so blames her for his own sexual frustration:

> A glow of desire kindled again his soul and fired and fulfilled all his body. Conscious of his desire she was waking from odorous sleep, the temptress of his villanelle. Her eyes, dark and with a look of languor, were opening to his eyes. Her nakedness yielded to him, radiant, warm, odorous and lavishlimbed, enfolded him like a shining cloud, enfolded him like water with a liquid life: and like a cloud of vapour or like waters circumfluent in space the liquid letters of speech, symbols of the element of mystery, flowed forth over his brain. (*Portrait* 223)

The poem is more conventional than enlightening, and even Stephen connects its failure to his employment of an outworn and ultimately nonreferential muse-trope: "the images he had summoned gave him no pleasure. They were secret and enflaming but her image was not entangled by them" (*Portrait* 233). Once again, dream maidens fail to satisfy him both sexually and artistically.

However, as with his verses "To E.C." and his vision of the bird-girl, Stephen's writing of the villanelle is followed by an uncanny set of imaginative associations involving the maternal body. Gazing at the birds in the heavens to make himself forget the "image of his mother's face," her "sobs and reproaches" (*Portrait* 224), Stephen at first seems to cling to the image of Daedalus, his spiritual father. Yet the words he uses to describe the experience emerge from the womb-like sea below:

> A soft liquid joy like the noise of many waters flowed over his memory and he felt in his heart the soft peace of silent spaces of fading tenuous sky above the waters, of oceanic silence, of swallows flying through the seadusk over the flowing waters.
>
> A soft liquid joy flowed through the words where the soft long vowels hurtled noiselessly and fell away, lapping and flowing back and ever shaking the white bells of their waves in mute chime and mute peal and soft low swooning cry; and he felt that the augury he had sought in the wheeling darting birds and in the pale space of sky above him had come forth from his heart like a bird from a turret quietly and swiftly. (*Portrait* 225–26)

In this layered meditation, Stephen associates the source of his creativity with the flowing waters of a vast and oceanic womb of poetry. Yet while this image is soothing and inspiring, it is also frightening. Almost immediately he tries to disengage his psyche from the all-encompassing, subtly incorporating waters, attempting to escape into the bodilessness and nonmateriality of Daedalus, the father. Yet the swallows, the birds he chooses to represent that father, make a troubling image. Traditional harbingers of death, they imply that this flight away from the oceanic waters of a female imagination is a step toward the loss of creativity or, perhaps more important, the loss of male identity.[7] Stephen wonders whether the swallows serve as a "symbol of departure or of loneliness" (*Portrait* 226); although the question remains unanswered in the text, Stephen's reveries suggest them both.

Stephen's failed attempts to repress the recurrent suggestion that he must identify with and incorporate a female component within his imaginative framework—not merely his psychological one—ultimately leads him to substitute the birth metaphor for the muse as a figure for his imagination. Like innumerable male artists before him, Stephen appropriates the female language of reproduction to represent the process of his artistic creation. Although many scholars have pointed this out, nearly all the discussion on this subject focuses on the degree to which his use of the trope is an appropriative or misogynistic gesture. Condemning the fact that Joyce "dispenses with the need for a female participant in what he sees as the quintessential creative act" (Perreault 304), many feminist critics tend to argue that he "attempts to reduce women to the processes of their body" (Friedman 76) and thereby "replicates the sexual division of labor and reinforces the mind-body split" (Friedman 79). At the other extreme, critics such as Robert Boyle label Stephen's use of the birth metaphor as an overtly feminist gesture by claiming that while the creator model in *A Portrait* appears to be exclusively male, Joyce intends "to effect a union between male and female acting as one in his final Creator, with the female not only consubstantial but finally predominant" (Boyle 126).

Yet debating whether or not this trope is or is not sexist does not help us understand the troubled manner in which Stephen engages it. Although—as Susan Stanford Friedman, Terry Castle, Mary O'Brien and others have noted—appropriating "female" terms of reproduction to refer to male artistic creation is certainly nothing new, what is different is that for this modern male artist it brings up a plethora of anxieties with which earlier writers simply did not contend, anxieties about ego-incorporation and engulfment which recapitulate those engaged by the experience of the sublime.[8] While on the one hand this appropriation invokes what Stephen has come to recognize as the powerful, transformative creativity of the female, the oceanic unity of vision, on the other hand it also threatens to incorporate him completely, to dislodge his male identity.

It is important to recall that Stephen insists that "when we come to the phenomena of artistic conception, artistic gestation and artistic reproduction I require a new terminology and a new personal experience" (*Portrait* 209). Despite the fact that Stephen is describing an old methodology (the birth metaphor), he is careful to point out that using these terms of reproduction to describe the workings of his imagination in this new age means something different than it did in the nineteenth century. Ultimately the most frightening thing for Stephen about this "male model of aesthetic creation" (Henke, "Stephen Dedalus" 101) is that it is not really "male" at all; given the fact that gender is now no longer even a remotely stable concept (as we saw in our discussions of the sex theories of Freud, Weininger, et al.), incorporating this female metaphor of reproduction into his creative mind generates heightened fears about being "feminized." We see evidence of this anxiety in the cautious manner with which Stephen treats the trope. While he does utilize the birth metaphor, he retreats from it—and indeed any mention of the body—as soon as he possibly can; attempting to invoke its power without becoming subsumed by it, Stephen believes he can escape the feminizing, ego-incorporating potential of the "womb of the imagination" by remaining "within or behind or beyond or above his handiwork, invisible, refined out of existence"—essentially by divesting himself of his sexual body altogether, insistent upon becoming a "priest of eternal imagination" (*Portrait* 215, 221).

Dissociating himself from his body is not the only evidence of Stephen's discomfort with his new imaginative model. It is no coincidence that at the same time that he attempts to incorporate this construction of female creativity within his mind, Stephen goes to extraordinary lengths to distinguish his creation—and implicitly his body—from hers. Like Plato, he insists that the male artist creates in his mind that which transcends the procreative progeny of woman. While Stephen admits that both man and woman possess generative abilities, he consigns female creations to the earthly and the physical realm of bodies, that which is "inferior" to his masculine mental poetic progeny—his "new soaring impalpable imperishable being[s]" (*Portrait* 169). Associating sex and the (female) body with an "undivined and squalid way of life," he boasts a "virgin womb of the imagination" in which life is "purified" (*Portrait* 78, 217, 215). While Emma has been "humbled and saddened by the dark shame of womanhood" (*Portrait* 223), Stephen thus escapes the defilement of the flesh in his bodiless creative powers.

Denying his link with or dependence upon his mother's body,

Stephen claims to be tied to his family only "in the mystical kinship of fosterage" (*Portrait* 98) and boasts a fresh, independent, and self-created identity. As Stephen explains, "The soul is born . . . first in those moments I told you of. It has a slow and dark birth, more mysterious than the birth of the body" (*Portrait* 203). Unlike the workings of the flesh-and-blood womb, the male artist's imagination is thus invested with the inscrutable power of the godhead. Assuming the role of his own progenitor, Stephen invokes the mythic artist Daedalus as his spiritual father. Not only is this identification with the paternal figure significantly less frightening or threatening than his relation to the mother, it is positively thrilling for Stephen. As we will soon see, he continues to cling to it as to a life raft.

If Stephen sounds desperate throughout his disavowal of the feminine or the maternal, it is because despite the enormous amount of time he spends trying to convince himself (and indirectly the reader) that his model of creation is separate from and superior to the female model on which it is based, he continues to experience agonizing moments of doubt concerning the transcendence of his physical and creative powers. Seeing the word "foetus" cut into the wooden desk makes him doubt the primacy of his creativity:

> It shocked him to find in the outer world a trace of what he had deemed till then a brutish and individual malady of his own mind. His recent monstrous reveries came thronging into his memory. They too had sprung up before him, suddenly and furiously, out of mere words. He had soon given into them and allowed them to sweep across and abase his intellect, wondering always where they came from, from what den of monstrous images, and always weak and humble towards others, restless and sickened of himself when they had swept over him. (*Portrait* 90)

Of course Stephen's reaction reflects his adolescent disgust with the physicality of his sexual desires and the impurity of a language that would express them. Yet the fact that the word that inspires his anti-epiphany is "foetus," as opposed to a more conventionally "dirty" term, suggests that Stephen's angst has multiple referents. Why would a developing writer, contemplating the powers of the womb of his imagination, balk at the linguistic representation of recently gestated progeny? Could it be that his shame at his sexuality extends to his procreative efforts? Does the word "foetus" remind him of his emergent but abortive efforts at imaginative fulfillment? Or, is what disturbs him that rather than a transcendent, aphysical source of poetic truths, the womb of his imagination, is an earthly "den of monstrous images" that bears remarkable resemblance to his description of the supposedly defiled female womb? That Stephen experiences such anxieties while walking with his father suggests that all the rhetoric about paternal identification masks a more deep-seated anxiety about his authority as a male artist. Instead of allowing this new version of his creative method to provide an influx of inspiration, "the letters cut in the stained wood of the desk stared upon him, mocking his bodily weakness and futile enthusiasms" (*Portrait* 91). Beyond feelings of sexual inadequacy, Stephen's thoughts—in the context of the rest of the novel—thus betray a perceived failure of enthusiasms that allude to the passion for the artistic as well.

Haunted by the possibility that this womb of his imagination is more monstrous than divine, more physical than spiritual, more feminine than masculine, Stephen nevertheless finds himself attracted to Cranly, whose "priestlike face . . . [and] dark womanish eyes" (*Portrait* 178, 247) mirror the image of himself that he has been consistently trying to repress. When Stephen looks at Cranly,

> he had a glimpse of a strange dark cavern of speculation but at once turned away from it, feeling that it was not yet the hour to enter it. But the nightshade of his friend's listlessness seemed to be diffusing in the air around him a tenuous and deadly exhalation and he found himself glancing from one casual word to another on his right or left in stolid wonder that they had been so silently emptied of instantaneous sense until every mean shop legend bound his mind like the words of a spell and his soul shrivelled up, sighing with age as he walked on in a lane among heaps of dead language. (*Portrait* 178–79)

Cranly's androgynous visage prompts Stephen to recall that terrifying "dark cavern of speculation," that womb-like imagination that he has been attempting to engender. Rather than experiencing empowerment or excitement, however, Stephen is suffused with fear and unease and "at once turn[s] away from it"; looking at his mirror-image, he feels a shriveling of the imagination, a kind of mental castration. Perhaps to a greater extent than any other in the novel, this passage reveals Stephen's ambivalence about his creative model; in particular, it reveals his fears that creative or imaginative androgyny will result in permanent feminization, homoerotic identification, and ultimately spiritual death.

Refusing what has become a sublime confrontation with the powerful yet attractive female principle he has constructed, Stephen, in *A Portrait,* instead chooses to escape into the aesthetics of the beautiful; sacrificing transport, he clings to the safety of an experience in which "the mind is arrested and raised above desire and loathing" (*Portrait* 205). As Stephen suggests, "beauty expressed by the artist . . . ought to induce, an esthetic stasis" (*Portrait* 206). But of course the sublime is anything but static, and without it one wonders how he will ever recapture "the lightnings of intuition . . . lightnings of so clear a splendour that in those moments the world perished about his feet as if it had been fireconsumed" (*Portrait* 177) that heretofore represent his ideal form of aesthetic experience. Stephen leaves the novel fleeing from all females—particularly from Emma and his mother—into the arms of yet another father he hopes will protect him, "stand [him] now in good stead" (*Portrait* 253). Yet while Stephen desperately tries to link "father" with "artificer," he never succeeds in doing so. The irony of his flight is that it will cement his failure. To be an artist, Joyce implies, he still must confront—and somehow incorporate—the mother in the mirror.

It is not surprising that at the beginning of *Ulysses* Stephen is still waiting to fulfill his artistic potential, and remains paralyzed with anxieties about his feelings for his mother. Images of May Dedalus appear early in *Ulysses* and continue to haunt the text; the first time we see her, she looks frightening indeed. Haunted by the vision of her agonized tortured face and "wasted body" (*Ulysses* 5), Stephen transforms it into a monstrous incarnation of his guilt which, on a conscious level, Stephen locates in his having refused to pray for her at her deathbed. Yet it becomes clearer and clearer that the true reason for his discomfort is not his supposed heresies against the church but against her sex; in contrast to the traditional oedipal drama, this son wants the *mother* dead—in order safely to possess her creative powers.

The contemplation of matricide becomes, for Stephen, even more terrifying than any oedipal desire to murder and to supplant the father. Unlike Freud, Stephen recognizes the debt he owes the mother—not only for giving him life but for preserving him from the destructive influence of a violent and numbing patriarchal culture.[9] Looking at one of his young students, Stephen thinks of the boy's mother and admits, "but for her the race of the world would have trampled him underfoot, a squashed boneless snail" (U 23). Nevertheless, such dependence annihilates individuation and identity; filled with "weak watery blood drained from her own" (*Ulysses* 23), Stephen—like Cyril—is frighteningly ill equipped to assert himself either personally or poetically.

As in *A Portrait*, Stephen tries to dismiss and ultimately deny his artistic dependency, or "womb envy" (Bettelheim), by once again consigning woman's creativity with the body, with the evils of sin and death. Obsessed by the contents of a midwife's bag, he muses on the miracle of birth, the ultimate "creation from nothing," and addresses a rhetorical aside to the female sex: "will you be as gods?" (*Ulysses* 32). Picturing the eternal image of Eve's protruding belly, "orient and immortal, standing from everlasting to everlasting" (U 32), Stephen attempts to deflate its power by associating it with "sin" (U 32) and mortality (the "allwombing tomb" [*Ulysses* 40]). Both in "Proteus" and "Oxen of the Sun," he imagines "monstrous births" (*Ulysses* 335) and birth defects, implying the comparative purity of his imaginative progeny.

Stephen's desire to deny the importance of the female to his creative process ultimately leads him to hypothesize that William Shakespeare identified with the ghost of Hamlet's father—and not Hamlet—in order to support a male model of artistic creation based solely on literary paternity:

> As we, or mother Dana, weave and unweave our bodies, Stephen said, from day to day, their molecules shuttled to and fro, so does the artist weave and unweave his image. And as the mole on my

> right breast is where it was when I was born, though all my body has been woven of new stuff time after time, so through the ghost of the unquiet father the image of the unliving son looks forth. In the intense instant of imagination, when the mind, Shelley says, is a fading coal, that which I was is that which I am and that which in possibility I may come to be. (*Ulysses* 159–60)

That sublime moment of empowerment, that "intense instant of imagination," would appear to be generated from the male poet's spiritual identification/merging with the father. Yet the comparative reference, at the beginning of the example, to "mother Dana" offers a not-so-hidden second account of the father-son equation. The fact that, for this male poet, it is the ghost of the unquiet *mother* who haunts him lends more credence to the first, if hastily revised, version of an androgyne imagination.

Despite the underlying contradictions of his paternity theory, Stephen continues to sublimate his link to the maternal by once more resurrecting the male birth metaphor for his imaginative model. As in *A Portrait*, he argues for its supremacy to female generative power: "In woman's womb word is made flesh but in the spirit of the maker all flesh that passes becomes the word that shall not pass away. This is the postcreation" (*Ulysses* 320). Claiming to experience "dread . . . in the mystery of his own body," Stephen turns the male artist's poetic production into a divine mystery rivaling the virgin birth; it is for him "a pregnancy without joy . . . a birth without pangs, a body without blemish, a belly without bigness" (*Ulysses* 168, 321). As critics R. Barrie Walkley and Suzette A. Henke suggest, Stephen invokes the couvade, a ritual in which the husband simulates his wife's experience of confinement and giving birth, as a metaphor for his own creativity. "Belonging to this turning point in society when the tie of parentage, till then recognized in maternity, was extended to take in paternity" (Walkley 57), modern anthropologists describe this custom as marking the transition between matriarchal and patriarchal societies. Stephen uses it to reassert a privileged realm of masculine discourse: "Fatherhood, in the sense of conscious begetting, is unknown to man. It is a mystical estate, an apostolic succession, from only begetter to only begotten. On that mystery and not on the madonna which the cunning Italian intellect flung to the mob of Europe the church is founded" (*Ulysses* 170). In his bizarre and increasingly desperate efforts to replace the powerful mother with a paternal power, Stephen charges that fathers and sons have been unfairly pitted against one another, "sundered by a bodily shame so steadfast that the criminal annals of the world, stained with all other incests and bestialities, hardly record its breach" (*Ulysses* 170)—presumably the taboo against father-son incest. Seeking, in effect, to subvert the Oedipus complex, Stephen rejects the theory that the son's "growth is his father's decline, his youth his father's envy, his friend his father's enemy" (*Ulysses* 170).

Nevertheless, with all these elaborate arguments about fathers and sons, Stephen cannot help wondering whether "*amor matris*, subjective and objective and objective genitive, may be the only true thing in life" (*Ulysses* 170). Unable completely to resist the identification between son and mother, male and female, he finds himself at the end of his narrative bitterly admitting that the human soul is, after all, inescapably androgynous: "The playwright who wrote the folio of this world and wrote it badly . . . is doubtless all in all in all of us, ostler and butcher, and would be bawd and cuckold too but that in the economy of heaven, foretold by Hamlet, there are no more marriages, glorified man, an androgynous angel, being a wife unto himself" (*Ulysses* 175). As a further sign of his confusion over his imaginative model, Stephen denies believing in his androgyny theory immediately after this pronouncement.

Joyce brings these alternating expressions of interest in and terror at the notion of any sort of creative androgyny to a climax in the chapter "Circe." In Stephen's nocturnal adventures in Nighttown, that long-delayed sublime confrontation between son and mother finally comes to pass. Instead of leading to an empowering influx of imaginative power, Stephen's attempt to identify with the female turns into a nightmarish fantasy of incorporation that results in Stephen's figurative murder of his mother, the ironic renunciation of his creative imagination, and his frenzied escape back into the safe world of the father.

In a moment of stubborn denial, Stephen pronounces at the beginning of the chapter that the father will save him from all these inner conflicts: "*Pater!* Free!" (*Ulysses* 466). Yet the father he imagines in the reverie, Simon Dedalus, is not exactly a *deus ex machina;* he "*swoops uncertainly through the air, wheeling, uttering cries of heartening, on strong ponderous buzzard wings*" (*Ulysses* 466). To be an artist Stephen still must confront his mother, incorporate a construction of woman into his identity. Yet May Dedalus's ghoulish figure—a product, we have seen, of her son's denial of her power and her sex—leaves Stephen "*choking with fright, remorse and horror*" (*Ulysses* 474). Calling her "Hyena" (*Ulysses* 474)—a ferocious, devouring beast mythically represented as both male and female—Stephen can only make sense of her as a hermaphroditic mutant, as opposed to a projection of the androgynous self-image he has attempted to repress.

Ultimately, Stephen chooses to forgo the sublime moment of confrontation and identification, crying to the figure(s) of woman, of mother, of hermaphrodite Hyena—"No! No! No! Break my spirit, all of you, if you can! I'll bring you all to heel!" (*Ulysses* 475). Smashing their images with his phallic walking stick, he finally kills them off and reasserts the primacy of the unadulterated male. However, refusing to merge with any construction of the female means renouncing altogether his new model of creativity, and this is precisely what Stephen does: "*Ah non, par example!* The intellectual imagination! With me all or not at all. *Non serviam!*" (*Ulysses* 475). Associating the oceanic merge with the female-androgyne with an emasculating enslavement to a not-so-liberated mother, Stephen once again postpones the sublime moment of identification and in doing so (at least for the time being) forfeits his imaginative powers. By the end of the episode we find him drunkenly reciting William Butler Yeats's early ballad "Who Goes with Fergus," a romantic, nostalgic, and conventional poem that invokes old images of the poet as mythic male hero and nature as the mystic muse whose "woven shade" he strives to "pierce." Stephen's mumbled recitation of these lines is both eerie and ironic, especially considering that he had begun his career rebelling against the inefficacy of these same tropes.

Prevented by fears of sexual engulfment and feminization from realizing an androgynous artistic subject position, Stephen thus retreats painfully back into an outdated and escapist brand of romanticism. While Joyce validates Stephen's fears about feminization as real, if culture-bound, he nevertheless exposes his protagonist's "solutions" to his crisis of authorship as bizarre and even absurd. He ironizes Stephen's retreat into Yeatsian myth, as well as his interest in the male birth metaphor. As Buck Mulligan sarcastically remarks, "Himself his own father. . . . Wait. I am big with child. I have an unborn child in my brain. Pallas Athena! A play! The play's the thing! Let me parturiate" (*Ulysses* 171). However, despite Stephen's failure to accept it, the idea of an androgyne imagination is still one Joyce wishes to explore further. In *Ulysses*, and particularly through Bloom's increasingly masochistic response to his own androgyny, Joyce finally finds a way to affirm this new creative model while at the same time critiquing and exposing the patriarchal politics that make its enactment difficult. Drawing on the work of contemporary sex theorists, this modern male artist ultimately makes clear the sources for his characters' and his own attraction to and anxiety about an androgynous model of creativity.

Diagnosed as "bisexually abnormal" by "sex-specialist" Buck Mulligan, Leopold Paula Bloom is presented in his Circean fantasy as "a finished example of the new womanly man" (*Ulysses* 402, 403). Yet while the language of anomaly parodies the sexual degeneracy theories of modern sexologists, in particular Krafft-Ebing and to some degree Ellis, Joyce also uses their rhetoric to make a more positive comment about Bloom's androgynous condition; specifically, we are told that he manifests something called "Hypsospadia" (*Ulysses* 402). While the disease sounds a lot like "hypospadia," a medical-sexual deformity that is characterized (in men) by an increased opening of the urethra on the underside of the penis that makes the external genitalia look more like a woman's, the addition of the "s" turns what might be read as a degenerate hermaphroditic condition into a transcendent and empowering one, as indicated by the term *hypsos*. As Paul Scorn points out, such an addition "strongly suggests that this combination of the masculine and feminine traits in a single individual is a higher form of human life," and that this kind of progressive "evolution" (114, 109) is what "Circe," and a large portion of *Ulysses*, is all about. I think, though, we can take the significance of this word even further, for "hypsos" is a term not only associated with height, or transcendence, it has an intertextual link as well with Longinus's treatise on the sublime, or as he calls it, "hypsos." Longinus associates the term "hypsos" with especially powerful, transportive discourse. That Joyce links it with androgyny suggests that sexual indeterminacy, not the possession of an indeterminate muse, is connected on a figurative level with heightened artistic ability.

Joyce does have a precedent for joining the potential for transcendent creative abilities with an androgynous consciousness: the same sex theory upon which much of the discussions in "Circe" are based. In a chapter rich with allusion to the work of Krafft-Ebing, Ellis, Carpenter, and Weininger, it is not surprising that Joyce builds on their universal belief that artistic aptitude is often concomitant with a kind of psychic hermaphroditism, or the "swift and constant interaction between [the mind's] masculine and feminine elements" (Carpenter 192) or "plasms" (Weininger 17) in the brain. Nevertheless, within a few moments the initial promise of Bloom's hypsospadia and its sublimity of sexual indeterminacy modulates into perhaps the most bizarre masochistic nightmare in modern fiction. Why this shift from transcendence to travesty?

Ironically, Joyce's problem lies in his creative solution. For while androgyny—which his contemporaries describe as the simultaneous coexistence of male and female cells or plasms in the brain—was believed to promote heightened sensitivity and greater artistic vision, it was also considered by some theorists (particularly, as I discussed in the first chapter, Krafft-Ebing, Ellis, and Carpenter) to be indicative of either overt or repressed homosexuality, a condition these scientists dubbed "sexual inversion." How to effect the former without the latter becomes the challenge for Joyce as a male heterosexual modernist writer. Recently, considerable attention has focused on Joyce's purported homophobia, with critics maintaining that to various degrees his "denigration of his own homoerotic energies" function as a "fundamental determinant" of his earlier narratives (Valente 169).[10] While I agree that both Stephen (in *A Portrait*) and Bloom struggle with anxieties about their gender and sexual identities, I will argue that Bloom's failure to fulfill the promise of his "hyspospadia" is due less to the nature of his "condition" than to the socially imposed directive to view that condition as a feminizing disease. In other words, Bloom's masochistic self-punishments operate as Joyce's critique not of androgyny but rather of the hierarchical sexual politics that prevent its realization in culture.[11]

In *Ulysses*, Bloom defines "metempsychosis" as "the transmigration of souls" (*Ulysses* 52). Throughout the text, he appears to harbor a not-so-hidden wish that gendered experience can be shared or even transgressed; in "Circe" that wish extends itself to the literal experience of childbirth as Bloom fantasizes about being able to give birth not just to a baby but to an entire race of "yellow and white" children (*Ulysses* 403). Yet while this womanly man craves what appears to be female experience, he "tends to fear what he most desires: woman as mother and fertile creator" (Henke, *James Joyce* 110). The tension between the attraction to and anxiety about female identification is evident early in the novel. Observing his genitals in the bath, Bloom sees "the dark tangled curls of his bush floating, floating hair of the stream around the limp father of thousands, a languid floating flower" (*Ulysses* 71). This hermaphroditic image reflects his confusion about his sexual and personal identity, as it suggests at the same time both impotence and transcendence. On the one hand, the limpness of the phallus indicates loss of masculinity and male procreative power. However, on the other hand, the fact that the penis resembles a wet "floating flower"—the flower being a traditionally positive metaphor for the female genitalia—reworks the initial symbol of impotence into one of potential luxuriant and fertile sexuality and beauty. The problem for Bloom is that he is unable to experience that latter without suffering (or at least assuming) the former.

Bloom's elaborate masochistic fantasies in "Circe" illustrate this basic anxiety that being androgynous or desiring access to a kind of bisexual shared experience comes at the cost of emasculation and social censure. Many critics have traced Bloom's reveries to his "psychic need for punishment" (Henke, *James Joyce* 113; see also Shechner) and particularly to his guilt over his transgressive sexual desires. They view the agent of his self-punishment, Bello/a, as the incarnation of the Phallic Mother to whom he must submit but ultimately overcome and subvert in order to reestablish his masculinity. Yet such readings, which tend to reduce Bloom's experience to an oedipal struggle, dehistoricize his reveries from the subtle but central social critique that Joyce makes in this chapter. This critique becomes clear if we compare in more detail Bloom's Circean visions to the text that inspired them, Leopold von Sacher-Masoch's novel, *Venus in Furs.*[12] While theorists such as Krafft-Ebing, Freud, and Ellis explain masochism as a degenerative condition characterized by "a manifestation of psychical characteristics of the feminine type transcending into pathological conditions, insofar as its determining marks are suffering and subjection to the will of others and to force" (Krafft-Ebing 211), I will argue that Joyce uses Sacher-Masoch's text to *subvert* rather than to affirm this "pathology" of effeminacy. More specifically, Joyce explores Bloom's masochism to elucidate the social and political obstacles that prevent most modern male artists from affirming an androgynous mode of creativity.

Venus in Furs is a novel within a novel that essentially showcases the "transcribed" textual confessions of a young, upper-class gentleman's masochistic experiences. Like Bloom, who thinks he is "a bit of an artist in his spare time" (*Ulysses* 533), Severin is a self-proclaimed "dilettante" who claims to suffer from an insurmountable creative blockage: "I never got far beyond the preparation, the plan, the first act, the first stanza" (*Venus* 24). Interestingly, Severin associates his dilettantism not only with his artistic failures but with his sexual repression as well; although claiming that his "shyness before women, was nothing but an excessive feeling for beauty," this self-proclaimed "suprasensual" man is in fact terrified of women and of sex, and at one point goes so far as to call himself a "great big donkey" (46, 44, 29). Preferring Greco-Roman statuary to flesh-and-blood females, Severin has admittedly "avoided all contact with the fair sex" (45) until the masochistic episode with widow-turned-dominatrix, Wanda. As for Bloom, we are told "there remained a period of 10 years, 5 months and 18 days during which carnal intercourse had been incomplete" (*Ulysses* 605); besides his onanistic experience with Gerty McDowell and post-office flirtation as Henry Flower, actual evidence of sexual activity is minimal.

In both novels, then, sexual repression and artistic failure are inextricably linked. While Severin and Bloom each fantasize about having heightened artistic abilities, whatever aesthetic sensitivities they do possess can only be channeled into their masochistic sexual fantasies. Both characters imagine being whipped, tortured, sexually humiliated, and trod underfoot by a powerful fetishized "woman." Both imagine (or experience) being treated as her slave, put under the yoke by her maidservants, obliged to help bathe her, forced to watch that beloved mistress have affairs with other men, and then being beaten, whipped, and/or humiliated by that man. Each is forced to change his dress and identity: Severin is made to wear his mistress's livery and be called "Gregor" and Bloom is coerced to wear a woman's maid outfit and be referred to as a woman or an animal. Both call their dominatrixes "Mistress!" in a suppliant and abased tone of voice; moreover, we are told that Bloom—like Severin—addressed at least one neighborhood woman (Mrs. Bellingham) as "Venus in Furs" (*Ulysses* 439, 380).

The most important thing about these experiences is that rather than truly nightmarish occurrences, they represent deep-set desires of both men. Severin insists to Wanda, "*I want to be your slave*" (*Venus* 42), while Bloom—whose desire for abasement is more unconscious—awkwardly announces to Bello/a, "Enormously I desiderate your domination" (*Ulysses* 430). Although Bloom is the only one who literally experiences a sex change, both men experience some form of emasculation. The apex of Severin's masochistic delight occurs when Wanda finally announces to him that "you must be a slave, and feel the lash, for you are not a man" (*Venus* 72). Similarly, Bloom's Bello insists: "What you longed for has come to pass. Henceforth you are unmanned and mine in earnest, a thing under a yoke. Now for your punishment frock. You will shed your male garments" (*Ulysses* 436). Why this overt desire to be "unmanned"? How does the experience of sexual humiliation affect the sexual and artistic blockages plaguing these characters?

The answers to these questions become clearer if we take a second look at Sacher-Masoch's novel. Rather than a mere exercise in erotic exhibitionism or titillation, this text puts forth a surprisingly liberal social critique. There is a moral to this story: "woman, as nature has created her and as man is at present educating her, is his enemy. She can only be his slave or his despot but *never his companion*. This she can become only when she has the same rights as he, and is his equal in education and work" (*Venus* 140). Ultimately, *Venus in Furs* is a story about the destructive effects of a patriarchal politics that is grounded in a system of sexual hierarchy.[13] In the first part of the novel, the frame narrator (an acquaintance of Severin) has a dream in which the dominatrix tells *her* side of the story: "Yes, I am *cruel*—since you take so much delight in that word—and am I not entitled to be so? Man is the one who desires, woman is the one who is desired. This is woman's entire but decisive advantage" (*Venus* 18). Placed in passive position of desire, woman is forced to use her only permissible role, that of erotic object, as a means of self-defense, thus ironically prolonging the sex-war. This sentiment is reiterated by Wanda—the widow Severin makes into his phallic mother par excellence. Yet as great as his desire for her to play this part is her reluctance to do so; indeed, the majority of the novel consists of her continued resistance to his entreaties. Desiring the "pleasure without the pain," Wanda exclaims: "You look at love, and especially women . . . as something hostile, something against which you put up a defense, even if unsuccessfully. You feel that their power over you gives you a sensation of pleasurable torture, of pungent cruelty. This is a genuinely modern point of view" (*Venus* 31). What Wanda categorizes as modern is a heightened anxiety about the status of woman, and, more particularly, an agonizing but nevertheless pleasurable wish to exchange roles with her, to be dominated and "feminized" and then to blame her for that wish.

The great irony of Sacher-Masoch's novel is that these fearsome phallic women are the creations of the men themselves. Severin is a slave less to Wanda than to a system of values that encourages male dominance and female *ressentiment*, which thus makes any efforts either toward coequal relations between the sexes or androgynous expression doomed to failure. That Severin and Bloom's masochistic fantasies become the only way they can express their artistic or creative impulses at all suggests not only that artistic inspiration is associated with androgyny but that the fear of merging with woman (sexual or otherwise) is linked to artistic blockage. Wishing to rid themselves of the paralyzing inhibitions of patriarchy, yet afraid of social censure, these "modern" men must create a scenario in which they are seemingly "unmanned" against their will, seduced by a powerful "manly" woman who simultaneously becomes the projection of their self-image, the scapegoat for their transgressive desire for that image, and the punishing agent of their self-directed guilt.

The grotesquely androgynous Bello is in many ways a distorted reflection of Bloom's sense of himself. Just as Bello is called "ma'amsir" so is Bloom referred to as "hrim" or "shis" (*Ulysses* 434, 440). Punishing Bloom for his desire to merge with her/him, Bello castigates Bloom for having transgressed traditional sex roles. Yet Bloom is put on trial not only for his sexual perversity but for "masquerading as a littérateur" (*Ulysses* 374). Mocking his artistic pretensions, Bello points to the "writingtable where we never wrote" (*Ulysses* 442). Unable to embrace his self-image, Bloom thus remains powerless to create anything, sexually or artistically.

That fetishistic masochism could reflect a deeply repressed desire to transcend or escape masculine social roles (sexual, artistic, or otherwise) is not an altogether new concept. Indeed, Gilles Deleuze argues that masochistic practice is ultimately directed toward the expulsion of the father from a man's conscious and unconscious self-identification: "*It is not a child but a father that is being beaten.* The masochist thus liberates himself in preparation for a rebirth in which the father will have no part" (58). In order to escape and expel the repressive legacy of patriarchy, the masochist attempts to construct a "New Man" by figuratively identifying himself with "the hermaphrodite" represented as the phallic mother (88, 60). In other words, "femininity is posited as lacking in nothing and placed alongside a virility suspended in disavowal" (59). The goal for the male masochist's ego is thus a kind of "resexualization [that] . . . allows it to enjoy the pleasures that the superego forbids" (113).

More recently, Marcia Ian has asserted that the phallic mother not "does not refer to women or to mothers" at all; instead, "she represents the wish for the end of contradiction and the end of ambivalence," particularly—although not exclusively—in the arena of sexuality (8, 9). As the figure of "embodied sexual nondifference," the fetishistic construction of the phallic mother becomes "an act of idealization by means of which some 'other' is endowed with transcendent wholeness, autonomy, and power the self presumably lacks" (59, 84). Interestingly, Ian argues that this project becomes a central one for early-twentieth-century male intellectuals terrified by the disruption of the old patriarchal order (164).

In the context of Joyce's aesthetics, Frances C. Restuccia utilizes these theories of the masochist to argue that "Joyce had a surplus of fathers and surrogate fathers, that their presumed authority was the problem, and that Joyce exhausted himself in attempting to subvert the law of the father/Father to achieve the pleasure of Nora, Molly, Mary, and 'Penelope'" (3). While I agree that Joyce is conflicted about his patriarchal inheritance, he is just as troubled by a response or solution that would merely reverse the sexual hierarchy. In other words, at least in *Ulysses*, Joyce exposes Bloom's fetishistic and masochistic solution as equally complicit in the patriarchal system of values from which he is trying to escape.

Joyce critiques this modern "masochistic solution" by comparing it to the transcendental experience of the sublime and exposing both modes as problematic. Although sublimity and masochism might initially appear irreconcilable, their similarities are striking. At the most obvious level, they inspire the same emotional responses. Describing his sensations, Severin repeatedly claims he "was enraptured and at the same time filled with a strange fear" by his mistress, and he often uses terms such as "tormenting bliss" (*Venus* 26, 26–27) to express the nature of his attraction to the idea of being punished or beaten by a beautiful woman. Bloom claims to "love the danger" of being close to a dominatrix, and, at least early on, he is "enthralled" by the "Magmagnificence!" of Bella/o (*Ulysses* 381, 433).

Even beyond the affective similarities between these descriptions of masochistic bondage and the commonly held emotions associated with sublime transport are the dynamic parallels between the two experiences: the perilous confrontation with an all-powerful and transcendent Other, the wish to merge with that Other, the terror of being overcome and inundated, and the pleasure associated with the knowledge that utter annihilation will not occur. Julia Kristeva, whose discussion of abjection serves equally well as a description of the masochistic urge, argues that this type of experience "is edged with the sublime" (11) because it forces the subject to make a transgressive and exciting identification with an infinitely powerful, however degraded, Other. The transportive pleasure afforded the masochist is thus "a repulsive gift that the Other, having become *alter ego*, drops so that "I" does not disappear but finds, in that sublime alienation, a forfeited existence. Hence a *jouissance* in which the subject is swallowed up but in which the Other, in return, keeps the subject from foundering by making it repugnant" (9).

The sublimity of abjection is that it allows us to inhabit two vastly different subject positions simultaneously: the one self-conscious and abased but the other transgressive and "sparkling" (Kristeva 12). In the context of the two novels we have been studying, such a strategy permits both Severin and Bloom to make androgynous identifications with their tormentors while at the same time forfeiting responsibility for their acts. In their elaborate fantasies, they essentially attempt to negotiate the narrow path between illuminating transgression and social censure.

To a degree they succeed in this endeavor; as we have seen, these sublime fantasies or scenarios lead to artistic inspiration, of sorts, for both men. When Severin succeeds in convincing Wanda to participate in his charade, this lifelong dilettante is able to write and complete a poem for her. Entitled "Venus in Furs," it is essentially a sordid version of a love lyric; it begins: "Place thy foot upon thy slave, / Oh thou, half of hell, half of dreams . . ." (*Venus* 36). One could argue that the text of "Circe," particularly the fantasies, is the one sustained exemplum of Bloom's "art" (Shechner 123). Yet this rather degraded "sublimity" is a far cry from the promise of "hypsospadia" with which "Circe" begins. As Virag suggests, "from the sublime to the ridiculous is but a step" (*Ulysses* 419). Although hungry for the experience of transcendence, Joyce is more and more suspicious of the idea of sublimity. Severin's insistence that "*It is possible to love really only that which stands above us*" (*Venus* 43) reminds us that the politics of the sublime are the politics of hierarchy, sexual and otherwise—a hierarchy that impedes complete self-expression. Even if—like Neil Hertz—we view the sublime as a pre-oedipal desire to merge with the maternal, it remains a vertical relation; for Joyce, it becomes just another form of masochism, and as such it is equally problematic.

Richard Brown suggests that Joyce read a translation of Mathilde Vaerting and Mathias Vaerting's *The Dominant Sex* shortly before completing work on *Ulysses* (in particular, "Circe") in 1922. The

Vaertings' argument is that any system of values that elevates one sex over the other creates a society which is both repressive and regressive, a culture that breeds unending cycles of seething *ressentiment* and violent revolution. It is no coincidence that Bloom's masochistic reverie begins with Bella's "patriarchal" assertion that Molly's independence can only be read as unnatural, a "petticoat government." Hierarchy and domination lead to rebellion and reversal; the cycle never ends. Joyce suggests that masochism and the sublime cannot help but participate in these patriarchal structures, and, instead, he attempts to subvert and therefore escape altogether the prison of hierarchies.

The suggestion of "Circe," then, is that whatever positive potential the trope of the androgyne imagination implies, it will never be reached as long as it is mired in the current politics of patriarchy. For Joyce, the real pathology of hypsospadia is not the "spadia," the androgynous condition, but the "hypsos," the sublime dynamic that forces the subject into a destructive cycle of transcendence and self-abasement. However, some feminist critics, most notably Sandra Gilbert and Susan Gubar, argue that rather than gesturing toward a "nobler and more vital androgyny," Joyce's "Circe" ensures that "men and women might learn the necessity for male dominant–female submissive sexual order" (Gilbert and Gubar 333, 334; see also J. Johnson 215; Henke, *James Joyce* 111). Reading Bloom's fantasies as essentially a wish that his "secret manliness may ultimately seduce and subdue insubordinate New Women" (336), Gilbert and Gubar argue that Joyce—like other male modernist writers—uses the theme of transsexuality to reaffirm patriarchal privilege. Rather than reasserting male dominance, however, Joyce seems to me to parody and curse the patriarchal system with which critics such as Gilbert and Gubar charge him to be complicit.[14] In a letter to his wife, Nora, on August 29, 1904, Joyce "cursed the system which made her [his mother] a victim" (*Letters* 48). Although Bloom's sex changes in "Circe" overtly link passivity, victimization, docility, and imbecility with the feminine, there are numerous indications in the passages that such implications are ironic. As one critic suggests, "the fact that Bloom-as-woman manifests all the negative connotations of the female role also works to accentuate the *unnaturalness* of the feminine stereotype" (Boone 77).

Comments such as Bello's mocking "with this ring I thee own" (*Ulysses* 439) offer scathing indictments of a system of bourgeois marriage that enslaves woman, a system in which Joyce refused to participate. Moreover, Bello's depictions of what accoutrements will accompany Bloom in his new feminine role further emphasize the "bondage" implicit in the social construction of femininity: "As they are now so will you be, wigged, singed, perfumesprayed, ricepowdered, with smoothshaven armpits. . . . You will be laced with cruel force into vicelike corsets of soft dove coutille with whalebone busk to the diamondtrimmed pelvis, the absolute outside edge, while your figure, plumper than when at large, will be restrained in nettight frocks, pretty two ounce petticoats and fringes and things stamped, of course, with my houseflag" (*Ulysses* 437). With its focus on modes of restraint, confinement, and ownership (branding), this description of women's clothing illustrates the extent to which even women's bodies have been reshaped, commodified, and exposed for what society accepts as a "normative" male gaze. Bello's demand that the now female Bloom "learn the smooth mincing walk on four inch Louis Quinze heels, the Grecian bend with provoking croup, the thighs fluescent, knees modestly kissing" (*Ulysses* 441) again highlights the degree to which women must not only dress but position themselves constantly so as to enhance their role as sexual objects and, more specifically, as the sexual property of men. No part of a woman's body is protected from male desire, as Bello proves when he brutally shoves his arm up Bloom's vulva and then threatens to auction her off as little more than a sexual receptacle. These passages certainly show Bloom's anxiety about being feminized, but, more important, they reveal the source of those anxieties in a system of values that associates being feminine with being a slave—sexual and otherwise.

If some critics argue that by the end of the episode "matriarchy has become patriarchy" (Walkely 65), others contend that Bloom finally succeeds in making peace with his androgyny and becoming an enlightened man "whose 'feminine' and 'masculine' traits are no longer in conflict" (Boone 80; Henke, *James Joyce* 120), even if "the vision falls short" (Boone 82) of its potential. This more utopian reading also rings false, for what strikes me most about the end of "Circe"—and the end of *Ulysses*—is how much Bloom does not change.[15] At the end of the Bello episode, Bella warns, "you'll know me the next time" (*Ulysses* 452), and indeed before the chapter is over Bloom is already caught in another masochistic reverie in which he becomes the Peeping Tom cuckold to the nocturnal escapades of Blazes and Molly. Once again, Bloom engages in behaviors directly out of *Venus in Furs:* he imagines that Molly wears a fur pelt (*Ulysses* 461), that he must bathe her (like Gregor/Severin) but be denied any sexual favors. By the end of the episode, Bloom is still enthralled and threatened by the woman as "sacred lifegiver" and has a nightmarish vision of her dark and dangerous powers: "on the altarstone Mrs. Mina Purefoy, goddess of unreason, lies, naked, fettered, a chalice resting on her swollen belly" (*Ulysses* 488, 489).

Even after "Circe," Bloom continues to be possessed by anxieties about being dominated or outdone by woman, anxieties that but thinly disguise a not-so-repressed wish to identify/merge with her. His "Utopian plans" (*Ulysses* 538), for example, include a determination to become a famous artist, most particularly a singer who would garner more admiration than his wife. While claiming to have found "instances of deficient mental development" in women, such as their "deficient appreciation of literature," Bloom nevertheless cannot help admitting that for him they possess the unequaled "power to enamour, to mortify, to invest with beauty, to render insane, to incite to and aid delinquency" (*Ulysses* 562, 583, 576).

Thus, in "Circe" Joyce still asserts the positive *potential* of an androgynous vision—of a Deleuzian New Man—while simultaneously presenting the social and political obstacles that ultimately prevent its realization. Not surprisingly, Joyce's artistic self-conception, according to his biographer Richard Ellmann, revolved around his theory that like Bloom, he was a womanly man (51). Yet what is surprising and ironic is that Joyce was also obsessed with the same kinds of masochistic fantasies that he presents in *Ulysses* as so tragically unnecessary and counterproductive. How does his complicity in the system he critiques problematize any argument for his "feminist" or at least "protofeminist" enlightenment?

In Joyce's 1909 letters to Nora, he unabashedly links his experience of artistic inspiration first and foremost with the maternal body. Being a writer involves identification with the female, in particular with the mother: "Guide me, my saint, my angel. Lead me forward. *Everything* that is noble and exalted and deep and true and moving in what I write comes, I believe, from you. O take me into your soul of souls and then I will become indeed the poet of my race. I feel this Nora, as I write it. My body soon will penetrate into yours, O that my soul could too! O that I could nestle in your womb like a child born of your flesh and blood, be fed by your blood, sleep in the warm secret gloom of your body!" (*Letters* 248). Anything but muse-like, Joyce's image of Nora in these letters is maternal and corporeal. Instead of using a phallic pen, Joyce envisages writing out of the maternal body, with maternal blood. Although at first the image is one of penetration and domination, it soon modulates into a fantasy of pre-oedipal merging with/into the (m)Other that recalls Hertz's description of a pre-oedipal sublime. Like his hero Bloom, Joyce becomes both "the childman" (*Ulysses* 606) who must (at least figuratively) return to the womb for his creative sustenance as well as the womanly man who must transcend the boundaries of single-sex consciousness in order to create. This deep-seated desire for identification and union with the mother becomes even more pronounced when Joyce describes *Dubliners* to Nora as "the child which I have carried for years and years in the womb of the imagination as you carried in your womb the children you love . . . fed it day after day out of my brain and memory" (*Letters* 308). Read alongside the previous passage we see that this is no ordinary birth metaphor, but rather it is an uncanny and transgressive attempt to write hermaphroditically.

As with Bloom, however, Joyce's ill-suppressed hunger for what can best be described as a pre-oedipal sublime experience precipitates acute oedipal anxiety. Even Joyce himself seems unable to gesture toward a kind of androgynous consciousness without engaging in masochistic fantasies of excuse and punishment. Ellmann notes that "his [James's] sense of his weakness and her [Nora's] strength persisted and grew in his mind" (287); I would argue that this dynamic becomes the means by which Joyce—like Bloom—is able to reconcile himself to his "feminine" qualities. In a letter to Nora written soon after the one (quoted above) in which he admits his desire to merge with her maternal body, Joyce writes: "I am your child as I told you and you must be severe with me, my little mother. Punish me as much as you like. I would be delighted to feel my flesh tingling under your hand. . . . I wish you would smack me or flog me even. Not in play, dear, in earnest and on my naked flesh. I wish you were strong, *strong* dear, and had a big full proud bosom and big full thighs. I would love to be whipped by you, Nora love!" (*Letters* 273).

This is only one of several letters in which he reveals his wish to be beaten by her, to "see [her] eyes blazing with anger" (*Letters* 243). Once again, the longing for a kind of pre-oedipal merging modulates into a masochistic wish to be punished for those desires. However, the pleasurable terror that such a wish evokes comes to resemble nothing less than a kind of degraded sublimity. Making Nora into his own Venus in Furs, Joyce even tells her in one letter that he wants to buy her a cap, stole, and muff in sable fur (*Letters* 254); then later he changes his mind to grey squirrel furs (258) and urges her to develop her breasts and wear black underwear. Insisting that she "study how to please [him]" (249), Joyce essentially desires her to fulfill not only the role of the sexual temptress but those of scapegoat, judge, and redeemer for transgressive carnal desires which are in fact his own.

By imagining Nora as this powerful demanding woman, Joyce is able to blame her for his transgressive desires, claiming "you seem to turn me into a beast. It was yourself, you naughty shameless girl who first led the way" (*Letters* 270). Yet almost at the same time he uses her to punish him for the desires that he finds unacceptable: "All day, since I received your letter this morning, I have felt like a mongrel dog that has received a lash across the eyes. I have . . . wandered about the streets like some filthy cur whose mistress had cut him with her whip and hunted him from her door. . . . Leave me. It is a degradation and a shame for you to live with a low wretch like me" (*Letters* 265). Finally, he makes her an agent of divine forgiveness: "You will take me now into your bosom and shelter me and perhaps pity me for my sins and follies and lead me like a child" (*Letters* 249). Joyce seems at least partially aware of the tension between these roles; in frustration he admits, "One moment I see you like a virgin or madonna the next moment I see you shameless, insolent, half naked and obscene!" (*Letters* 243). While I agree that "Joyce saw clearly that an important part of the relation between him and his wife depended upon a reversal of accepted male-female roles" (Gose, *Transformation* 12), we have seen that such a reversal is an appropriative gesture that makes Nora into the agent of Joyce's self-directed guilt. Moreover, although merging in such a way with his wife may have helped "generate a vision of a deity who would be divided and variable, in accord with Bruno's theories" (Brivic, *Joyce* 35), such an inspirational union is not nearly so idyllic or effortless to achieve and sustain.

Yet what if, as Froula suggests, "Joyce-as-Molly transforms history's nightmare, sexual difference, into fiction's dream—a wish fulfilled" ("History's Nightmare" 868)? Can we agree with Restuccia that by the end of the novel "Joyce positions himself to write bisexually, to oscillate constantly throughout *Ulysses* between the (phallic) referential and the (feminine) nonreferential and ultimately to disseminate linguistic play" ("Molly" 115)? In other words, does Joyce succeed—*at least in his text*—in ridding himself of the (patriarchal) politics of sexual hierarchy?

The answer to these questions must inevitably be "yes and no," depending upon one's definition of sexual difference. In the sense that the chapter "Penelope" represents a significant attempt by a male artist at letting the female object become a conscious subject, at supplanting the muse's face with the "woman's" voice, and at transgressing the rigid boundaries of "male" consciousness, we must accord Joyce his due. Moreover, there is significant evidence that at least part of his motivation for writing the chapter was to challenge and disrupt a literary tradition insisting on the absolute difference between men's and women's writing, between the male sex and the female.[16] However, we must also note that once again Joyce can only achieve this "ideal" state of androgynous consciousness through yet another appropriative gesture, one which is not merely intrusive but violent as well. The only way he can comfortably express his androgyny without resorting to the absurdities of masochism is to conceal himself behind a woman's skirts, to displace his voice onto a woman who once again becomes objectified. In addition, as most feminist critics point out, Joyce's portrayal of Molly is informed and suffused by assumptions about the female mind and body that originate from the patriarchal culture against which he is attempting to rebel.

Sometime in the early 1930s, Joyce told a surprised Frank Budgen that he resented "woman's invasiveness and in general her perpetual urge to usurp all the functions of the male—all save that one which is biologically pre-empted, and even on that they cast jealous and threatening eyes." He admitted, reluctantly, that "women write books and paint pictures and compose and perform music. . . . And there are others who have attained eminence in the field of scientific research. But . . . you have never heard of a woman who was the author of a complete philosophic system. No, and I don't think you ever will" (Budgen 318–19). Rather than using such comments to condemn Joyce for failing to slough off his patriarchal inheritances, we ought to view them as part of his lifelong struggle to come to terms with radical cultural change. Inhabiting a newly gendered world, he found himself in the difficult position of having to authorize and justify his personal and intellectual standing without reference to familiar sexual commonplaces. Despite all his efforts to challenge gender hierarchies, Joyce never claimed to be morally superior to his contemporaries. Based on his critique of sublimity, such a notion of transcendence would have seemed to him, one can imagine, completely farcical at best.

3

"The Perfection of the Fiery Moment"

H. D. and the Androgynous Poetics of Overmind

> I lost the early companions of my first writing period in London, you might say of my "success," small and rather specialized as it was. I was rather annoyed with the Professor in one of his volumes. He said (as I remember) that women did not creatively amount to anything or amount to much, unless they had a male counterpart or a male companion from whom they drew their inspiration. Perhaps he is right and my dream of "salting" my typewriter with the tell-tale transference symbol is further proof of his infallibility.
>
> —"Advent," H. D.

IF H. D. CANNOT seem to reconcile her respect for and frustration with her analyst Sigmund Freud, she makes at least one thing clear: being a woman and an artist means being engaged in a constant battle for authority. Torn between her creative ambitions and her desire for acceptance and connection, H. D. finds herself, even at the age of sixty-two, struggling for empowerment and recognition and plagued by a writer's anxiety, guilt, and self-doubt. Her troubled insecurity is striking considering that by this time (1948) H. D. was the accomplished author of six novels and several books of poetry, not to mention numerous unpublished manuscripts. Nevertheless, this passage from "Advent" suggests she still lacks a stable sense of herself as a woman writer and has not, as virtually all readers of her vast oeuvre have argued, emerged or begun to emerge as a confident female artist triumphantly proclaiming "the power of her own (pro)creativity" (Friedman, *Penelope's Web* 253–54).[1]

H. D.'s efforts to solidify her personal and artistic identities engaged her in a lifelong conflict not only with her own fears and doubts but with virtually every important male figure in her life. From the beginning of her professional artistic career, that famous moment in the tea room of the British Museum when Ezra Pound invented the great poet "H. D., Imagiste" with a broad scrawl at the bottom of her poem "Hermes of the Ways," H. D. found herself surrounded by literary and intellectual men who supported her work but nevertheless challenged her sense of artistic independence and authority.[2] Like Freud, who believes—according to H. D. in the epigraph to this chapter—that it is the phallus, not the womb, that can add the life-giving, enhancing, semen-like "salt" to art, her male literary contemporaries left her troubled about her personal and professional identity, and, most particularly, about her creative powers. That H. D., in this same passage, connects the memory of her painful abandonment by two men who "seemed to like [her] writing" ("Advent" 149)—Richard Aldington and D. H. Lawrence—with a muted but visible rebellion against Freud's insistence that a female artist cannot stand alone betrays her intense ambivalence about her need for the support and guidance of these and other male "initiators" (*Compassionate* 35). In this rare moment, H. D. allows herself to challenge the powerful intellectual men in her life and admits to the frustration and anguish their engagement with her career has engendered. In the following pages, I will examine her anxiety-ridden response to this crisis of authorship and, more specifically, her attempts to claim artistic authority and self-worth without either alienating the (male) literary establishment that promoted her or sacrificing her female self.

Rachel Blau DuPlessis calls H. D.'s troubled attraction to the men in her life "romantic thralldom," a "transfixed attention to heterosexual romance" (*Writing Beyond* 66, 67) from which she constantly struggled to free herself. While it is true that H. D. wrote a considerable amount about her personal and professional relationships with men, that which enthralls her has much more to do with her desire for the power and recognition they offered than with any kind of romantic or sexual addiction. In one of her first works of autobiographical fiction, *Asphodel* (1921–1922), H. D.'s artist-heroine laments, "Women can't speak and clever women don't have children. So if a clever woman does speak, she must be mad. She is mad" (113). Unable to reconcile her creativity and intelligence with her womanhood, Hermione is on the verge of the abyss until she remembers her poet-husband (a character based on H. D.'s real-life husband, Richard Aldington). Admitting that it was he who "had given her words and the ability to cope with words, to write words" (*Asphodel* 114), H. D.'s protagonist reveals her dependence not upon her husband's body but upon the specifically artistic authority that he grants her.[3] Although she later tries to deny it, Hermione cannot completely quell the inner certainty that "men could mar or make her" (162).

That Hermione experiences such a contingent existence as both agonizing and humiliating is made painfully clear by her identification with Joan of Arc: "They had trapped her, a girl who was a boy and they would always do that. They would always trap them, bash their heads like broken flowers from their stalks, break them for seeing things, having 'visions' seeing things like she did and like Fayne Rabb. This was the warning" (*Asphodel* 9). The images of bashed and broken heads suggest that Hermione has, like Joan, martyred herself to remain true to her visionary powers. Yet what is particularly interesting about this modern woman's interest in the fifteenth-century French saint is not only her identification with the latter's suffering but with her androgyny. Splitting herself in two, H. D.'s protagonist (and, ultimately, H. D.) imagines herself as both female and male, as "a girl who was a boy." Despite the fact that it comes at the cost of social and cultural alienation, persecution, and—as we shall see later—a cloudy sense of her identity as a woman, Hermione's androgynous identification offers the possibility of heightened creativity and spiritual power.

For H. D., the link between androgyny and creative or artistic empowerment extended well beyond the Joan of Arc legend. Ironically, sexual indeterminacy—which threatened to make H. D. a prisoner of her male peers—also held the potential key to her liberation from them. While patriarchal prejudices against the transgression of sex roles were still very much a part of early-twentieth-century culture, modern scientists—as we have already seen—were beginning to paint a more attractive picture of androgyny. Not only did the vast majority of researchers (including Freud) believe in the inherent bisexual nature of human beings, a few even went as far as Otto Weininger, who, as we saw in the introduction to this study, postulated the existence of gendered cells in the body and a universally "permanent bisexual condition" (7).[4] A common denominator among these new theories of gender differentiation was the hypothesis that sexuality had a function beyond the reproductive, that of "furthering the higher mental and emotional processes" (Morris 107)—most notably, the artistic. As we saw in chapter 1, the most well-known proponent of this concept in Britain was Havelock Ellis, a close friend of H. D.'s and whose oeuvre, *Studies in the Psychology of Sex*, she read between 1915 and 1920. Like many of his contemporaries, Ellis noted that heightened creative abilities were characteristic of the sexual invert (or homosexual), who as a "psychic hermaphrodite" mirrors most closely the androgynous condition of the child. Considering herself to be both androgynous and bisexual, H. D. found in Ellis's discussions a potential solution to her "anxiety of authorship" (Gilbert and Gubar, *Madwoman* 49). In providing her with fresh and more fluid models of gender as well as a new vocabulary with which to describe them, Ellis's inquiries into the relations between sexuality and creativity helped H. D. transform her androgynous self-conception into an empowering aesthetics. Not only does she assume a gender-neutral name, she will also attempt (at least figuratively) to incorporate a construction of "the male" within herself, to represent her imagination as an androgynous and empowering union of sexual opposites.

H. D.'s first significant effort to reconceptualize her creativity was made between 1919 and 1920. Suffering from severe psychic stress after the stillbirth of her first child, her husband's series of extramarital affairs, her brief affair with Cecil Grey which resulted in an unplanned pregnancy, the deaths of her father and brother, and a case of Spanish influenza that nearly killed her and her unborn child, H. D. was on the brink of total mental collapse. It is at this moment of utter exhaustion, alienation, and powerlessness that she sets forth her boldest claims about her art and her powers as an artist. In the Scilly Isles and in Corfu in July 1919 and the spring of 1920, while on a trip to recuperate from her illness and losses, H. D. had a series of visionary experiences which led her to envision and describe an androgynous "state of transcendental imagination" ("Advent" 182) that she believed would restore and empower her, and which she would painfully attempt to recapture in her autobiographical fiction.

Called *Notes on Thought and Vision*, H. D.'s lyrical and personal manifesto begins with a declaration of the three states of consciousness—body, mind, and "over-mind" (later referred to as sub-conscious, conscious, and over-conscious minds)—and argues that the "aim of men and women of highest development is equilibrium, balance, growth of the three at once" (17). Yet it is soon clear that the over-mind is what most interests the author, for "the realization of this over-conscious world is the concern of the artist" (40). A kind of super-imagination, it is described by H. D. as a "cap, like water, transparent, fluid yet with definite body, contained in a definite space . . . like a closed sea-plant, jelly-fish or anemone" (18–19). However, it can also be located in the "love region of the body . . . or placed like a foetus" (19). The overmind thus promotes two kinds of "sight," or "knowing"—that of the womb and that of the brain—both of which, according to H. D., are "equally important" (20, 21). Ultimately, she argues, one must use both "lenses . . . [to] bring the world of vision into consciousness" (23).

Although some of the imagery H. D. uses is grounded in the female body, this is not, as some critics maintain, a truly gynocentric model of creativity.[5] Representing the overmind as something which must be appropriated, put on like a hat or fertilized like a human egg, H. D. suggests that rather than being self-generated this heightened state of consciousness is something separate from her (female) body, or at least something that depends upon an external agent to activate. Moreover, of the two sites of this superconsciousness, mental and genital, H. D. insists that the brain is most necessary for the creation of art—"there is no way of arriving at the over-mind, except through the intellect"—and goes on to argue that "most of the so-called artists of today have lost the use of their brain" (21), not their womb or "love region," as one might expect from someone advocating an aesthetic grounded solely in a uniquely female anatomy. Although H. D. does assert that she became most aware of this elevated level of consciousness while pregnant, she claims that the experience was centered in her brain (an organ she does share with men), not her womb (20); further, she declares that different people will find their overminds in different ways, and even gives examples of three male "artists"—the Galilean (a Jesus-like figure), Leonardo, and the Chinese poet, Lo-Fu—who engage it through moments of erotic epiphany (47).

What does seem crucial to the visionary experience of overmind is that it mirrors the experience of erotic union. However, this union is forged between psychic not physical entities. Recapitulating Plato's *Symposium* almost verbatim, H. D. explains that as "the minds of the two lovers merge, interact in sympathy of thought . . . the brain, inflamed and excited by this interchange of ideas, takes on its character of over-mind" (22). But what is most interesting about her paradigm is that the love sensation is not directed outward but rather inward to the self—the two "lovers" are masculine and feminine parts of the same psyche; while H. D. observes that the erotics of overmind may be initiated by gazing at the statue of the Charioteer of Delphi, or an apple branch, or the body of a young Greek boy, these are "impersonal" objects that become "a means of approach to something else . . . as a means of approach to ecstasy" (47, 45). That something else takes place within the self as the body "casts off the spirit, a concentrated essence, not itself, but made, in a sense, created by itself" (51). H. D. elucidates: "But as it takes a man and woman to create another life, so it takes these two forms of seed, one in the head and one in the body to make a new spiritual birth. . . . They are really two flecks of protoplasm and when we are 'born again,' we begin not as a child but as the very first germs that grow into a child" (50). In this metaphor, H. D. represents the self as an androgynous composite of a "masculine" intellect and "feminine" body and represents the overmind, or transcendental imagination, in terms of a confrontation between rarified male and female elements that recall Weininger's gendered plasms.

This confrontation has for H. D. an unusually transformative effect. As Albert Gelpi points out in the preface to *Notes*, "the impulse behind 'Notes' is to account for those mysterious moments in which the polarities seemed to fall away, or—more accurately—to find their contradictions lifted and subsumed into a gestalt that illuminated the crosspatch of the past and released her to the chances of the future" (12). What Gelpi calls a gestalt experience—that moment "in which the polarities seemed to fall away"—can better be described in terms of the sublime. For behind the idealistic eroticism of H. D.'s overmind model is an intense, almost Nietzschean, will to power, a thinly repressed wish for the authority to "bring power and irresistible might to bear, and reign supreme over every hearer" (Longinus 76). While other critics, most notably Susan Stanford Friedman, Cassandra Laity, and Eileen Gregory, have identified H. D.'s interest in androgyny and the androgynous artist,[6] none have responded to the intense undercurrent of power-lust that accompanies these images; looking more closely at the language H. D. uses to describe this experience—the overmind, overconsciousness—we can see that her objective is not simply to move beyond gender difference. Using the language of hypsos, height, and transcendence, she wants to construct or imagine an imagination that can burst upward through blockages, transgress boundaries, and authorize itself by "over"coming the paralyzing power of literary fathers such as Pound, Freud, Aldington, and Lawrence by incorporating it within herself, by creating an "over"mind and joining it to her womb. Achieving the sublime state of overmind is neither easy nor safe; H. D. admits that "the swing from normal consciousness to abnormal consciousness is accompanied by grinding discomfort of mental agony" (19), and she later warns that "it is very dangerous" to reach beyond, to venture out of the "dull little houses" of our minds (41, 40).

Nevertheless, H. D. insists that once achieved, this act would open possibilities which are not merely empowering but world-changing: "Two or three people, with healthy bodies and the right sort of receiving brains, could turn the whole tide of human thought, could direct lightning flashes of electric power to slash across and destroy the world of dead, murky thought" (*Notes* 27). To use Longinus's words, such "sublimity flashing forth at the right moment scatters everything before it like a thunderbolt" (76). Ultimately, the androgynous dynamics of overmind lead H. D. to identify with nothing less than the godhead; the last line of *Notes*—"Christ and his father, or as the Eleusinian mystic would have said, his mother, were one" (53)—makes it clear that the fusion of male and female leads to the power of the divine.

When the exhilarated H. D. finished *Notes on Thought and Vision*, she gave a copy to her friend Havelock Ellis. This would seem a natural choice given Ellis's interest in the connection between sexual and artistic characteristics. Contrary to her expectations, however, Ellis hated the book. His rejection continued to trouble H. D. for years afterward; she refers more than once in her personal papers to her "disappointment in Havelock Ellis," the man she admits to having deified into "a saint as well as a savant" ("Advent" 147). Crestfallen, she writes: "I thought he would be so interested. But he appeared unsympathetic, or else did not understand or else may have thought it was a danger signal" ("Advent" 130). While H. D. does not expressly state what Ellis would have found so "dangerous" about her book, she seems to suggest that it has something to do with her defiant and transgressive assertion of sexual and artistic empowerment. Just as she links her abandonment by mentors Aldington and Lawrence to Freud's comment about the absurdity of the female artist trying to stand alone (in this chapter's opening epigraph), so does she associate Ellis's rebuff with the excess of her ambition.

Thus while *Notes on Thought and Vision* is a dizzying text, full of energy and enthusiasm that would seem to provide H. D. with unlimited access to the overmind, its reception leaves her once again feeling deflated and defeated, tied to the opinions of a male authority figure. Again and again her efforts to authorize herself will lead to the realization that her strategy for empowerment is dangerous, for internalizing this male "principle" reinforces her feelings of intellectual and physical failure as a woman. Increasingly unable to escape this crisis of artistic identity, H. D.—as we will soon see in our discussion of her novels—finds that what was supposed to result in the freeing up of her creativity has led to the imprisonment, punishment, and devaluation of the woman within. Putting on the "cap" of the overmind soon starts to feel like putting on a straitjacket; rather than assimilating it, her body starts rejecting the "jelly-fish consciousness" as it might a false limb.

Ultimately, this new blockage has to do with what Henry Hart describes as the central limitation of the sublime experience: "the newly empowered bystander seems to have subverted the hierarchical relations that once trapped him, but his revolutionary act is a delusion, an example of what Freud called 'the omnipotence of thought' or 'wish fulfillment'" (497). Promising the complete reversal or at least full equalization of the power dynamic between the self and the all-encompassing Other, the sublime masquerades as the ultimate aesthetic of empowerment. However, the perceived victory of the mind is at best only temporary; as Longinus points out, the sublime experience enables us for a brief moment to feel "as if" we have produced what we heard. In psychoanalytic terms, we feel "as if" we have subverted, conquered the infinitely powerful Father, but not for long. At the end of his famous essay, Longinus argues that the perverse social, psychological, and political situation of his times effectively cancelled the possibility for prolonged connection with such greatness; Kant would later argue that the experience of the sublime rested in the nearly instantaneous moment at which human reason succeeds in apprehending the infinitude that has surpassed the power of the imagination to describe. By its definition, the sublime consists in a transitory and, ultimately, impalpable experience of transcendence that invariably leads the subject to the disillusionment and despair of lost vision.

When the subject is female, the emotional cost of such efforts are even more dramatic and painful. For if "the sublime is a genre the woman writer needs" (Yaeger 192), it is also one which for her is most difficult to achieve and most agonizing and traumatic to forfeit. The reason is that the sublime experience, which psychoanalytic critics have described in terms of the oedipal confrontation between the father and the son who seeks to usurp him, alienates and excludes the woman. Edmund Burke, one of the earliest theorists of the sublime, argues that the experience differs from that of the beautiful by virtue of its emphasis on "terror" over "love," and power over "weakness" (100). Throughout his *Philosophical Enquiry*, Burke associates the beautiful with the "feminine partiality" (101) and, by implication, the sublime with the masculine. The problem with this, as Joanne Feit Diehl points out, is that "if authority is associated with the patriarch, then the woman poet cannot so easily experience the identity between self and all-powerful other" (*Women Poets* 3) that the moment of sublimity entails.[7] Thus, while both male and female writers who seek out the sublime experience risk the wrath of the father they wish to surmount, the woman's transgressive act of overreaching makes her femaleness vulnerable to incorporation by the patriarchal force with which she attempts to identify. In other words, figuratively merging with the father means the possibility of losing a stable sense of her identity as a woman. Even if she does manage to survive the initial confrontation, her sublime victory does not and cannot last; in order to sustain it, she must go through this most transgressive and nearly impossible act over and over again as she faces more and more symbolic "fathers," all the while fearing greater and greater repercussions to her selfhood. Not surprisingly, many women writers who quest the sublime find themselves feeling hollow and empty, experiencing brief moments of empowerment only to fall into the morass of self-alienation, confusion, and despair (Yaeger 201). H. D. more often than not ends up feeling like a freak when she tries to merge "masculine" and "feminine" aspects of consciousness; all too often her female self is what ends up getting sacrificed and repressed.[8] As a result, H. D. often feels alienated both from contemporary culture and her own body. For despite her will to power, "nothing . . . changes the external structures of society that initiated [her] interior conflicts" (Friedman, *Penelope's Web* 251).

In the following analysis of H. D.'s failed efforts to regain the empowering overmind of *Notes on Thought and Vision*, I will focus primarily on a representative selection of H. D.'s prose works because they most directly and fully explicate and confront these personal and artistic struggles. That H. D. chose to publish only a few of her novels and novellas in her lifetime suggests that they divulged more about herself than she was willing to share. As H. D. wrote in *Tribute to Freud*, "Yes, the poems are satisfactory but unlike most poets of my acquaintance (I have known many) I am no longer interested in a poem once it is written, projected, or materialized. There is a feeling that it is only a part of myself there" (149). Despite the fact that she claims her prose works reveal a whole or united self, that whole is always on the verge of falling apart. Rather than leading toward sublime unification, her novels indicate a consciousness split into more and more fragments. That explosion of selfhood is expressed most graphically by the myriads of characters she invents to represent herself in her autobiographical works of fiction. From the seemingly endless string of pseudonymns she uses as her signature (H. D., John Helforth, Rhoda Peter, Alex Dvorat, D. A. Hill, Delia Alton, Helga Dart, Helga Doorn) to the appellations she assigns her self-modeled heroines (Hermione, Hedyle, Raymonde Ransome, Midget, Julia, Natalia, Helen), Hilda Doolittle is unable to locate a singular, human identity. In a short piece called "H.D. by Delia Alton" (1949–1950), the narrator, yet another mask for H. D., argues that these various personae "all are, the same woman . . . seeking, as one woman, fragments of the Eternal Lover" (181). Recalling the Egyptian myth of Isis and Osiris and, implicitly, H. D.'s troubled sense of her androgynous selfhood, Delia Alton explains that her female heroines must redeem "not so much the fragments of Osiris, as of his sister, twin or double, the drowned or submerged Isis" (182). Although she argues that both halves are equally important, social and cultural pressures have made women's female side the most shadowed and repressed. Despite this confident claim, however, the message of nearly all of H. D.'s novels is precisely that the "lost Isis" remains missing, an ironic casualty of the sublime dynamics by which she seeks to free herself.

H. D.'s most complete autobiographical novel, *HERmione* (1926–1927), dramatically outlines the sexual and artistic conflicts that plague her throughout her career. In its equivocal ending, this narrative vividly foreshadows the psychic and artistic agony of works such as "Murex" (the central chapter in *Palimpsest*), "Narthex," *Kora and Ka*, and *Nights*, texts to which we will turn later. Unpublished until after her death, *HERmione* condenses the events of H. D.'s life between 1906 and 1911—among them her failure at Bryn Mawr, engagement to Ezra Pound, and love affair with Frances Gregg—into a nine-month gestational period that never quite results in the unqualified spiritual birth described in *Notes*. Exploring her feelings of alienation, frustration, and confusion about her sexuality and identity, this roman à clef focuses on its heroine's problematic relationships with her distant father, frustrated mother, overbearing fiancé, and transgressive female lover in the context of their disastrous effects on her writer's self-consciousness.

The novel opens with young Hermione already feeling alienated from her femaleness as a result of her creative and intellectual ambitions. Whirling about in the backyard as she tries desperately "to hold on to something" (3), presumably to stabilize her identity, she "crie[s] in her dementia, 'I am Her, Her, Her,'" (3). But who is "she"? A tall, literary girl who feels she "was a disappointment to her father, an odd duckling to her mother, an importunate overgrown, unincarnated entity that had no place here" (10). Viewing a domestic existence abhorrent and suffocating, she vows to "get away from Eugenia sitting in the dark like a great moth" (80); yet her coldly scientific, intellectual father has no sympathies for her creative talent. Here is a girl who adores her mother, finds in her "more power than textbooks, than geometry" (89). As H. D. later wrote of her own mother in *End to Torment* (1958), "the mother is the Muse, the Creator, and in my case especially, as my mother's name was Helen" (41). Yet at the same time, as we will see in the last chapter of this study, she is also like Mrs. Ramsay in Woolf's *To the Lighthouse*, a threat to the emergent artist-daughter's sense of identity in her acceptance of repressive cultural norms. Unable completely to reject the mother whose patriarchally inscribed domestic role she despises, Hermione has a hard time finding the inner strength and license to create.

Being a woman, in the cultural sense, is thus incompatible with creative confidence. However, unlike the artist-hero Stephen Dedalus, this modern artist-heroine cannot even try to escape the repressive destiny that her mother has modeled for her by an easy identification with the father (Friedman, *Penelope's Web* 113). Alienated from and oblivious to his daughter, Carl Gart can only lament that "Hermione has some odd way of seeing . . . she had failed him" (100). Rather than leading her to epiphanies of spiritual vision, he reacts to her entreaties by peering more directly through the narrow lense of his microscope, leaving Hermione feeling "defeated" (100). The other man in Hermione's life, George Lowndes (a representation of Ezra Pound), while seductively interested in the workings of her imagination, is finally dismissive as well. Characteristically, he sees not Her (Hermione) but "her" (objectified female). Wanting "a Her that he called decorative" (172)—a muse, not a colleague or partner—George is always threatening to leave Hermione "smudged out" (73).

To him she "was Dian or Diana, never Artemis. To George, she was the Queen of Love, never white Aphrodite" (172–73). Realizing that she "can't be called Lowndes" (112) and still call herself an artist (here figured as the almost sexless "white" version of the love goddess), Hermione painfully recognizes that in place of the talented Arachne her lover sees a sensual wood nymph, "Dryad," or a voiceless little mermaid, "Undine" (190)—or in real life, the derivative student—"Imagiste" with initials "H. D." Soon even she loses track of who she is—is she Hermione out of Shakespeare's *The Winter's Tale*, or "the word AUM," a mantra from the *Mahabharata*, or a "Tree" (32, 70)?

Hermione's self-defeating connection with her mother and her self-effacing connections with men result in a heightened sense of self-dislocation that inhibits her attempts at poetic production by destabilizing her sense of identity and authority. Trying to escape from the repressive maternal and paternal influences that she compares to the dual horrors of Scylla and Charbydis, Hermione often experiences a paralyzing vertigo of consciousness and loss of vision. Seeking to prevent herself from being "broken like a nut between two rocks" (81), Hermione comes up with a strategy that is almost as dangerous as the repression from which she is seeking to escape. In desperation, she contemplates the possibility of directly confronting, rather than evading, the powerful patriarchal forces—incarnated by her mother and father—that threaten to destroy her creativity: "She wanted to see through reaches of sea-wall, push on through transparencies. She wanted to get away, yet to be merged eventually with the thing she so loathed. She did not struggle toward escape of the essential" (7). Already linked in the text to "a biological-mathematical definition of the universe, a world known to her as Pennsylvania" (6), the "thing she so loathed" represents her astronomer-father, Carl Gart, and patriarchal repression. That Carl has come to represent far more to her than a biological parent is suggested by her description of him as an enticing but threatening force: "'Father' was a run forward, a plunge backward; that thing had now no visible embodiment" (16). In the "sea-wall" passage just quoted, Hermione associates imaginative vision precisely with the merging of that inhibiting paternal factor with her female self. To put it another way, she imagines here the generation of creative vision through her sublime confrontation with the father whom she both admires and fears.

Hermione's meditations on her emergent creative consciousness soon begin to sound a lot like the experience of overmind H. D. depicts so vividly in *Notes.* At one point Hermione explains, "Some plants, some small water creatures give a sort of jellyfish sort of birth by breaking apart, by separating themselves from themselves" (118). She describes her creative mind as an "amoeba giving itself another amoeba, a sort of birth, a sort of twin repeating itself" (120). This moment of twinning suggests again that the overmind or sublime imagination is a separate consciousness which becomes powerful precisely when it is no longer connected to her original (female) self. Envisaging a creative mind or consciousness independent of her female body, Hermione attempts to escape her vulnerability to patriarchal demands. Although George patronizingly labels as "rot" her attempts to recreate herself, Hermione refuses to "sell this inheritance . . . of amoeba little jellyfish sort of living creature separating from another creature (120). Resisting his attempts to silence her, to turn her into the voiceless Undine, Hermione resolves that she "shall have a new name" (119), shall transcend her aesthetic and psychic blockage by constructing an imaginative self that incorporates the perceived power of the other gender.

My reading of *HERmione* challenges the standard interpretation, put forth by Friedman, DuPlessis, and others, that it is the lesbian subplot of the novel, and not the gestures toward an androgynous overmind, that allows H. D. to escape her paralyzing anxieties over her self-conception as woman and artist.[9] These scholars read the unconventional, exotic Fayne Rabb (Frances Gregg—H. D.'s first female lover) as representative of an alternative female community in which Hermione's (and, ultimately, H. D.'s) creative self could be recognized and accepted. Hermione does at first bond with Fayne in a way which suggests that their relationship permits her to resurrect her "lost Isis" or strong female component: "I am Her. She is Her. Knowing her, I know Her. She is some amplification of myself like amoeba giving birth, by breaking off, to amoeba. I am a sort of mother, a sort of sister to Her" (158). Hermione describes her attraction to Fayne as thus a kind of positive self-love; she exclaims "I love—I love Her, only Her, Her, Her" (170), recognizing the part of herself that George nearly succeeded in smudging out. By virtue of psychic sisterhood, they have a kind of "concentric intimacy" (164) that sanctions Her to surmount for a time her sense of this violation; throughout the narrative, passages from Swinburne's poem "Itylus" (179)—about the rape of one sister and the other sister's killing of her son in revenge—surface, often amidst the dialogue between Her and Fayne. As Cassandra Laity proposes, the sisterly association of this intertextual link—which is sustained through much of the novel—helps allow Hermione (H. D.) to free herself from the patriarchal politics of George Lowndes (Pound). Indeed, while George sees Hermione and Fayne's attraction as narcissistic, H. D. represents it as an important means toward self-recovery. Love for Fayne allows her to protect herself: "I will not have Her hurt. She is Her. I am Her. Her is Fayne. Fayne is Her. I will not let them hurt HER" (181). The association between Hermione and Fayne is not only sisterly, however. The fact that Hermione names Fayne (and implicitly herself) Itylus in the text (181), as Cassandra Laity argues (*H. D.* 37), transforms a purely female or lesbian aesthetic into a much more androgynous one by transgressing the gender boundaries of both subjects.[10] Hermione has already described Fayne as a kind of amoeba-like, protoplasmic twin; that she is figured also as a boy implies the dual, ambiguous sexual nature of Hermione's self-definition.

Even if we ignore this complication in the gendering of Hermione and Fayne's relationship, evidence that H. D. here successfully evokes a female-centered model of creativity wanes as Fayne's female loyalty (as well as her potential for inspiring her imagination) soon begins to look feigned, or at least ambiguous, when Hermione discovers that, like Frances Gregg, the flesh-and-blood Fayne has had an affair with George. Once again, about to be "defeated" by the same old patriarchal plot, Hermione finds herself on the brink of total mental collapse. However, she finally transcends her despair by appropriating the repressive element, incorporating it within her psyche and transcending her aesthetic blockage. On a snowy walk, Hermione begins at last to anticipate her writer's vocation, and she comes to a kind of victory through her experience of a sublime moment: "Last summer the Creator had been white lightning brandished against blackness. Now the creator was Her's feet, narrow black crayon across the winter whiteness. . . . She trailed feet across a space of immaculate clarity, leaving her wavering hieroglyph as upon white parchment"

(223–24). This lightning, previously associated in the text with Hermione's mother (90), the whims of American culture (101), and the same George that would efface her, had seemed only to illuminate the factors leading to the void within herself. Yet here Hermione turns her own nothingness into positive power; black smudge becomes magic symbol—poetic feet—writing against what now becomes the white void of the blank page. At the nadir of emotional and aesthetic blockage she begins to make her mark by appropriating and then repressing the "suffocating" (83) power of patriarchy (symbolized as the lightning) and, for a moment at least, the hierarchies are reversed, sublimity and transcendence are possible. In order to complete this experience, to push away a final moment of visionary blockage, Hermione does call up the image of Fayne; it is important to note that this time, however, the image Hermione chooses to summon is not that of the real-life femme fatale but of the imagined androgyne. Hermione finds herself at the brink of overmind consciousness but at first cannot find access:

> The stars are shining all of them, but I can't see any. She felt like a star invisible in daylight. Then her thought widened and the tension snapped as swiftly. It's like a violin string. It's like Fayne exactly.
>
> When she said Fayne a white hand took Her. Her was held like a star invisible in daylight that suddenly by some shift adjustment of phosphorescent values comes quite clear. Her saw Her as a star shining white against winter daylight. (225)

Although once again identifying with Fayne, here Hermione represses the body of the warm sexual woman in order to link Fayne's image with a whiteness that both Laity and Gregory identify as a code for androgyny and late-Victorian male homoeroticism that H. D. appropriated from decadent writers such as Swinburne and Pater.[11] The catalyst for H. D.'s sublime moment of creativity (here figured as the resonance of a "violin string") involves a "shift adjustment" in her artistic self-image, an identification with the figurative white hand of an androgyne imagination.

Yet, as in most of H. D.'s texts, this potentially sublime moment of becoming ends up leaving her not only psychically deflated but alienated from her female body. For just when it appears we will leave Hermione "at one with herself, with the world, with all outer circumstance" (234), the next—and last—line of the novel consists of Hermione's servant announcing the return of the irresistible Fayne. Rather than the imagined "Her" or Fayne-as-Itylus whose white androgynous body provides Hermione visionary access, this visitor is clearly the real, living, female body of a duplicitous sexual rival now transgressively occupying Hermione's "little workroom" (234) without the poet-worker's permission. That H. D. abruptly ends the novel here, omitting Hermione's response to the news of Fayne's return, implies its ambivalent effect upon her protagonist's newfound personal and artistic self-confidence. Thus, despite her importance in initiating the reassertion of Her's essential female identity, the part of her that George "doesn't know" (84), the flesh-and-blood Fayne's insistence on and privileging of her womanhood proves to be extremely troublesome for Hermione. For while on the one hand Fayne's sexual license with George seems like a betrayal, on the other hand, her flirtation and seduction reminds Hermione of the cost of her androgynous model of creativity: her alienation from her female body and female desires. A haunting presence, Fayne Rabb as femme fatale reappears in many more of H. D.'s novels in various guises as the one who "could jab through war-battered, none too reliable intellectual armour" (*Usual Star* 84).[12] While Laity asserts that H. D.'s "inscriptions of the fatal woman articulate a specific phenomenon of some lesbian relationships that too closely replicate the mother-daughter bond" ("Introduction" xxv), the texts suggest that Fayne's "fatal" effect is to expose the repressiveness of H. D.'s model of creativity. Forcing her female friends to remember their bodies and desires, Fayne is portrayed as a "spiritual gynecologist" who mercilessly "rip[s] souls from bodies" ("Narthex" 231) in an effort to reconnect them at a more earthly level. Susan Friedman points to the way H. D. represents this figure as one who "tampers," "blights," and "withers" her "spiritual flowering" ("Narthex" 231) by privileging the "feminine" realm of the body (*Penelope's Web* 262). Yet if H. D. and her heroines often rail against this "Hellenistic monster" with "the instinct of a Harpy" ("Narthex" 231), they nevertheless cannot silence her or the voice of the physical, sexual woman whom she represents. As the heroine of "Narthex" reluctantly admits, the voice of these so-called fatal women "wouldn't be negated" (282).

Fayne's is not the only female voice to challenge H. D.'s sublime strategies for artistic empowerment. Just as *HERmione* ends with Fayne's troubling arrival, *Paint It To-Day* (one of *HERmione*'s companion novels) concludes with the appearance of Althea, who represents Winnifred Bryher, H. D.'s friend and lover for nearly forty years. While Fayne criticizes Hermione's alienation from her body, Althea warns Midget—the aptly named, vulnerable H. D. character in this novel—about becoming too alienated from the "visible world" (81), fearing that her friend has become too lost in those nebulous "poetic isles" and Artemesian mysteries of her imagination. Yet just as Fayne's insistent sexuality threatens painfully to destroy Hermione's androgynous self-image, so Althea's pragmatic presence leaves Midget feeling "defeated" (87). Rather than the jubilant homoerotic vision that critics have labeled it, the dream of the goddess Brindel that ends *Paint It To-Day* seems to me an ambivalent one: "She is one with the white future. She says, 'I do not like Midget's arguments but Althea's.' She is one with the past, trailing purple and vanity and despair and tragedy and dirth. She is one with the small people with hummingbird claws that are so hard for me to realize. She understands and explains them to me" (89). In its simplistic repetition of sentence structure, this vision sounds more like the forced rehearsal of a catechism, like a statement of a new and self-deprecating initiate than that of a confident and enthusiastic believer. Like Hermione (and H. D.), Midget shows herself assaulted from both sides; in attempting to prevent the male artistic establishment from silencing her poetic voice, Midget adopts an imaginative model—that of the androgynous overmind—that draws criticism from the female community upon which she depends for emotional support.

In her efforts to resolve this dilemma, H. D. attempts to metamorphose the two most important women in her life into a single image of the androgynous self she has tried over and over again to envision and embody. Calling Frances Gregg "Katherine" and Bryher "Gareth," she transforms their disapproving and inhibiting presences into inspirational, self-reflecting ones: "Katherine, Gareth, they were two antique coin sides, Katherine one side, towered head, some Asiatic goddess, many breasted, something monstrous that yet holds authenticity, Gareth the other side, boy Emperor, slightly undershot little chin that gave a baby frailty to the hard clear profile, clear line of profile, short hair and boy-turn of chin and that frightening intensity; power, power and that tyrannical forceful head-line somehow negated by the child chin . . . of some pre-Byzantine emperor, authentic but late, late Greek" ("Narthex" 262). In these powerful descriptions, H. D. turns both visions of womanhood that her friends represent into caricatures—one of unbridled, perverse, Medusan sexuality; one of repressive, tyrannical intellectualism. Yet the passage emphasizes the authenticity of these figures, despite their distastefulness. Moreover, by making them literally two sides of the same coin, H. D. attempts the reconciliation of these sexual and intellectual representations of womanhood. At one point later in the novel, Raymonde comments that "we're not three separate people. We're just one" ("Narthex" 273)—suggesting that these coin sides represent disparate parts of her androgynous self.

Yet no matter how hard she tries, H. D. never remains comfortable for long with her sexual or artistic identities. Twinship becomes a trap: is she man or woman or freak? "You give your soul to one thing, you can't give to another. Yet is this true? She had given herself to abstraction, little crystal boxes, she had given her soul to loss of identity, a snail outside an aquarium sort of window. Soul putting out feelers was lost without crystal boxes to confine it . . . soul shut in crystal boxes too long and too deliberately is in psychic danger" ("Narthex" 282). Representative of the world of the mind, the crystal boxes are both enticing and repressive. On the one hand, to give herself completely over to her creative impulses means "loss of identity." To live for the imagination is, for this woman writer, to repress her female body. Yet at the same time, on the other hand, "soul putting out feelers was lost without crystal boxes"; in other words, to resist the construction of some kind of authorized artistic space within her consciousness means psychic death as well. H. D.'s challenge thus becomes how to explore her imagination without becoming its prisoner.[13]

By the early 1930s, H. D. has become so anxious about her ability to negotiate the treacherous path between competing abysses of her creative model that she starts conceptualizing her artistic imagination as a separate entity that she can "put on" and "take off" whenever necessary. Among the most troubled of H. D.'s works, the Raymonde Ransome series—which includes "Murex" "Narthex," *Mire-Mare*, and *The Usual Star*—concerns an H. D. character, now herself a recognized writer, who is consumed by painful memories of her failed marriage, her stillborn child, and her growing sense of alienation from the workings of her imagination. Although her real name is Raymonde Ransome, she has an alter ego, or writer-identity, as well: "Beyond Raymonde there was another Raymonde. She called it Ray Bart" ("Murex" 149). More than just a pen name, however, Ray is an androgynous, individual presence, a third-sexed alter ego that functions, parasitically, as her imagination; when she wants to be inspired, she invites it to possess her consciousness. Yet the price of Ray's success is Raymonde's insecurity and failure; unable to feel empowered as a woman, she must create a super-self that only serves to increase her personal sense of alienation from her readership. Raymonde explains: "People called her Ray Bart, to distinguish the things she wrote from the things they found wanting in her. Ray Bart, on many occasions, sufficed to jerk back Raymonde" (*Usual Star* 73). In these novels, success as an artist reminds the protagonist—a thinly veiled mask for H. D. herself—of her own insecurity and inferiority as a woman. Making the transition from the woman Raymonde Ransome to the artist Ray Bart is agonizing, and, as we shall see, it is often not worth the cost of those fewer and fewer sublime moments of overmind.

We first meet Raymonde Ransome in "Murex," of *Palimpsest*. Events in "Murex" take place in postwar London and concern Raymonde's coming to terms with the stillbirth of her child and the extramarital affairs of her former husband. Terribly insecure about her woman's body and its generative powers, Raymonde recalls her failed pregnancy as a creative failure as well; rather than a perfect being, she has birthed "a beautiful little—body" (111). In contrast to the fragility and vulnerability of Raymonde, the creative entity Ray Bart is fierce, hard, and invincible—much like the images in the verses s/he creates: "Raymonde's double . . . the poet, the young spearman who was Raymonde's genius. Ray Bart held a sword of pure steel" (127). Significantly, Raymonde genders her poet-self predominantly masculine (although the names Raymonde and Ray both remain ambiguously androgynous), a strategy which appears to guarantee its/his empowering authority.

In keeping with my argument that H. D.'s androgynous model of the overmind is becoming increasingly difficult to recapitulate in practice, the transition from Raymonde to Ray—essentially the transition from female self to the sublimity of the poetic self—is excruciating and even dangerous. Reluctant to leave her protective, self-effacing "ghost world" (138) for the world of electrifying vision, Raymonde at first resists the "devastating spiritual passion" (128) of Ray's art. Only by painfully forcing herself can "the icy glamour of the thing she knew was Ray Bart's helmet [close] above her" (148); only then will she approach the enlightened vision of overmind she earlier described in *Notes*. Rather than liberating and soothing, however, this militant, hardened version of the "jellyfish consciousness" metamorphoses into a helmet or cap that does not seem to fit her: it "bit and scalded into Raymonde's forehead but it must be borne" (150). At one point Raymonde describes it as "a small painful grub that sank deep and gnawed into one's forehead and burrowed painfully deeper," a parasite that threatens to take her over and ultimately has to "be prodded out like some festering splinter" (149). Her character's stoic masochism underscores the agonizing dichotomy between H. D.'s woman and artist selves; forced to sacrifice the former to achieve the latter, Raymonde finds that writing becomes a kind of self-mutilation, a self-torture, and, at moments, she considers giving up her artistic project altogether.[14]

Nevertheless, Raymonde finally convinces herself that "one must take up a standard, take up a banner, take up an attitude" (136) in order to be recognized and heard, even if it means sublimating a large part of one's identity. For despite the fact that imagining this androgyne imagination or overmind is becoming more and more painful and "tiresome" (150), it seems to be the only way she can authorize her creativity. The few moments when Raymonde does succeed in assuming Ray's helmet, she is able to experience sublime moments of vision that open her potential for outdoing, overcoming, and transcending the paralyzing influence of the male artistic establishment:

"Perceptions like lightning and lightning flash of bird-wings flashing up, up, up to the sun of inspiration. Banalities were the real facts. Fortunes in tea leaves. James Joyce (she had found that the advance-guard of the intellectuals was usually on the right track) was in her inmost searching mind, repudiated" (171). The irony in this passage is that up until this point, and even at the beginning of this paragraph, Raymonde has continually been asserting that "Joyce was right" (157) in his belief that the most ordinary, mundane object or situation can serve as the site of transcendent epiphany. Despite the obvious fact that Raymonde continues to subscribe to this theory, she, nevertheless, makes a point of repudiating her artistic dependence upon the man who originated it.

This moment in "Murex" is pivotal because it is one of the few times in H. D.'s fiction that the sublime overmind model actually works. Raymonde's experience of aesthetic blockage is followed first by identification with the power of the paternal predecessor, or in this case the literary rival, then, more important, by an appropriation of his power and an accompanying sensation of the brilliant "lightning flash" of sublimity. Becoming Ray Bart, the personification of Raymonde's androgynous overmind, allows her to equal and remain independent of Joyce or any other of her male literary peers. Figuring her imagination as androgynous leads to a murex (160)—essentially, a hidden underwater stash—of creative "treasures" that help Raymonde to generate multiple epiphanies of vision. The rest of the narrative of "Murex" consists of her sustained creative effort of composing an actual poem.

Although Raymonde would seem to have triumphed, the fact that she presents the verses of her completed poem as the song of the male Greek oracle Helios, "who was competent to deal with a broken pencil, [and] whose laws held inviolate over the merest dust heap" (151), suggests that she has relatively little confidence in her own, broken female voice. Like the rest of the pieces in the Raymonde Ransome series, "Murex" emphasizes the painful process of constructing an imagination that works; always at risk is the destruction of the feeling woman underneath.[15] "Raymonde still with the drift and obliteration of her past three months in London didn't want so to repudiate herself. Maybe Ray Bart the poet was a flaming white sword of the spirit. But who wants white swords nowadays and who wants spirit?" ("Murex" 128). Tired of "repudiat[ing] herself," of sublimating her femaleness to the merciless demands of her art, Raymonde soon begins to lose faith in her project. Frustrated and self-hating, she finds that "writing was no inspiration . . . it was pages and pages and sometimes one got out of oneself because one wrote" ("Narthex" 266). Rather than blessing her like a divine visitation, Raymonde's creative genius soon comes to threaten her like a "plague" ("Murex" 150).

While appropriating the perceived power of her "masculine" intellect is often a difficult and painful task in the Raymonde Ransome series, H. D.'s artist protagonist does experience some sublime moments of empowerment at the end of each work. At least Raymonde and Ray Bart inhabit the same body. But in two later novels, *Kora and Ka* (1930) and *Nights* (1931–1934), H. D. splits these two sides of herself—woman and artist—into two different people. Gendering her artist-self male, she describes "his" systematic psychological destruction of the fragile female companion (Friedman, *Penelope's Web* 270) or subject. At a deeper level, she depicts the failure of her over-mind model to prevent her female identity from being overpowered and erased. Unable to reconcile her "masculine" and "feminine" halves, H. D. essentially kills the latter off, sacrificing not only her femaleness but her precarious psychic stability in a simultaneously murderous and suicidal effort to capture, if only for a moment, the transformative power of the sublime. What is particularly important about these two texts is that unlike H. D.'s earlier novels, they do not even attempt to entertain the possibility of a successful female artist. Instead, they reveal a woman writer guiltily but inescapably complicit in her own victimization.

In *Kora and Ka*, a shell-shocked war vet named John Helforth and his lover Kora are both writers and are both perilously close to madness. Similar to the characters in the 1930 film in which H. D. starred under the direction of Kenneth McPherson, these are "borderline social cases, not out of life, not in life" (*Borderline* 5). Like H. D., both have undergone severe war trauma—Helforth has lost his two older brothers in the war; Kora is separated from her two children and has been abandoned by her husband—and are utterly alienated from themselves, society, and each other. With them resides the enigmatic entity, Ka. Like the overmind or Ray Bart, Ka represents the visionary potential of the imagination. Unlike these earlier imaginative models, however, Ka is an externalized, palpable presence with a strong and independent will of its own that narrates the first section of the novel. A kind of spiritual double, Ka exists as a shadow or shared soul between Kora and Helforth, although it is more connected with the male character; periodically Helforth's "eyes will go blank, staring straight in at the light and mine [Ka's] will see" (11).

Being possessed by Ka is even more dangerous than putting on Ray Bart's helmet. Manipulative and tyrannical, it rules its host with utter abandon: "Ka weeps, waits for attention and then must be put to sleep like any tired infant . . . [but] like most infants, is never really tired. Ka wears me to a shred" (26). The jellyfish consciousness of *Notes* has become a dirty parasite that has contaminated consciousness; at times, Helforth wants to "let red flares eat out my mind, red Verey light shall burn up Ka who is a jelly fish, who is a microbe, who is (a specialist all but told me) a disease" (28–29). Yet for this malady there is no cure, even from "this new sort of analysis stuff" (40). Indeed, Helforth experiences the androgyne imagination as torture, not triumph: "Who gave me this broken duality? Who gave me this curse of intimate perception? I curse Ka" (29). This sense of "broken duality"—the imperfect, painful combination of "masculine" and "feminine" within the consciousness—becomes even more poignant when one considers Helforth's similarity to H. D.'s female artist characters, such as Raymonde Ransome, and ultimately, of course, to H. D. herself.[16]

Yet what about the woman, Kora? At one point, Helforth suggests that "Kora is everything. Without Kora, Ka would have got me. Sometimes I call Kora, Ka, or reverse the process and call Ka, Kora. I am on familiar terms with Kora, with Ka, likewise. We are, it is evident, some triple alliance, primordial Three-in-One. I am Kora, Kora is Helforth and Ka is shared between us. Though she repudiates affiliation with Ka, and refuses to discuss it, yet the fact remains. Ka is Kora, Kora is Ka. The waif must be shared between us" (26). This linguistic substitutability or consubstantiality—at least for Helforth—supports the theory that Kora, Ka, and Helforth are all aspects of the same being whose psychic and creative health is predicated on the delicate balance of opposites contained within it. Yet it is important to note that the connection, as described by the male component, depends upon female sacrifice. Despite Kora's obvious discomfort with Ka, Helforth demands the she continue to protect him from the destructive force of this ego-incorporating, parasitic creature, even, presumably, at the cost of her psychic well-being. Susan Friedman's observation that "the three represent a psychic ménage à trois . . . that echoes Aristophanes's myth of the Androgyne" (*Penelope's Web* 268) seems to me an over-optimistic reading. Unlike Plato's theory in the *Symposium*, which postulates a transcendently balanced androgynous being, the psychic entity that is Kora, Helforth, and Ka is anything but stable. For one thing, one of the components—the female aspect—is significantly weaker than the others and is the one most easily sacrificed.

Kora's reluctance to participate in this strange trinity underscores the violence of Helforth's attempts to appropriate her into his artistic consciousness; if we assume that Helforth is also a mask for H. D.'s artist self, Kora's lament echoes H. D.'s guilt about repressing the woman within. Viewing Helforth's aesthetics as more banal escapism than divine visitation, Kora scoffs, "isn't your over-world as you call it, simply substitution . . . for this world?" (40). Like Althea in *Paint It To-Day*, who warns against too much mysticism, Kora views Ka as a kind of trauma-induced neurosis or disease, reminding Helforth "conclusively, that the war is over" (41). However, when Kora's reproaches become too strident, H. D. shuts her up and essentially kills her off. This novel ends with "Helforth's rebirth, not Kora's . . . the 'masculine' side is restored to speech and sanity, while the 'feminine' side remains unreconciled and mad" (Friedman, *Penelope's Web* 270).

Helforth finally achieves some psychic balance by willingly appropriating Ka for himself, effectively destroying Kora's significance to him in the process: "Ka, it appeared however, still belongs to Helforth, his personal little dragon; it seemed, with the assistance of this personal little pest, that I could see around and, as it were, through walls and into tree-trunks" (52). His "over-mind or other-mind or other-world experience" (40), once claimed and tamed, becomes a useful and empowering tool. That H. D. manages to channel her own "personal little dragon of war-terror" (*Tribute* 94) into creative vision suggests that she too is complicit in Kora's demise. Discarded once she threatens to silence Helforth's and ultimately H. D.'s androgynous vision, by the end of the narrative Kora "has gone to bits" (49), collapsed like "a drowned girl from the water" (47). The novel concludes with Helforth's transcendent visionary experiences—he sees the Holy Grail and the androgynous image of a Kore-Persephone—and boasts in the last line of the novel that "We were Kora of the Underworld and Dionysus, not yet risen. . . . Now we are Kore and the slain God . . . risen" (54). Dionysus was—like Osiris—torn to bits, then restored as a deity. But the irony once again is that while this Osiris is reassembled, made whole, his Isis essentially remains unresurrected, in pieces, subsumed within the male figure as part of himself, the "Kore," or male youth. *Kora and Ka* does emphasize the importance of the androgyne imagination to the creative process, but more than any other of H. D.'s novels it shows the terrible cost to the woman writer behind the text, a cost so terrifying that in her next novel she ends up a suicide.

In this later work, *Nights*, the conflicts of *Kora and Ka* are transferred from the psychic to the sexual sphere. Narrated almost exclusively from the bed in which the sexual encounters that inform the text occur—a "tomb; womb" (71) obliterating consciousness—this manuscript records with diary-like intimacy the ultimate destruction of its author, Natalia Saunderson. Abandoned by her husband, Neil (loosely based on Kenneth McPherson), Natalia is living with her former female lover, Renne (Bryher), and is having an affair with a new lover, David. Increasingly, however, sex is no longer either generative or pleasurable for her; instead, she frequently resorts to masturbation in an effort "to get out of [her] body" (64), to deny her vulnerability and her femaleness, imagining "herself only a sexless wire that was one wire for the fulfillment. She was sexless, being one chord, drawn out, waiting the high-powered rush of the electric fervor. It crept up the left side, she held it, timed it, let it gather momentum, let it gather force; it escaped her above the hip-bone, spread, slightly weakened, up the back-bone; at the nape, it broke, distilled radium into the head but did not burst out of the hair. She wanted the electric power to run on through her, then out, unimpeded by her mind" (51). Here, the androgynous experience of overmind, the cap of jellyfish consciousness, can only be initiated through an onanistic act. While it does bring Natalia "nearer than she had ever been to the source of this power" (52), its potential remains unfulfilled, blocked by fear and guilt. Wondering whether "all her fervor, after all, [was] an illicit escape" (53), Natalia voices H. D.'s concern that the erotics of overmind are only a degraded form of autoeroticism and not a transcendent experience after all. Leaving her "not so much healed as shocked back, re-vivified, for fresh suffering" (53), her masturbatory experiments prompt Natalia to return to the suffocating bed of her lover David as a kind of masochistic punishment for her perceived transgressions.

For returning to David means returning to a power struggle that she knows she will lose. Like the failed sublimity of her overmind model, this sexual merging results in the annihilation of the female host when the man supplants her energy and power with his: "She would lie in his arms, die, be so blotted into darkness. His lips would open her mouth, breathing the darkness that was sleep, that was oblivion; his rooted-stalk would push down. Those other lips would be penetrated by the slow poison of that beating earth-flower, down and down, into her drugged body. He would break anew a wound, work into a cauterized wound, to renew and re-create. He would work into her, fertilize, invoke that flower" (65). Rather than energizing or life affirming, this is "rape out of stone-age" (74). Her passive, drugged body is the clay into which he plants, renews, and reaffirms himself; in the process, however, his "earth-flower" poisons the soil upon which it grows. Like Kora, Natalia is left "in so many pieces" (72), "dynamited to bits" (73), while the man is reborn, empowered. Rather than a productive merging of male and female which, however frightening, results in the sublimity of heightened vision for the woman artist, this union does not go beyond "the unfulfillment and the terror" (65). Instead of stimulating Natalia, David's "kiss was death" (79): "Personality was a thing that didn't matter. The first time she had said that, she had thought, 'David will break between us and make him-me, a fissure or a chasm.' There was no chasm in this . . . her mind went out, out" (72). There is no Ka here to preserve the delicate balance of opposites, no androgynous "him-me," just a complete evaporation of identity as she is flooded and subsumed by his sexuality.

Ironically, Natalia's only positive sexual experience with David occurs at the moment of his sexual failure; after he ejaculates prematurely, she suddenly masters her fear and tentatively begins to be more aggressive sexually—a response that shocks her lover. Because David is unable to sustain his erection, Natalia is able to experience the fusion without the engulfment, and at least for a few seconds draw strength from that precarious balance of masculine and feminine between them. She is able to use him as "the bridge" (87)—the approach to ecstasy; she for a moment escapes from the paralyzing cycle of self-annihilation: "she didn't, now, want David. . . . She could explain it, as she had that other time, say, 'you excite me and, after you left, I excited myself more.' But she didn't want to explain it. She must get away, must lie alone, must get away . . . she wanted to be a parallel, running to infinity and never touching that twin other line. She wanted David there. But she must be free" (89–90). Envisioning the masculine and feminine elements as parallel rather than intersecting lines is safe, but it infinitely postpones any real transformative union with the Other. Finding refuge from the agonies of the body and sexuality in her geometrical abstractions, Natalia finds some peace but no real fulfillment.

Regardless of its empowering or saving potential, Natalia's new strategy does not last for long. A postcard from her estranged husband announcing his return draws Natalia back into the bedroom, renews all her anxieties about being subsumed, "smudged out," incorporated by male desire. Recalling how "her humanity had been shattered" (99) by Neil's rejection, she becomes more and more "troubled" (104) by his return and finally concludes that "the dream is greater than reality" (88), looking to the still frozen waters "to draw her—out—" (106). Natalia drowns herself, leaving only a borrowed watch, a muff, and a manuscript behind her. In her twelve-night sexual odyssey, fusion with the masculine and feminine ends not with an influx of strength but rather with self-annihilation.

Yet while this energizing duality eludes Natalia in her narrative, it comes close to being realized in H. D.'s novel, which prefaces her heroine's tale with the commentary of a rather unremarkable male author-critic, ironically named John Helforth. Unlike the hysterical war veteran of *Kora and Ka*, however, this Helforth is a "reader, travelling-salesman, and general under-paid, overworked utility man, to a publishing firm of semi-popular scientific brochures" (5–6). Hoping one day to "be rich enough to write a sort of second-rate best seller" (7), Helforth's critical acumen is questionable. Although he claims to be an expert on psychoanalysis (he says he has worked with the famous "Dr. Frank" of Vienna), his "power of psychoanalytic dissection" (23) is somewhat overstated. Impressed by the luminous quality of Natalia's writing, he nevertheless finds it too mysterious, too dark, too ephemeral to comprehend, decrying that "she wouldn't project herself, materialize herself, for any sort of public" (24). Admitting that when Natalia was alive he "never took her seriously, and didn't really like her" (15–16), Helforth finds her narrative "too terribly, too blazingly true, to be quite bearable" (21–22); like the sublime moment, "every line seemed to bleed fire. Or ice. Ice and fire" (21). While Helforth's comments about Natalia's art are mostly naive, they are occasionally on target. Sensing the anguish and the pain behind the prose, it is he who recognizes and reports the truth about Natalia's feelings about her art: "she didn't get any fun out of her writing, any more than we may have said to have got any fun out of our separate infernos or inquisitions of analysis" (10).

Could H. D.—as the third "author" of the narrative—exist as a more positive Ka that unites Helforth and Natalia? Certainly the frame narrative liberates the text from the spiraling subjectivity of the suicide; it creates an androgynous space (between male and female speakers) that reaches beyond the individual narratives. Yet if the structure of the novel achieves any victory, it is at best an ambivalent one, as this unity between male and female only occurs after the female is dead. Unable to keep their Isis, or female, identity from being sacrificed to what is increasingly envisioned as a "masculine" intellect, or a writer's consciousness, H. D.'s writer-heroines fail to work through their author's crisis of authority. Stripped of its potential for transcendence, the sublimity of overmind becomes all terror; as H. D. remarked, "the 'glasses' of *Nights* are very dark" (*Compassionate* 82).

In the early 1930s, H. D. had an experience that some critics—chief among them, Rachel Blau DuPlessis and Susan Stanford Friedman—argue did much to unblock this creative impasse: her analysis with Sigmund Freud. By allowing H. D. to "link her bisexuality to her creativity—both to its block and to its flowering" (Friedman, *Penelope's Web* 310; see also DuPlessis, *H.D.* 83), Freud was able, these scholars claim, to alleviate much of her sexual and artistic insecurity.[17] In many ways, Freud's theory that all humans are inherently bisexual, at least in the beginning stages of development, did prove liberating for H. D. In a now-famous letter to Bryher, she wrote: "I have gone terribly deep with papa. He says 'you had two things to hide, one that you were a girl, the other that you were a boy.' It appears I am that all-but-extinct phenomena, the perfect bi— . . . it seems the conflict consists partly that what I write commits me—to one sex, or to the other, I no longer HIDE" (letter to Bryher, November 24, 1934). The term "perfect bi—" recalls H. D.'s conception of the androgyne imagination—one that had begun to lose much of its transcendent potential after *Notes.* However, while Freud's acceptance of her bisexuality helped ease her anxieties about her split nature, it did little to alleviate her anxiety of authorship, of creative authority. If anything, H. D.'s relationship with the "Professor" served more to underscore her own sense that power—physical, intellectual, or artistic—was a masculine privilege.

This more problematic message was directed at H. D. even before she walked into Freud's office. Having complained to Hanns Sachs that she was convinced that her then-analyst, Mary Chadwick of Bloomsbury, "could not follow the workings of [her] creative mind," she was told "it would be better to continue the work, if possible with a man and preferably one superior to myself" ("Advent" 150). From the beginning, then, the dynamics of the relationship between H. D. and Freud involved a hierarchy based not only on expertise but on gender as well. Moreover, when H. D. does go to see the professor, his diagnosis is essentially that she desires a kind of power that is forbidden and unnatural to a woman. Having failed to transfer her sexual desires to her (distant) father ("Advent" 175), H. D., said Freud, was still obsessed with latent pre-oedipal longings for her mother, and she was hiding a secret wish to be a boy. We know from the epigraph at the start of this chapter that in his effort to explain and diffuse what he saw as her unresolved penis-envy, this "blameless physician" makes a point of showing her his statuette of Athena: "'She is perfect,' he said, 'only she has lost her spear'" (*Tribute* 69). As Norman Holland suggests, the intended message of Freud's comment is that woman is perfect only when she recognizes and accepts her castration, and reconciles herself to her female position. By subtly emphasizing woman's inferiority to man, her powerlessness, Freud perpetuates H. D.'s fears that authority (artistic and otherwise) is inherently a masculine province; if we recall the epigraph opening this chapter, according to Freud it is the phallic, not the feminine, that adds the empowering "salt" to art. In *Tribute*, H. D. does attempt to ignore the true import of the "spear" story, choosing to read the statue of Athene as the prized and triumphant "wingless victory" of Athens; later, when Freud's supposedly temperamental dog nuzzles against her, H. D. thinks to herself about the power of her intuition, and allows herself to admit, for a second, that "the Professor was not always right" (98).[18]

Almost all major critics of H. D.'s oeuvre have argued that such moments mark the beginning of the triumphant emergence of H. D. as a confident woman writer, free of the artistic identity crisis that had plagued her throughout her career. In "The Master," a poem she wrote during her analysis but which she refused to publish at the time, H. D. does express a much deeper rebellion against this powerful man "beyond all-men" (1. 44), and she admits, "I was angry with the old man / with his talk of the man-strength. . . . I could not accept it" (l. 17–18). Seeming "to disregard the prescriptions for 'normal' femininity implicit in Freud's general theory of female development" (Friedman, *Psyche Reborn* 135), H. D. argues in the poem that woman is "herself perfect" (l. 43).

Yet despite this evidence for H. D.'s ability to challenge—at least privately—the more repressive aspects of Freud's theories about women, I stop short of arguing that the "gift of the Primal Mother that Freud had given (back to) her" ultimately allowed H. D. to let "the Mother/Muse figures inspire and authorize" (Friedman, *Penelope's Web* 326, 327) her work. The "mother" Freud leads H. D. to recapture does little to erase her anxieties about her authority as a woman writer because Freud layers all their discussions of motherhood and femininity with not-so-subtle assertions of sexual hierarchy. One of the most blatant of these is his reaction to H. D.'s confession that she had begun to feel maternal transference toward him (letter to Bryher, March 10, 1933). Although transference was an important part of Freud's analytical method, he reacts to this admission almost as if insulted, admitting "'I do not like to be the mother in transference—it always surprises and shocks me a little. I feel so very masculine'" ("Advent" 147). Femininity or female-identification, while recommended for H. D., is portrayed as degrading, even disempowering for the male.

It is thus not surprising that while H. D.'s later novels and poem sequences are somewhat bolder and more articulate in their expression of her artistic ambitions and desires, they are still very much invested in efforts to appropriate that "masculine" power, to experience the sublimity of an androgynous overmind rather than in developing a truly gynocentric model of creativity. Despite occasional bursts of self-confidence, these texts continue to be anxious, nervous, and even apologetic at times, particularly with regard to those same male "initiators" that have haunted and rejected her. Although touted by many critics as a triumphant assertion of newfound selfhood,[19] *Bid Me to Live* is in many ways as troubled as *HERmione*. Begun in 1918 but rewritten over a number of years following her analysis with Freud (1939–1950), this novel confronts once again H. D.'s war experience, particularly her relationships with Aldington (Rafe), Grey (Vane), and D. H. Lawrence (Rico), and in it she struggles unsuccessfully to reconcile herself with their attitudes about her body and her oeuvre.

Although the book revisits her abandonment by Aldington and her affair with Grey, it is Lawrence who becomes the major focus of H. D.'s musings about yet another one of her male "initiators." During and immediately after the First World War, Lawrence and H. D. maintained a close relationship; she even harbored him and his wife in her home after they were accused of spying for the Germans. Yet while she deeply admired his genius, his vocal assertions about the relationship between sex and art—as well as his representation of women in much of his fiction—deeply troubled and confused her. Most critics have read *Bid Me to Live* as a response to two of Lawrence's particularly misogynist texts: *St. Mawr* and *Aaron's Rod*. However, of all his writings, H. D. "particularly disliked and distrusted his books on the unconscious" (*Compassionate* 50), books which did everything to reinforce her own anxieties about her authority and ambition as a woman writer.

The most strident of these works is Lawrence's *Fantasia of the Unconscious* (1921–1922). A brief look at its major themes will illustrate why H. D. found it especially threatening to her androgynous self-conception. For unlike H. D., Lawrence is rabidly determined "to keep the sexes pure" (188) from the concept of gender mutability, insisting that "Every single cell in every male child is male, and every single cell in every female child is female. The talk about a third sex, or about the indeterminate sex, is just to pervert the issue" (96). Deeply disturbed by the conclusions of sex theorists such as Ellis and Carpenter, Lawrence interprets the modern breakdown of gender divisions as a problematic feminization of culture and loss of male dominance. Bemoaning the fact that "man has assumed the gentle, all-sympathetic role, and woman has become the energetic party, with the authority in her hands" (97), he preaches a return to more conventional delineations between the sexes. Because of changes in the social and cultural landscape, Lawrence argues, modern man "begins to imagine he really is half female. And certainly woman seems very male. So the hermaphrodite fallacy revives again. But it is all a fallacy. Man, in the midst of all his effeminacy, is still male and nothing but male. And woman, though she harangue in Parliament or patrol the streets with a helmet on her head, is still completely female" (100). Blaming all this gender confusion first and foremost on "a dynamic spiritual incest" between mothers and sons which results in the perversion of the male sex, Lawrence asserts that the remedy for "the actual state of affairs to day, when the poles are reversed between the sexes" (141) is for men to "drive her [woman] back to her own true mode. Rip all her nice superimposed modern-woman and wonderful-creature garb off her. Reduce her once more to a naked Eve, and send the apple flying" (191).

Lawrence's ardent protests betray more than a fearful misogyny. The fact that he so adamantly decries the reality of gender indeterminacy, the existence of a "third sex," suggests not only its prominence in cultural debate but also his ambivalence about his sexuality. Nevertheless, Lawrence's comments, like Freud's theories of sexual development, proved extremely destructive for H. D. In *Bid Me to Live,* she refers to a real-life conversation she had with Lawrence about her plans to write a new poem: "Rico could write elaborately on the woman mood, describe women to their marrow in his writing; but if she turned round, wrote the Orpheus part of her Orpheus-Eurydice sequence, he snapped back, 'Stick to the woman-consciousness, it is the intuitive woman-mood that matters'" (62). While this passage reveals Lawrence's dependence upon some form of "woman-consciousness" for his creativity, it also graphically underscores the double standard imposed on H. D. as a female artist, the underlying assumption of the male's superior intellectual powers. Although she rebels enough to expose their conversation in her novel, the real-life H. D. ended up writing only the "Eurydice" portion of the poem sequence she had envisioned.

It is not surprising that H. D. "could not swallow D. H. L. whole, after studying Sigmund Freud and reading the Fantasia" (*Compassionate* 59). In *Bid Me to Live,* the heroine Julia ultimately comes to this conclusion: "What did Rico matter with his blood-stream, his sex-fixations, his man-is-man, woman-is-woman? That was not true. This mood, this realm of consciousness was sexless, or all sex, it was child-consciousness, it was heaven" (62). In this passage, H. D. returns to her conviction, first expressed in *Notes on Thought and Vision,* that both male and female writers are creatively bisexual and can approach imaginative pursuits from both gender perspectives. By now, however, this H. D.–surrogate realizes that women have a far greater stake in the concept of the androgynous vision than do men:

> Why this vaunted business of experience, of sex-emotion and understandings that they made so much of? It might be all right for men, but for women, any woman, there was a biological catch and taken at any angle, danger. You dived up and were an old maid, danger. You drifted into the affable hausfrau, danger. You let her rip and had operations in Paris (Poor Bella), danger.
>
> There was one loophole, one might be an artist. Then the danger met the danger, the woman was man-woman, the man

> was woman-man. But Frederico, for all his acceptance of her verses, had shouted his man-is-man, his woman-is-woman, at her; his shrill peacock-cry sounded a love-cry, death-cry for their generation. (135–36)

Interestingly, H. D. portrays art as woman's only possible escape from the paralyzing demands of sex consciousness, her only possible freedom from a culturally imposed biological destiny. Again, she hopes that by assuming this androgyne imagination she can achieve a kind of empowerment that is denied to the woman-as-woman. Yet H. D.'s frustrated musings admit the failure of her efforts to transform the power structure within the artistic world. Like Freud and Pound, Lawrence patronizingly "accepts" her verses while continuing to proclaim and reassert old sexual hierarchies.

At one point near the end of the novel, Julia (once again) does seem to come close to realizing the empowering sublimity she has sought so desperately. Realizing that "something had to come of this, of this war" (141–42), she finds herself walking alone in a strangely sublime landscape: "The whole place was out of the world, a country of rock and steep cliff and sea-gulls" (144). Exhilarated by the scene, Julia imagines she is "Medea of some blessed incarnation, a witch with power. A wise-woman. She was seer, see-er" (146). Rescuing her from the abyss, the power of the Overmind asserts itself so that "every breath she drew was charged with meaning. . . . She was filled literally now with that divine Spirit, as remote, as beautified as a Yogi in a mountain temple. . . . If her mind had lowered its vibration, its mood, to the mere mechanical act of thinking, she would have understood the symbolism of manna falling from heaven" (147). To this experience Julia attaches the term "*gloire*," which recalls an expression Lawrence used to describe moments of heightened beauty and power in poems such as "Gloire de Dijon," "Glory," and "Lord's Prayer." Appropriating this symbol of the male artist's authority, H. D. attempts to create a sublime moment extended through time:

> Perhaps you would say I was trespassing, couldn't see both sides, as you said of my Orpheus. I could be Eurydice in character, you said, but woman-is-woman and I couldn't be both. The gloire is both.

> No, that spoils it; it is both and neither. It is simply myself sitting here, this time propped up in bed, scribbling in a notebook, with a candle at my elbow.
>
> The child is the *gloire* before it is born. The circle of the candle on my notebook is the *gloire*, the story isn't born yet.
>
> While I live in the unborn story, I am in the *gloire*. (176–77)

The bed, which in *Nights* was the site of her annihilation, becomes the nexus of psychosexual self-renewal when Julia shares it with her pen. Like the "very first germs that grow into a child" (*Notes* 50) which are simultaneously female and male, the *gloire* of Julia's artistic inspiration (which she asserts above is both and neither female and male) is connected to an archetypal sexual unity. Although H. D. did not read much of Carl Jung's work, she became fascinated by the mystical writings of Robert Ambelain and Jean Chaboseau, which "all posited the primal existence of a divine One, a latent androgynous Whole" (Friedman, *Psyche Reborn* 179).

Unlike the terrified, self-hating Raymonde Ransome or the suicidal Natalia Saunderson, Julia "hugged her old coat tight, hugging herself tight, rejoicing in herself, butterfly in cocoon" (151). Yet her moment of rejoicing, of self-realization, does not last long. When Julia returns from her solitary walk, back to the house of her cold and distant lover, Vane, back to the memories of rejection and abandonment by Rafe (Aldington) and Rico (Lawrence), she experiences a huge deflation of ego. Picking up a pad and paper, she begins a letter to Rico in which she tries to explain her avoidance: "I thought I was someone but he [Vane/Grey] calls me *Personne*, Nobody. I am nobody when it comes to writing novels. But I will find a new name. I will be someone. I will write these notes and rewrite them till they come true. Maybe you haven't tuberculosis. [paragraph break] I don't mean the T.B. would make any difference to me. Only, I am susceptible, would catch something. I would catch your mannerisms, your style of writing, your style of thinking, even" (176). That Julia compares Rico's genius, as well as his paralyzing assertions about women and art, to an infectious disease suggests the degree to which she is still vulnerable to expressions of patriarchal power; even the idea of seeing him becomes more pressure than she can stand. More than anything, Julia fears Rico's censure, his disapprobation, his dismissal: "You might be angry with me. You might shrivel my hope" (176). Thus the paradox: to achieve the moments of sublimity that would empower her, Julia must confront the father figure, yet to do so is also to risk the utter obliteration of her selfhood. Although determined to pursue her artistic vocation, Julia still cannot shake the fear that she has no being, that she is a "nobody" both as a woman and as a writer.

Throughout the novel these fears only get worse; struggling to assert herself, Julia more often than not falls into the mode of hesitation and self-deprecation. At one point, she even starts to agree with Rico: "You are right about man-is-man, woman-is-woman, I am wrong. But it's no good. My work is nothing. But, Rico, I will go on and do it. I will carve my pattern on an altar because I've got to do it. You jeered at my making abstractions of people—graven images, you called them. You are right" (164). Whatever momentary infusion of the *gloire* Julia has experienced vanishes almost without a trace, replaced by a painful and embarrassing obsequiousness and the tears of frustration and despair.

So terrified is Julia by Rico's response that she decides not to send the letter (164). Yet even without the immediate threat of his censure, she is still too frightened to voice her resentment; while she knows that "the thing that kept me from you wasn't only your genius" (182), she nevertheless is unable to "explain my revulsion to your writing, nor why it bored me. . . . I wanted to know why I was overwhelmed and angry" (179). By the end of the novel, the most Julia can come out with is the understated, watered-down, "I don't really know if this man-is-man, woman-is-woman means all that you think it does" (183).

If Julia cannot imagine creative transcendence without some connection to the male, neither can the heroines of H. D.'s most famous sequence poems, *Trilogy* and *Helen in Egypt.* Once again, the feminist critics who have written on the poems conclude, with Donna Krolik Hollenberg, that they thematize "the de-idealization of the father and recovery of the mother's power" (125).[20] Yet despite the appearance of the seeming muse-like Lady in *Trilogy* ("Tribute to the Angels," verse 25), the legacy of Freud means that H. D. shows Mary Magdalene (in *Trilogy*) and Helen (of *Helen in Egypt*) as needing to unite with Kaspar and Theseus/Achilles in order to reach their imaginative potentials. While the poet of *Trilogy* desires to "recover the secret of Isis" (54) in order to experience "union at last" within her consciousness (57), what she ends up with is the "unsatisfied duality" (72) of Kaspar and Mary Magdelene (modeled at least in part on Freud and H. D.). While Kaspar does come to see the falsity of his sexist attitudes, the absurdity of believing that "one jar was better than the other" (168), it is he—not Mary—who is granted the moment of vision at the end of the poem:

> he saw what the sacrosanct legend
> said still existed,
>
> he saw the lands of the blest,
> the promised lands, lost;
>
> he, in that half-second, saw
> the whole scope and plan
>
> of our and his civilization on this,
> his and our earth, before Adam.
>
> ("The Flowering of the Rod," verse 31)

Having, by the end of the poem, seen "deeper, apprehended more / than anyone before or after him" (verse 40), Kaspar serves as a marked contrast to the "shy and simple and young" Mary Magdelene (verse 43). Moreover, it cannot be ignored that it is ironically he who recognizes her potential, not Mary herself. For when she remarks that Kaspar's gift to the Christ child has "a most beautiful fragrance / as of all flowering things together," she does not realize that the magical, transcendent scent comes from her own gift:

> but Kaspar knew the seal of the jar was unbroken.
> he did not know whether she knew
>
> the fragrance came from the bundle of myrrh
> she held in her arms.
>
> ("The Flowering of the Rod," verse 43)

Whatever inner powers Mary possesses are still nascent and unselfconscious. Although H. D. gestures toward the possibility of female authority and power, she is still unwilling to discard her male persona. Even in her last major work, *Helen in Egypt*, which H. D. considered essentially the "same story" (*Hirslanden Notebooks* 3: 27) as *Trilogy*, the union of Helen and Achilles, made possible by Theseus (Freud), is what restores and reconciles the female protagonist to life.

In *End to Torment* (1958), H. D.'s memoir about her relationship with Ezra Pound, she admits to being shocked when one of the doctors at the rehabilitation hospital in which she is staying (Dr. Eric Heydt, who would later become her friend and analyst) asks her about the first of her "initiators." Associating the doctor's query with the shot he has just given her, H. D. finds herself "injected . . . or reinjected with Ezra" (11). Repeating the needle metaphor several times, H. D. associates Pound's influence with a painful "jabbing" (20) but nonetheless energizing infusion of patriarchal power, conceding that "to recall Ezra is to recall my father" (48) and also D. H. Lawrence.[21] At first, H. D. recollects the danger of this potentially suffocating influence, and she admits that "Ezra would have destroyed [her] and the center . . . of [her] poetry" (35) just as he destroyed another one of his initiates, May Sinclair (who, H. D. remembers, ended up in a mental hospital).

However, these anxious thoughts soon give way to an intense excitement when H. D. recalls the other half of Pound's legacy, her own creative method: "*Séraphita.* A story by Balzac. The Being, he-her, disappears or dies in the snow. Séraphitus. Ezra brought me the story. [paragraph break] The perfection of the fiery moment can not be sustained—or can it?" (11). What Pound, and, indirectly, Freud, Lawrence, Aldington, Ellis, and the rest, suggested for H. D.—through their ideas about sexuality, art, and androgyny—was a new way of thinking about her imagination in a world unwilling to grant a woman artist authority on her own terms. Like Balzac's mystical, androgynous figure—half man, half woman—who haunts the sublime Alpine peaks, and possesses superhuman strength, transcendent wisdom, and magical powers, the persona these intellectual men left for H. D. to adopt was ultimately unsustainable. Yet while Séraphitus/Séraphita, like many of H. D.'s own artist-heroines, ultimately cannot survive for long in the world of men, H. D.—even at the end of her life—still wonders if her fiery moment of overmind can one day be made to last.

4

"A Perversion That Builds Chartres and Invents Lear Is a Pretty Good Thing"

Psychic Incest and Haunted Hermaphroditism in Faulkner

> "These young girls . . . they scare me," he admitted. "Not as a possible or probable chastity you know."
>
> Do you remember the pictures you used to get in packages of cigarettes, or that you saw in magazines in barber shops? Anna Held and Eve Tanguay with shapes like elegant parlor lamp chimneys? Where are they now? Now, on the street, what do you see? Creatures with the uncomplex awkwardness of calves or colts, with two little knobs for breasts and indicated buttocks that, except for their soft look, might well belong to a boy of fifteen. Not satisfying any more; just exciting and monotonous. And mostly monotonous. . . . But still, they are kind of nice, these young girls: kind of like a thin monotonous flute music or something.
>
> —*Mosquitoes*, William Faulkner

In his contemplation of the female body, Dawson Fairchild, the novelist in William Faulkner's second novel, *Mosquitoes* (1927), laments far more than a change in women's fashions. What is at stake for this male artist is the possibility not only of "satisfying" his sexual fantasies but, more important, of expressing his creative impulses. For what bothers him the most about the boyish-looking "creatures" he sees on the streets is that they have displaced familiar, predominantly male constructions of femininity—the hourglass shapes displayed on magazines, advertisements, and theater bills—with a provocative and transgressive sexual indeterminacy, thus fundamentally changing the nature of female representation. These young girls are no longer compliant and reassuring muses; instead of inspiring him with images such as "elegant parlor lamp chimneys," their bodies leave him at a loss for words. The once glib man of letters struggles to come up with even the most inarticulate trope, mumbling that they seem "kind of like a thin monotonous flute music or something." Torn between feelings of fear, excitement, and boredom at the sight of what he finally can only characterize as sexless, vaguely animal-like organisms, Fairchild cannot decide what to do with them.

Although he is clearly satirized throughout the text as "a babe in that wood" of modern culture (251), Fairchild's troubled response to this vastly changed sexual landscape distinguishes much of Faulkner's fiction. The degree to which sex and varying constructions of sexuality haunt Faulkner's narratives, especially those written between 1925 and 1940, is striking. Filled with references to androgynous men and women, these texts return again and again to subjects such as hermaphroditism, incest, twinning, and pregnancy. Critics have identified the recurrent blurring of gender distinctions among Faulkner's characters and his fascination with the "epicene" woman. They have traced Faulkner's obsession with androgyny to his early interest in romanticism (Brooks); his small and effeminate physique (Karl); his sexual preference for women (Blotner); his rejection by those women (Broughton); his struggle against patriarchal constructions of gender (Jones; Duvall; Chakovsky; K. Johnson); his neo-Hegelian interest in merging (Harrington; Snead; Slatloff); his recognition of the "oneness" of all nature (McHaney, *Faulkner's* 147); and his attempt to recuperate his masculinity and narrative authority (Irwin).

While these explanations contribute volumes to our understanding of Faulkner's work, they ultimately fail to account for the pervasive influence of new cultural constructions of femininity and sexuality on this modernist author, constructions shaped by a number of factors, including late-nineteenth-century sex theory, Freudian psychoanalysis, the First World War, the suffrage movement, and the entry of women in the workforce and their establishment in the world of arts and letters.[1] To an even greater extent than writers such as Woolf and Joyce, Faulkner's early novels are full of references to the groundbreaking work of sex theorists, such as Richard von Krafft-Ebing and Havelock Ellis, who exploded age-old gender divisions by asserting that "each sex . . . is latently hermaphrodite" (Ellis 79–80) and argued for a direct link between androgyny and creative ability.

For Faulkner, as for his character Dawson Fairchild, the most immediate legacy of this sexual "revolution" was a profound crisis of artistic identity. How can he engage or even "imagine" his imagination when traditional tropes for the creative consciousness—tropes which are rooted in patriarchal constructions of the feminine—can no longer be employed? Or, to put it another way, how can he claim the power of language when the male writer's privileged relationship with the muse has disappeared? We find Faulkner's often troubled solution to these dilemmas in a crucial fact that other critics have ignored: in Faulkner's novels, sexual indeterminacy is consistently linked to the artist and to creativity. In response to a lived crisis of authorship, Faulkner ironically rereads the source of his aesthetic blockage—the breakdown of gender divisions—as precisely his solution. Drawing from the modernist scientific association between androgyny and creativity, he endeavors to envision his process of poetic production as generated from a double-sexed imagination.

In my readings of several of Faulkner's early literary efforts and then in extended treatments of three novels that most dramatically highlight his struggle for literary authorization and artistic empowerment—*Mosquitoes*, *The Sound and the Fury*, and *The Wild Palms*—I will illustrate the ways in which Faulkner imagines his creative consciousness as both "male" and "female" in response to modern changes in the cultural constructions of gender. Abandoning the muse-trope, he—like Joyce, a writer after whom Faulkner would model his work in his first attempts at novel writing—instead envisions an androgynous consciousness "infinitely dynamized by an incessant process of exchange" (Cixous 254) between its masculine and feminine elements. Although two recent feminist critics have identified Faulkner's association between androgyny and creativity, each essentially locates the extent of Faulkner's "'bisexual' artistic consciousness" (Gwin 4) in the interaction between his male psyche and the "subversive deconstructive" (Gwin 25) presence of some of his female characters. For Minrose Gwin, these include Caddy Compson, Rosa Coldfield, and Charlotte Rittenmeyer; Frann Michel focuses on *Mosquitoes*'s lesbian poet, Eva Wiseman. I agree that Faulkner sometimes identifies with his female characters in order to direct his narrative toward transgressively "new and unknown spaces" (Gwin 25) or to dissociate himself from the culturally ascribed image of the artist as "feminized male invert" (F. Michel 16). However, what both these critics leave out is the most central and transgressive part of Faulkner's creative strategy: his efforts to envision his imagination as both male and female in response to a culturally motivated crisis of artistic authority. Rather than safely projecting the female aspect of his imagination upon his female characters, Faulkner self-consciously claims it for himself, and, in doing so, he ironically chooses a creative model that has the potential both to empower and threaten him sexually and artistically. Although he does invent various strategies to resolve this dilemma, the tension between Faulkner's attraction to and fear of his imaginative model remains unresolved; as we shall see, incorporating any construction of the female within his consciousness generates anxieties about feminization, homoeroticism, and, especially, the female body that constantly threaten to make the minds of his artist-heroes and artist-heroines the sites of sublime experiences finally more terrifying than transformative. What I hope to offer here is an explanation for why Faulkner nevertheless keeps trying to make his protagonists endure such agonies. Although these characters are rarely able to transcend this new point of blockage, we will see how Faulkner rereads their failure as inspiring and empowering. Thus, while Joyce would eventually dismiss the sublime as an essentially masochistic exercise in futility, his American counterpart would ultimately find his triumph in its elusiveness.

Having begun his career writing romantic verses, Faulkner early on showed signs of worry about their antiquated irrelevance to contemporary culture. In particular, Theodore Gautier's 1835 novel, *Mademoiselle du Maupin*—a text we know Faulkner read (Brooks

120)—appears to have significantly influenced Faulkner's decision to modify his aesthetic approach. The text chronicles a young nobleman's consuming passion for a cross-dressing, seductively androgynous woman who ultimately abandons both him and his mistress. Searching in vain for this lover of his dreams, D'Albert can never again be satisfied. More than a simple romance, this story offers an ironic critique of what happens to the romantic hero who predicates his sexual and spiritual survival on a relationship that cannot be fulfilled and is no longer even culturally valid since it depends upon a construction of the female that no longer exists. Mlle. du Maupin, like the more liberated women of Faulkner's era, refuses to be caught, categorized, and objectified, and, instead, she enjoys the freedom of transgressing traditional gender boundaries by posing as a man. Stripped of the object of his desire, D'Albert is left with only a museless absence and is rendered effectively impotent and imaginatively dead.

It is more than coincidence that at the beginning of his artistic career, Faulkner rejects this painful and, ultimately, anachronistic romantic legacy in order to adopt a more accessible conception of authorship. That he dedicates his first novella, appropriately entitled *Mayday*, to his real-life Mlle. du Maupin—the boyish and ever-elusive Helen Baird—suggests the depth of his fears and the strength of his resolve. Allegorical and written in the eclectically combined style of medieval romance and romantic quest-narratives, *Mayday* is far removed in setting and technique from any of Faulkner's later works. A fable of unrequited love, the text can also be read as a story about the danger of the romantic model of inspiration, specifically the problem of predicating artistic empowerment on an "economy of desire" between poet and muse that eventually can never be fulfilled; on a relation based on rejection and abstinence (Broughton 162); and on a mythic and ever-elusive dream maiden "whom he dare not touch" (*Mayday* 74).

At the beginning of the tale, young Sir Galwyn—accompanied by his ever-present sidekicks, Hunger and Pain—sees in a magic pool the watery image of a lovely maiden. Ever in search of his mystical muse, Galwyn refuses to be satisfied with three of the most beautiful women in the world (including the mythic Isolde), whom he meets and seduces along the way. Instead, he remains addicted to the experience of desire, admitting that "it is not the thing itself that man wants, so much as the wanting of it" (71). Following the lead of other romantic poet-heroes such as Shelley's Alastor and Keats's Endymion, Galwyn finally chooses to pursue the image of his dream maiden into the Lethe-like waters of oblivion. Although given the chance to live the mortal life of hunger and pain and hope and despair, he chooses death by drowning, or, as St. Francis—the Lord of Sleep—says, "little sister Death" (87).

We will see how both the images of drowning and deadly little sisters return to haunt Faulkner's fiction. However, the most immediate message of this brief book is a stern warning against following in the footsteps of romantic literary precursors who predicate artistic inspiration on an externalized relation with the female muse. In her recent book *Romantic Androgyny*, Diane Hoeveler argues that "the Romantics wanted to create female characters with whom their male heroes (often slightly veiled versions of themselves) could merge in a sort of apocalyptic union that would transform both the political and psychic realms" (6). While she does not use the term "imagination," Hoeveler chronicles the historical and cultural factors that contribute to the romantic model of creativity. Although Faulkner rejects the externalized model of the romantic muse, he does not completely abandon the idea that male artistic inspiration is generated from a transformative union with the female.

Yet the androgynous union this male modernist writer envisions reflects the unique cultural anxieties of his age, anxieties that are most dramatically represented in his first published novel, *Soldier's Pay* (written 1925). In this text Faulkner records the tragic odyssey of the wounded, impotent, and nearly unconscious World War I veteran Donald Mahon, who is carried home to die. This soldier's "pay," however, is a homecoming that is anything but familiar, or comforting. Instead, Donald returns to an alien landscape where "boys of both sexes swayed arm in arm" at dances (186)—a community of manly women such as Margaret, who upset "nice fixed ideas about women" (157), and womanly men such as Januarius Jones in whom "the feminine predominated so . . . [that he is essentially] a woman with a man's body and a cat's nature" (218). Even Donald's betrothed,

Cecily, in her short revealing dresses and "slim epicenity" (139) is anything but the chaste and loyal Penelope (Karl 210); she has transformed into the ultimate tease, into "something you want and can't get" (286). Thus, rather than celebrating the "romance of battle" (37) and the cult of the man-hero, this culture proclaims itself "the day of the Boy, male and female" (192).

In important ways, the dizzying culture shock awaiting Donald Mahon mirrors Faulkner's own.[2] Just as the once glorified, wounded war-hero becomes essentially an unconscious, empty shell in this environment, so does the romantic muse—however attractive—become an anachronistic and powerless imaginative trope. It is indeed hard to imagine Shelley's dream maidens in the decade of flappers and speakeasies. Faulkner, like Joyce, was attracted to the romantics' solution to the crisis of authorship—their attempts at transformative union with the male-identified female figure—but he ultimately rewrites it using the ambiguous sexual iconography of the modern period. Although the feminine remains intricately important to Faulkner's model of the imagination, he does not project it outward upon the figures of the Mother, Sister, Beloved, Femme Fatale, Muse (to use Hoeveler's terms). Rather than externalizing the source of his creativity and then trying to re-internalize it through the drama of quest romance (and risk succumbing to the endless cycle of unfulfilled desire), he envisions a creator who is self-fulfilled, who—like the subjects of Ellis's and Krafft-Ebing's case studies—becomes a kind of psychic hermaphrodite.

In *Elmer,* the unfinished novel the youthful Faulkner wrote on his European excursion in 1925, he first explores this possibility. Modeled after Joyce's *Portrait of the Artist,* this *Künstlerroman* revolves around a young painter named Elmer Hodge, and from the beginning he connects his sexual and artistic development in a manner that self-consciously links androgyny with creativity. As a child, Elmer exhibits a tremendous fondness for phallic objects, such as cigar stubs and screwdrivers and buggy whips, and for a time indulges in a crush on an older boy, "slender and beautiful as any god, and as cruel" (31). Yet what makes a lasting impression on Elmer's consciousness is his attraction to androgynous women. As a boy, Elmer embellishes his most prized possession—a Joan of Arc lithograph—with a moustache and imperial jacket, and he is fixated by an incestuous attraction to his androgynous-looking teenage sister, Jo-Addie, whose naked, breastless body he longs to touch. Although the incestuous overtones in the early part of the novel are more than subtle (every night he begs his sister to allow him briefly to touch her thigh), Elmer's transgressive desires for his sister's boyish body stem more from a narcissistic and even onanistic attraction to the feminine in himself. Resembling in many ways "a small boy in his larger brother's short pants" (12), Jo-Addie becomes a kind of twin with whom Elmer can indulge in a fantasy of amorphous sexuality and autoerotic desire; it is more than coincidence, for example, that she calls him Ellie and he calls her Joe.

Although Jo-Addie leaves home at a young age, she continues to be of central importance to Elmer's imagination. As he begins to make use of the paintbox that she gave him, Elmer transforms his "fierce and dark and proud" sister (17) into a powerful, and strangely violent, muse: "That shape, that image within him had become quite definitely alive: a Dianalike girl with an impregnable integrity, a slimness virginal and impervious to time or circumstance. Darkhaired and small and proud, casting him bones fiercely as though he were a dog" (47). Panthea Reid Broughton points out that Elmer's fixation with the girl's "impregnable integrity" sets up a problematic relation with the female, a relation based on a desire which by its very nature cannot be reciprocated or fulfilled (166). Yet this dynamic is more than frustrating; it is frightening and perverse. Inspiration here depends upon the whim of a childlike dominatrix to whom he has abased himself. This strange mixture of the romantic and the masochistic recalls Joyce's characters and their attempt to reconcile themselves to their inner femininity by externalizing it as an inescapable, powerful presence; suggestive of anxiety about and attraction toward the female presence, the dog in Faulkner's text is used alternately as a symbol of powerless dependency and transcendent wisdom. While Elmer distinctly associates the dog with his own passivity and helplessness in this passage, he later correlates the canine image with the transcendent indifference of both Jo-Addie and the boy with whom he falls in love; the androgynous Jo, for instance, is compared to "a dog that both suffered man and ignored him in the face of higher and more perfect things to do in the world" (15). Faulkner seems unsure as to the exact relation between artist and muse, and he ultimately leaves it unresolved. Nevertheless, it is clearly the female who retains the power and control and who exhibits a kind of fierceness and independence that is alternately presented as frightening and arousing.

As a result of this tension, Elmer (and indirectly, Faulkner) eventually abandons his Diana-like girl altogether: "Somewhere a fierce proud Dianalike girl, small and dark and impregnably virginal, waiting to cast him through the window of her arrogance, a bone as though he were a dog—but still waiting. Perhaps he was holding her by sheer strength. He could remember once when he did not have to hedge her in, when on a time the unbroken gold of his body had attracted the virginal silver of hers as metal calls to metal anywhere" (114). While the end of the passage suggests that it is she who now eludes him, there is also the hint that he resists her—she is "still waiting," perhaps for him to admit her fully into consciousness. Apparently this muse-figure poses a threat to him, so that he must "hedge . . . in," a threat that goes unnamed but has something to do with the dichotomy between her ageless beauty and strength and "that dusty reminder of his once curling yellow hair" (114); and it also harkens back to his repressed fear of her unusual power over him. This is no dream maiden whispering in his ear, but rather it is a strong and independent woman who holds the keys to his artistic success in her often disdainful hands. Externalizing (and controlling) the "female" source of one's creative energy is even more dangerous in this modern cultural climate than in the romantic one, as the graphic images of her independence and ferocity suggest.

Elmer finally transcends his creative blockage, however, by repressing the source of his fear and amazement—the new and powerful construction of the female-muse—only later to identify with it and reclaim it for himself. In other words, he recapitulates the sublime experience, in which the mind becomes overwhelmed by an object of unfathomable power and magnitude only to reread its ability to apprehend it at all as empowering and transformative; the subject thus represses the threat of ego-incorporation by identifying with the source of that imperilment. Psychoanalytic critics such as Thomas Weiskel, Mary Arensberg, and Neil Hertz describe this experience in terms of the oedipal struggle. Instead of confronting the father, however, Elmer must face the feminine "'source" of his creativity. Although this novel fragment just records the empowering end point of the process, the graphic descriptions of Elmer's early encounters with this Diana-like muse indicate that attempting to identify with her would be exceedingly risky. Nevertheless, he appears at this point to have survived it; in a crucial passage at the beginning of the novel, the now grown-up artist takes out his paint tubes and sees in them a fresh metaphor for his creative consciousness: "Elmer hovered over them with a brooding maternity, taking up one at a time those fat portentous tubes in which was yet wombed his heart's desire, the world itself—thickbodied and female and at the same time phallic: hermaphroditic" (4). Although critics have dismissed this strange image as merely a masturbation fantasy,[3] the paint tubes—as both phallus and womb—become symbolic of the artist's imagination, a self-contained, double-sexed creative consciousness that permanently escapes the pitfalls of the elusive romantic muse and the frightening Diana-like girl. While the male romantics "consistently presented Women as 'Other' to man—an idealized mother, a second self, a submerged double, an inspirational muse or mentor, or a demonic *femme fatale*" (Hoeveler 2), this modernist author makes "her" a part of "him." By internalizing the "feminine" within his "masculine" creative mind, Elmer—and through him, Faulkner as well—ensures that his heart's desire will always be available to inspire him, and thus it will allow him to recreate the world itself in his imagination. By figuratively granting him the procreative power of both male and female, this "hermaphroditic" or "androgyne" imagination frees him from the tyrannical whims of a threatening modern muse.

Yet would it really work? In a letter Faulkner wrote to his mother on September 22, 1925, he gave away his intended ending, revealing that his artist-hero "gets everything a man could want—money, a European title, marries the girl he wants—and she gives away his paint box. So Elmer never gets to paint at all" (quoted in Karl 150). For all Elmer's attempts to master her, the woman ironically gets the last word as she restores herself to power and the male artist to abjection. Although he initially had high hopes for the novel, Faulkner ultimately gave up writing *Elmer* because "the story was not funny enough" (quoted in Meriwether 81). In addition to questioning the degree to which he had distanced himself from his subject, it is probable that Faulkner was beginning to get disturbed by the direction it was taking. Nevertheless, as Thomas L. McHaney points out, "his continued use of the material indicates that 'Elmer' remained important for Faulkner, even though he could not bring it off in the form he had originally projected" ("Elmer Papers" 283).

Indeed, Faulkner's second published novel, *Mosquitoes* (1927), in many ways takes up where *Elmer* left off. Like *Mayday*, this text is dedicated to Faulkner's second lost love, the androgynous-looking Helen Baird, and it too offers a warning to himself about the perils of the romantic muse as well as the possibility for a saving alternative to it. *Mosquitoes* is not considered by most contemporary critics to be very important in the history of Faulkner's literary development.[4] I believe, on the contrary, that it is crucial, and it necessitates careful study because of its foregrounding of Faulkner's sexual and artistic anxieties. Extremely troubled and self-conscious, the text is concerned with the world of artists, and, more specifically, with the fate of art and imagination in the modern age. Highlighting the failings of traditional models of creativity, the text also shows the frightening underside of Faulkner's modern version of the imagination and the painful crisis of authority that leads to it.

Focusing on a four-day cruise hosted by Mrs. Maurier, a philistine widow who longs to venture into the society of the creative, *Mosquitoes* functions as a showcase for the modern artist. While not strictly allegorical in the style of *Mayday*, each character does represent a certain artistic "type," and, interestingly, each "type" involves a particular sexual stance. Virtually all the artist characters in *Mosquitoes* are satirized; yet, there is a hierarchy among them that, as Frann Michel suggests, reflects Faulkner's anxieties about this vastly transformed literary landscape and centers in particular on "feminization" and male homosexuality (16). Characters such as the pale and effeminate poet Mark Frost and the foppish dilettante and Prufrockian ladies clothing salesman Taliaferro are exposed as failed artists, while Gordon, the hypermasculine and misanthropic sculptor who some critics have argued is a representation of "the author's idealized self" (Bleikestan 32; Warren), is portrayed as the most authentic. Of the women, the sex-starved and man-hungry painter Dorothy Jameson is clearly set up as the repressed spinster, but her companion, the suggestively lesbian Eva Wiseman, is depicted as a serious, if enigmatic, modernist poet. Fairchild, the novelist who was modeled on Faulkner's friend and mentor Sherwood Anderson and represents the pre-modernist, late-nineteenth-century man of letters, is a little overwhelmed by contemporary revolutions in sex, style, and taste. While Julius, the sardonic, cynical "semitic man" and modern critic, serves as Dawson's foil, neither are able in their lengthy conversations to reconcile the relation between sex and art.

If this partial guest list suggests a great deal of confusion about artistic and sexual identity, it also raises questions about the position of the female figure in relation to the male artist. The fact that two of the artist characters are women obviously breaks down the gendered dynamic of "male" artist and "female" muse. Yet so does the strange opposition between two young girls who also take part in the trip. One is the vapid, blonde sexpot Jenny, a traditionally "feminine" figure exuding "supine abandon, soft and oblivious and terrifying" (128). Yet while the failed artist Taliaferro cannot stop drooling over Jenny, it is Mrs. Maurier's boyish-looking niece Patricia Robyn, the epitome of the androgyne with her "flat breast and belly, her boy's body" (24), who becomes the obsessive object of the "successful" sculptor's desire. Rather than being his muse, Pat comes to represent what is essentially the feminine aspect of Gordon's creative self. The degree of Gordon's reluctance to part with his headless, breastless statue of the young woman suggests that it represents much more to him than just a sculpture; indeed, in Pat's face, Gordon finds a "grave and sexless replica of his own attitude" (269)—an attitude which is specifically androgynous.

John Irwin suggests that Patricia becomes a "symbol of his love for, the work of art . . . that is simply the embodiment of the feminine aspect of the artist's masculine self" (161). Frann Michel insists that what is feminine is the process of authorship (7). Both critics overlook the fact that Faulkner presents the artist's imagination as double-sexed. To use the terms of the novel, the artist's creative stance is characterized by a kind of "emotional bisexuality" (251); artistic creation involves erotic union with both male and female aspects of the artist's psyche. Rather than as single-sexed, Gordon describes himself, in part, as a "woman who conceives without pleasure bears without pain" (48). While, on the one hand, it is a sterile image, on the other hand, it suggests a painless model of imaginative production that is geared toward eliminating the troublesome factor of desire. For while Fairchild argues that all male writers locate their inspiration in a female figure who "ain't always a flesh and blood creature . . . [but] may be only the symbol of desire" (250), Gordon ensures that his creativity will no longer depend upon the whims of an elusive muse. Like Joyce's Stephen Dedalus, Gordon constructs a "virgin womb of the imagination" (*Portrait* 217) in which to create a transcendent work of art. Through the autoerotic interaction between "male" and "female" elements of consciousness, the artist generates the inspiration necessary to create.

However, while this construction removes the factor of desire, it does not totally eliminate anxiety; it is not coincidental that Gordon is blatantly presented as a rough and tough he-man, quintessentially virile, replete with sweaty, bulging muscles. Incorporating any construction of the female within this version of the male self (including the appropriation of the birth metaphor) thus poses a significant threat of "feminization" unless one takes the proper precautions: in this case, assuming a particularly "masculine" stance. In addition, the autoerotic overtones of this conception of an androgyne imagination recurrently trigger the anxiety that this kind of creation is sexually transgressive, perverse, and even taboo; instead of a fertile union, the relationship between male and female within Faulkner's consciousness seems always on the verge of turning into a sort of "psychic incest" (Irwin 163) between twin halves of the artist's split psyche. In *Mosquitoes*, as in *Elmer*, the image of the artist's imagination is frequently juxtaposed against an image of real incest, in this case the unhealthy attachment of the androgynous twins, Pat and Josh. As we shall see later, Faulkner's artistic characters—especially Quentin Compson—regularly conflate the creative desire to merge the feminine half of their androgyne imagination with a carnal desire for the external twin, or sister, often allowing themselves to be devastated by their own misdirected and misconceived guilt.

Thus, while this new model of the imagination promises to reauthorize the male artist by saving him from the prison of desire, it also threatens to "feminize" and destroy him. Unless the perfect balance is achieved between male and female elements, one might end up like Mark Frost, the slight, ephemeral, and ghostly poet whose secret ambition is to be published in magazines such as the *Dial*, which to the more "masculine" artists is the same as "immolation in a home for old young ladies of either sex" (209). Clearly, Faulkner betrays here an intense anxiety about a literary establishment increasingly run by, and patronized by, women; however, what also precipitates this panic is the association—made famous by Krafft-Ebing—among androgyny, homosexuality, and genetic degeneracy.[5] Incorporating the feminine or the female into one's model of the imagination has strikingly different implications in this new cultural landscape, and this threatens, at times, to create more problems than it solves. Faulkner's worst fear seems to be that the male artist could end up like the pathetic Taliaferro—impotent, effeminate, and merely a dilettante. The suggestion at one point in *Mosquitoes* is that the artist must either be a muscled misogynist such as Gordon or participate in "an endless gabbling of esthetic foster sisters of both sexes" (51–52).

Some of Faulkner's paranoia can be traced to a crisis of audience, specifically to his difficult position as a writer in the postwar South. Frederick Karl points out that "Although writing was not itself anathema, it was not considered a fully masculine endeavor. . . . The South lauded soldiers and other doers; it tolerated writers. . . . Faulkner's desire to be only a writer and to pose as 'the writer' with bohemian abandon led not only to outright rejection but to steady ridicule. He was early on called 'the Count,' 'Count no Count,' and 'queer' as signs of his difference; even when he was becoming famous in the North and abroad, Oxford was slow to recognize him" (19). These attitudes were not merely a southern phenomenon. As I mentioned earlier, the link between artistic genius, psychic hermaphroditism, and homosexuality had been made commonplace by late-nineteenth-century German sex theorists. The prevailing belief among them was that "there are . . . certain avocations to which Inverts seem especially called. One of the chief of these is literature" (Ellis 293).

Perhaps this explains why Faulkner took such great pains to proclaim his masculinity and heterosexuality in both his life and his art.

As several of his biographers note, Faulkner carefully fabricated personae to present to the world, the most blatant of which was his youthful pose as a wounded hero of a war in which he never fought (Karl; Blotner). In *Mosquitoes,* Faulkner goes so far as to write into the novel a defense of his heterosexual virility. At one point, the seductive Jenny meets "a little kind of black man" (144) whose name turns out to be "Faulkner": "He was a white man, except he was awful sunburned kind of shabby dressed—no necktie and hat. Say, he said some funny things to me. He said I had the best digestion he ever saw, and he said if the straps of my dress was to break I'd devastate the country. He said he was a liar by profession, and he made good money at it, enough to own a Ford as soon as he got it paid out. I think he was crazy" (145). This is a bizarre self-portrait, revealing William Faulkner's insecurities and frustrations at being obscure and marginalized, although the passage certainly exhibits a large degree of self-parody as well. When Jenny tells Pat his name ("Faulkner"), the latter announces "with finality" (145) that she has never heard of him. What is most interesting about this completely abrupt interlude, however, is that its emphasis on Faulkner's "attraction" to Jenny reveals a strikingly defensive—and ambivalent—attitude toward his sexual and writer's identity.

In addition to openly proclaiming his heterosexuality, Faulkner defends the manliness of his vocation by showing the "superiority" of masculine artistic endeavors to female procreativity. Mrs. Maurier, for instance, is humiliatingly derided by the "creative" Gordon for her barrenness (154). Yet even Jenny's blooming fertility is represented as inferior to the outpourings of the male psyche; as Julius points out, women only "bear geniuses" (248). However, these misogynistic jibes are ambivalently undercut by what appears to be Faulkner's sympathy toward Pat's resistance to her culturally destined role as wife and mother; dismayed by the fact that her brother, Josh, is the only one who gets to go to Yale, Pat tells the ship's steward, David: "I wish I were a man, like that. I bet it's all right, going around wherever you want to" (123). Furthermore, at the same time that the novel appears to valorize the "masculine" domain of art, its central artist-critics, Julius and Eva, reveal a remarkable pessimism in the value of words. Despite the novelist Fairchild's romanticism, even he often comes to the conclusion that language is essentially sterile, meaningless, and inferior to nature. Having brashly defended the bearing of the word from accusations of effeminacy, Fairchild—and through him, Faulkner as well—is continually troubled by the relative worth of the literary enterprise in the first place.

In working through these contradictions, we must not confuse any of the characters' voices with Faulkner's own. Although Fairchild's character remains central to the work, he is self-consciously presented as the nostalgic, late-Edwardian artist assaulted and perplexed by the waves of modernism. Put off by the new epicene women, frightened by their awkward and "strange sexless shapes" (240), Fairchild prefers instead his ephemeral muse or else the old view of women as "merely articulated genital organs with a kind of aptitude for spending whatever money you have" (241). Yet unlike Julius, Fairchild admits some women have written good things; poetry for him is still "put down with the ultimate intention of impressing some woman that probably don't care anything at all for literature, as is the nature of women" (250). Terrified both by the emergence of women on the literary scene and the deconstruction of traditional gender categories, Fairchild is rebuked for this by Julius: "But you, staying trustfully about this park of dark and rootless trees which Dr. Ellis and your Germans have recently thrown open to the public. . . . You'll always be a babe in that wood" (251). To Fairchild, modern art and modern artists are disturbingly subjective and frighteningly androgynous. Julius's insistent message is that there is no going back. In their representations of an androgynous and artistically inclined third gender, modern sex theorists have forever destabilized traditional delineations between male and female, artist and muse; as long as Fairchild refuses the implications of this shift for his artistic method and preserves his trust in old sexual hierarchies and imaginative tropes, his creative power will remain in its infancy.

With whom does Faulkner agree? His psyche seems split among these characters. Julius proclaims the cultural reality of which we know Faulkner was very much aware, but Fairchild clearly voices some of Faulkner's troubling and lingering anxieties. A provocative poem (echoing the sentiments of verses bearing the same title by the decadent poet A. C. Swinburne) attributed to Eva Wiseman, Julius's sister, illuminates these tensions:

"Hermaphroditus"

Lips that of thy weary all seem weariest,
Seem wearier for the curled and pallid sly
Still riddle of thy secret face, and thy
Sick despair of its own ill obsessed;
Lay not to heart thy boy's hand, to protest
That smiling leaves thy tired mouth reconciled,
For swearing so keeps thee but ill beguiled
With secret joy of thine own woman's breast.

Weary thy mouth with smiling; canst thou bride
Thyself with thee and thine own kissing slake?
Thy virgin's waking doth itself deride
With sleep's sharp absence, coming so awake,
And near thy mouth thy twinned heart's grief doth hide
For there's no breast between: it cannot break.

(252)

Essentially, this poem has two conflicting messages. On the one hand, the hermaphroditic figure comes closest to validating the state of the imagination toward which we have seen Faulkner repeatedly gesture, however transgressive or "perverse" it appears to the frustrated speaker of the poem. The image is of the balance and wholeness of the hermaphroditic imagination generating art, figuratively making love to itself. Reminiscent of Elmer's paint tubes, the hermaphrodite metaphor comes to represent the epitome of the artist without muse, free from the demands and pain of external desire. Thus one can read the poem as a kind of reproach to the cast-off muse who alone assumes that the hermaphrodite figure is lonely, and thus keeps trying to re-seduce it. It is, after all, the lover and not the hermaphrodite who is speaking.

But, on the other hand, the poem indicates a much more troubled, darker side of Faulkner's model of the imagination. Its twinned heart—which reminds us of the twins, Pat and Josh, and their unhealthy attachment—suggests a more troubled kind of psychic incest, painful and empty, spinning inward unstoppably toward a transgressive and narcissistic desire that can never be fulfilled or eased. Ironically, the poem ends up recapitulating the frustrating muse model that Faulkner was trying to escape in the first place; with the repetition of "weary" and "ill," the speaker of the poem implies an overwhelmingly oppressive mood of disappointment and sick despair. This tension never gets resolved in the novel, and, as we shall see, it becomes a significant problematic throughout Faulkner's fiction.

Fairchild calls the poem and all of modern poetry a "dark perversion. Like a fire that don't need any fuel, that lives on its own heat" (252). As a metaphor for authorship, the hermaphrodite signifies danger for this novelist who argues that contemporary male writers are "not masculine and lusty enough to tamper with something that borders so close to the unnatural. A kind of sterile race: women too masculine to conceive, men too feminine to beget" (252). Fairchild's indignant objection is ironic, however, considering that Faulkner not only wrote the poem but published it in a separate collection of his verses, *The Marble Faun.* This elaborate cloaking suggests that Faulkner attributed these verses to Eva, a marginalized female character, in order safely to embrace his attraction to the hermaphroditic image.[6] By putting distance between himself and his ideas, Faulkner strategically manages to express them without claiming them directly, thus freeing himself from Fairchild's (and indirectly, his own) charges of perversity. Moreover, by figuratively becoming Eva, Faulkner models his conception of the androgyne imagination, creating the poem from both "male" and "female" aspects of his creative consciousness. Finally, Eva is presented as the androgynous artist; she is both the quintessential woman, Eve, as well as the "Wise Man."[7]

It is interesting that despite Fairchild's objections to the poem, he later describes the process of his imagination in hermaphroditic terms, referring to it as a "perversion," albeit an excusable one. Fairchild notes that "Women can do it without art—old biology takes care of that. But men, men . . . in art, a man can create without any assistance at all: what he does is his. A perversion, I grant you, but a perversion that builds Chartres and invents Lear is a pretty good thing" (320). This appropriation of the terms of feminine reproduction for male artistry is not new, but the intense anxiety that surrounds it is. For Fairchild goes on to ask if all artistic creation is essentially "reproduction from within," whether "the dominating impulse in the world [is] feminine, after all, as aboriginal peoples believe?" (320). Here Fairchild makes reference to the widespread modern anthropological debates centering on the issue of primitive matriarchy, or "mother-right." Initiated by the work of J. J. Bachofen, a nineteenth-century Swiss historian who argued that early civilizations were dominated by women, controversy over these issues erupted with the growth of the women's movement in the early twentieth century as both male and female social scientists began to recognize its implications for the modern political and sexual landscape.[8]

For Fairchild—as for many real-life male intellectuals—the reality of female dominance was extremely disturbing. What is most striking about Fairchild's response is that he connects these debates to his attitudes toward his art; if, as he suggests, "the dominating impulse in the world is feminine," if art is "reproduction from within" (320), then how can a male artist claim artistic privilege? Moreover, if he does appropriate or incorporate a construction of this feminine reproductive power in order to create, how can he ensure the preservation of his male identity? In a memorable simile, Fairchild compares the consumption of the male spider by the female during sexual intercourse to the male artist standing beside his physical, temporal self and the moments of his life, "killing them [the male spiders; later also "all the charming things that ever happen to him"] for the sake of some problematical something he might or he might not ever use" (320). In this complex recasting, the male artist's imagination thus becomes part devouring female, the feminine dark twin of the self, both powerful and terrifying. The male artist is thus engaged in a constant battle to maintain a balance between "masculine" and "feminine" parts of his imagination and thus avoid being subsumed or "feminized" by the artistic enterprise. One might argue that this tension explains Gordon's intense attraction to but also violence toward the symbol of the feminine aspect of his imagination, Pat. He beats her at one point for calling him a dirty name with the "genders backward" (271)—in other words, for calling him a woman.

Yet if this model of the imagination is that dangerous, why do Faulkner and his characters continue to attempt it? One could suggest, as does John Irwin, that Faulkner's early aesthetic efforts reflect his regressive, narcissistic, and self-destructive wish to destroy gender difference; alternatively, one could imply, as does Frann Michel, that Faulkner simply had no other choice in an environment in which "authorship was defined as feminine" (Michel 7). Such readings, however, oversimplify and significantly understate Faulkner's attraction to the concept of a double-sexed consciousness. The culturally fashioned iconography of the androgyne as an imaginative trope offered him a solution to the crisis of artistic authority generated when modern reconfigurations of sexual categories made the male artist–female muse model obsolete. Conceptualizing his creative mind as third-sexed and thus artistically endowed, according to the prevailing belief of the time, provided the possibility of expanded subjectivity and heightened vision free from the perils of the writer's now unfulfillable desire for his female muse. That constructing an androgyne imagination is worth the risk of feminization and psychic incest is evidenced by the fact that Faulkner will keep trying to represent and achieve it over and over again. But at the same time, the safety of the artist is soon called into question. "Hermaphroditus," in its attempt to reconcile "male" and "female" aspects of Faulkner's imagination, reveals a sublime dynamic that is often perilously out of control and ever ready to self-destruct into a narcissistic nightmare.

At the end of *Mosquitoes*, Fairchild talks about an "instant of timeless beatitude"—a moment of genius as "that passive state of the heart with which the mind, the brain, has nothing to do at all, in which the hackneyed accidents which make up this world . . . brought together by chance in perfect proportions, take on a kind of splendid and timeless beauty" (339). It is true that Faulkner makes fun of this high rhetoric—the drunken Fairchild vomits after his epiphanic meditation—and yet, at the same time, his aesthetic is geared toward making these moments of vision possible. In *Mosquitoes*, for instance, the only successful realizations of such "timeless" works of beauty are Gordon's statue of the androgyne and Eva's poem. Nevertheless, how to sustain this idea of an androgyne imagination, or what we might call "artistic" bisexuality, and thus ensure poetic power without becoming trapped by the cycle that was established to produce it appears to be Faulkner's lifelong dilemma. As André Bleikastan remarks, it "is not so much the 'ecstasy' of artistic creation as its 'agony'" that this author emphasizes (29).

Mosquitoes ends on a troubled note, as the pathetic Taliaferro—after failing to seduce Jenny—decides that the singular way to get women is to "dominate them from the start" (348). After eagerly expounding his new theory to Fairchild on the telephone, Taliaferro finds himself humiliated again when he discovers that his audience was in fact the novelist's female lover who mockingly replies, "'You tell 'em, big boy; treat 'em rough'" (349). Thus, not only does Taliaferro fail to control women, he ends up being rebuked by them for his pitiful attempts at masculinity, as is Joyce's Leopold Bloom by Bello/a. Although Taliaferro is a relatively minor figure, considered pathetic even by the other characters in the novel, his confusion, failure, and emergent misogyny signal trouble for Faulkner's imaginative model. As in the projected ending of *Elmer*, the resurgent ascendancy of the female is juxtaposed against the failure of a male artist. In his biography of Faulkner, Frederick Karl suggests that Taliaferro is what Faulkner feared he himself might become: effeminate, pathetic, a failure—like one of the throngs of mosquitoes in the novel, that annoy and buzz and hover but are never capable of real power, that kill passion rather than inspire it (273). Not all the artists in *Mosquitoes* fail so miserably but neither do they especially triumph. In later years, Faulkner would attempt emotionally to abandon his second novel, just as he had literally abandoned *Elmer:* "That one, if I could write that over, I probably wouldn't write it at all. I'm not ashamed of it, because that was the chips, the badly sawn planks that the carpenter produces while he's learning to be a first-rate carpenter, but it's not a—not an important book in my list" (*University* 257). Although *Mosquitoes* displays little of the poised and mature brilliance of later works, it reveals a little more of Faulkner's conflicted psyche than he was comfortable in claiming.

It is, of course, dangerous to base any broad argument about Faulkner's aesthetics on one or two texts. Yet like *Elmer* and *Mosquitoes*, Faulkner's other early novels—*Soldier's Pay* and *Flags in the Dust*—also have androgynous characters, among them would-be artists (Horace Benbow, Januarius Jones) who just do not seem able to get it right, who become painfully—in the novel's terms—"feminized," even "victimized" by the story's end. Perhaps the most striking example of the failed artist who becomes feminized and dies, who is unable to maintain the precarious balance between male and female elements that characterizes Faulkner's construction of the imagination, is Quentin Compson. Although *The Sound and the Fury* is, in part, a tale of the destruction of a Mississippi family and the disintegration of the Old South, it also chronicles the difficulty of achieving what Fairchild describes as that "instant of timeless beatitude." Quentin's self-inflicted death by drowning—a death that recalls Sir Galwyn's watery demise—can be read to some extent as the result of a sexual and artistic relation that, rather than empowering the male artist, ends up annihilating him.

While Quentin does not actively pursue an artistic career in either novel in which he appears, he does exhibit characteristics that suggest both an artistic temperament as well as a veiled but important connection to Faulkner. A number of critics have commented on the erudition of Quentin's imagination and his artistic nature;[9] even Rosa Coldfield, the spinster-poet and often hysterical narrator of *Absalom, Absalom!*, recognizes Quentin's artistic capabilities when she summons him to hear her story. "So maybe you will enter the literary profession . . . and maybe some day you will remember this and write about it" (6). As Jackson Benson points out, "Faulkner endows [Quentin] with the equipment of the artist—the awareness, imagination, conscience, and civilized burden—so that Quentin comes to represent both the modern artist in general and also, in many revealing ways, the agony of Faulkner in particular" (143). Not coincidentally, Faulkner remarked, in a 1955 interview with Jean Stein, that "'Ishmael is the witness in *Moby Dick* as I am Quentin in *The Sound and the Fury*'" (Blotner 213). Although Faulkner's analogy is muddled, it suggests that Quentin represents far more to Faulkner than just a troubled youth. This character becomes, as we shall see, "undeniably the most complex portrait of the artist as a young man" (Bleikestan 142).

Much of that portrait echoes the problematics laid out in Faulkner's earlier works. Like *Mayday*, the second section of *The Sound and the Fury* is in part another warning about the dangers of romantic desire, and, more figuratively, the romantic imagination. Quentin, like Galwyn, cannot rid himself of the need for an idealized female figure—in this case, Caddy—whom he wishes to possess within his consciousness forever; significantly, both Quentin and Galwyn choose watery "little sister Death" (87) over a life of empty desire for a woman they dare not touch. This "woman," however, is for each of these men revealed to be a projection of a part of his self-image that he has refused to recognize. Just as Galwyn sees his lady's face when he looks into the pool, so does Quentin find Caddy when he looks into the mirror. Not coincidentally, the first picture to enter Quentin's memory—his sister on her wedding day—suggests that he experiences Caddy's departure as a terrifying loss of self: "*She ran out of the mirror like a cloud, her veil swirling in long glints her heels brittle and fast clutching her dress onto her shoulder with the other hand, running out of the mirror the smells roses roses the voice that breathed o'er Eden. Then she was across the porch I couldn't hear her heels then in the moonlight like a cloud, the floating shadow of the veil running across the grass, into the bellowing*" (81). This ephemeral and ghostly spirit bears little resemblance to the strikingly human, intensely physical woman that we know Caddy to be. That Quentin pictures her as this mysterious essence "running out of the mirror" into a darkness that echoes with the eerie cries of Benjy's despair indicates far more than that she has finished primping and has departed for the marriage ceremony. At a deeper level, Quentin experiences Caddy's departure as a terrifying loss of an integral part of his reflection, a specifically feminine part that he cannot claim directly.[10]

Having projected the "feminine" aspect of his being onto Caddy, Quentin finds his sense of wholeness and identity destroyed when she refuses to return his gaze; over and over again, he laments that "she wouldn't look at me" (94). Quentin repeatedly refers to his sister as a "blackguard" (121, 123, etc.) suggesting her participation in nefarious acts and villainous betrayals. But Caddy's crime is not so much that she has lost her virginity than that in doing so she has destroyed the intimacy of their connection and has stolen away an integral aspect of his identity. His rage and violence toward her are always spurred by his recognition that she will no longer mirror back the part of his self-image that he has projected upon her. For instance, Quentin slaps Caddy for flaunting the fact that she wanted to be kissed by Dalton Ames, but later he associates the incident with the memory of her sitting "across the table not to look at [him]" (134). At another point in the novel, Quentin remembers smearing himself and Caddy with mud after she walks in on him kissing Natalie, but what had provoked him the most was that "she had her back turned" (137) and indifferently refused to face him until he forced her to do so. Still later, Quentin holds a knife to Caddy's throat after she convinces him of her passion for Dalton, but what appears fundamentally to disconcert Quentin is that throughout the episode "her face looked at the sky" (151), and when, later, "she lifted her face I saw she wasn't even looking at me at all I could see that white rim" (157). When Quentin forces Caddy to say Dalton Ames's name she finally does look at him, but "everything emptied out of her eyes and they looked like the eyes in the statues blank and unseeing" (163); to Quentin's horror, he can no longer recognize himself in her face.

Although he has tried to repress the image of her prior sexual adventures, the moment Caddy runs out of the mirror and into Herbert's arms represents for Quentin a fall comparable to the loss of Eden, as Benjy's mourning cries suggest. While on the surface this is a fall from sexual innocence into carnal knowledge—the rose smell that surrounds Caddy in the wedding passage is later associated with sexual experience—it is more importantly from wholeness into separation and division. Strikingly similar to Aristophanes' version in Plato's *The Symposium*, this expulsion from paradise amounts for Quentin to the permanent split of an original androgynous being—a being which, of course, he has created.[11] By disrupting the intensely self-reflexive nature of their connection, Caddy's promiscuity thus condemns her brother to a life of frustrated desire for his other half, a desire that prevents Quentin from functioning sexually, emotionally, and artistically.

Essentially, Quentin's incest fantasy amounts to his final and, ultimately, futile attempt "to isolate her out of the loud world" (177) and thereby put Caddy back into the mirror. By doing "something so dreadful that they would have fled hell except us," Quentin hopes to make hell a heaven and recover his sense of wholeness, "walled by the clean flame" with "nobody else there but her and me" (79, 117, 79). The pleasure of the incest idea is associated with a kind of possession and connection that is mental, not sexual; Quentin's fantasies take place after and, indeed, repress the carnal act. As his father points out, what Quentin really wants is nothing less than an "apotheosis in which a temporary state of mind will become symmetrical above the flesh and aware both of itself and the flesh it will not quite discard [he] will not even be dead" (177). What Quentin wants is a sublime moment—much like the moments of timeless beatitude that Fairchild recalls in *Mosquitoes* or the moment in which Elmer incorporates the world within himself through his hermaphroditic paint tubes—in which he can transcend the confines of the body and reintegrate into one consciousness both himself and the part of himself that he has projected upon his sister.

That sublime apotheosis never comes about, however, because unlike Elmer, Quentin cannot identify with and incorporate the feminine aspect of his psyche into the androgyne imagination that he thinks would empower him. One reason for Quentin's hesitancy is an acute fear of being "feminized," of becoming "nothing but a girl" (138). Although Gordon, the sculptor in *Mosquitoes*, is able to master this anxiety by emphasizing the strength and masculinity of his body, Quentin still "look[s] like a kid" (160). Yet by projecting the integral "feminine" part of his selfhood onto Caddy, Quentin precipitates the destructive experience of emasculation that he wished to avoid in the first place. Now dependent upon her self-reflecting gaze for psychic balance and survival, Quentin is relegated to a passive position of desire that destroys his sense of independence and autonomy and leaves him feminized and impotent. Although he tries to deny it, repeatedly admonishing his sister that "I'm stronger than you" (149, 154, 163), Quentin continually must confront the fact that in many ways he is more of a "girl"—in the terms of the novel—than is Caddy.[12]

When Caddy becomes pregnant, it is Quentin who cries helplessly "against her damp blouse" (151), not so much for his sister's misfortune as for his recognition that she will no longer be there to sustain him. Indeed, it is Caddy, not her brother, who takes the active role in everything, including sex; while Caddy is defiantly "unvirgin" (78), Quentin is unable to act on his desires, for fear of offending the one woman he cannot afford to lose. The single time Quentin does kiss another girl—Natalie—he is discovered by Caddy, and then he proceeds to throw himself in a hog wallow in utter self-abasement. Yet by avoiding other women, Quentin risks being considered "queer"; this happens at Harvard, when Spoade calls Shreve Quentin's "husband" (78). Increasingly, Quentin begins to wonder if Spoade is right:

"if it was that simple to do it wouldn't be anything and if it wasn't anything, what was I" (147). By the end of the novel, at least on a symbolic level, Quentin has turned into a woman. Yet the female Quentin that represents the legacy of his misplaced desire is an alienated, unhappy mistake, forever unattached, marginalized, and disempowered; as Faulkner explains in the appendix to the original 1929 edition, Quentin was "fatherless nine months before her birth, nameless at birth, and already doomed to be unwed from the instant the dividing egg determined its sex" (424).

Not only is Quentin "feminized," he is finally condemned and destroyed by the castrating guilt of his desire for what is essentially the kind of imagination he cannot admit to possessing. In projecting his androgynous, fertile, desirable, artistic self onto his sister, Quentin conflates an androgyne imagination with the most taboo form of sexual transgression and becomes obsessed with the "concept of its eternal punishment" (1929 edition, 411). As in *Elmer*, *Mosquitoes*, and even *Flags in the Dust* (with Horace and Narcissa), psychic hermaphroditism is associated with a problematic form of "psychic incest"; the other side of "Hermaphroditus" is a consciousness that is monstrous, perverse, and diseased. Quentin's guilt over his desire for what his sister mirrors back to him turns even his attempts at standing up to vulgarians such as Dalton Ames and Gerald Bland into occasions for self-punishment and humiliation. In the both instances, Quentin purposely picks a fight with a man much stronger than he could possibly hope to master, and then—it seems purposeful—he "passe[s] out like a girl" (162).

Despite the fact that waiting for it has almost completely destroyed him, Quentin keeps hoping for that sublime apotheosis of androgynous consciousness to occur, even up until the final moments before his death. In a brief and tightly layered moment, Quentin strives to work through his psychic crisis for the last time, conflating a recent experience on the evening train during which he "couldn't see anything except [his] own face [his reflection on the opposite window] and a woman across the aisle with a hat sitting right on top of her head, with a broken feather in it" (169) with Caddy's wedding and his perceived psychic split:

> While I was brushing my hair the half hour went. But there was until the three quarters anyway, except suppose *seeing on the rushing darkness only his own face no broken feather unless two of them but not two of them like that going to Boston the same night then my face his face for an instant across the crashing when out of darkness two lighted windows in rigid fleeing crash gone his face and mine just I see saw did I see not goodbye the marquee empty of eating the road empty in darkness in silence the bridge arching into silence darkness sleep the water peaceful and swift not goodbye.* (172)

At the last minute, Quentin hesitates in his suicidal resolve. Figuratively recalling the loss of his "feminine" side—the reflection he sees on the glass is no longer paired with the woman's face—he at first sees the void as permanent. Yet for a moment, he speculates: "unless two of them but not two of them like that." Here again, Quentin longs for some kind of union with Caddy, but a union which unlike that between Caddy and Herbert is psychic not sexual.[13] However, when Quentin recalls the two lighted windows, he is making a veiled reference to the moment in which Caddy confessed her love for Dalton and stopped being Quentin's "mirror," a moment which occurred at night, outdoors in front of his mother's and Benjy's illuminated rooms (150, 156). After Quentin recollects this night, he fully realizes that his fantasy is hopeless; Caddy will never again come back into the mirror. Unable to survive his fragmented consciousness, Quentin finally can only see his reflection in the "black, secret, friendly gaze" (138) of "little sister Death." The silent Italian girl who had refused to leave his side becomes her incarnation; her stare—"still and black and unwinking" (133)—ultimately merges with images of the river water "dark and still and swift" (138). Although Quentin has tried to evade her, she follows him like a shadow until his broken psyche eventually joins with the "tideflats [that look] like pieces of broken mirror" (170).

In suggesting this reading of Quentin's section in *The Sound and the Fury*, I do not wish to deny the validity of more conventional psychoanalytic interpretations. A share of Quentin's motivations does stem from a need to challenge the authority of the father (Irwin, Bleikestan) as well as a wish to relive the safety of his childhood world, especially his privileged relationship with Caddy, who is in part his mother-surrogate (Karl; Bleikestan 112–15). However, such readings do not take into account the tremendous affinities between this novel and Faulkner's earlier artist novels, affinities which are all the more significant considering that Faulkner began work on *The Sound and the Fury* barely one year after the publication of *Mosquitoes,* and only two years after he abandoned the *Elmer* manuscript. Although acknowledging that "Quentin's love for Caddy is from the outset an ambivalent form of self-love" (Bleikestan 117), many critics do not trace his narcissism to an unresolved crisis of imagination. Yet Quentin's "doglike" dependency upon that elusive sister who has become frighteningly "cunning and serene" (*Sound and the Fury* 77) strongly echoes Elmer's experience with his romantic muse. Unlike Quentin, however, Elmer is at least temporarily able to separate art from life, freeing himself artistically from his fierce "Dianalike girl" and, indirectly, from her prototype, the sister who also abandons the family and becomes a whore, by replacing her image with the hermaphroditic paint tubes that represent his artistic consciousness. Moreover, like Patricia Robyn, Caddy is another androgynous woman who scales fences, climbs trees, and is full of "'manly' courage and audacity" (Wittenberg 239); even in Caddy's fantasies, "she never was a queen or a fairy she was always a king or a giant or a general" (*Sound and the Fury* 173). Yet while Gordon—although attracted to Patricia—is able to recognize his interest in her as merely reflective of his androgynous artistic "attitude," or imagination, Quentin is not. What, then, is the significance of Quentin's suicide? Is Faulkner suggesting, in this work which he later said "caused me the most anguish and is to me the finest failure" (*Lion* 146), that for the male artist a truly androgyne imagination is forever "unachievable"?[14]

Minrose Gwin argues that Caddy represents "the feminine within" (27) that Quentin must deny in order to participate in the patriarchal world; however, Quentin's crisis—like Faulkner's—is specifically that he cannot deny his feminine side, nor does he wish to do so. As we have seen for Faulkner, artistic creativity requires more than mere "phallic generative power" (Irwin 159). Yet representing the imagination as both male and female, as both phallus and womb, means confronting the female body, and Faulkner is often troubled about that. Although Elmer is fascinated by the uterus, many of Faulkner's other male "artists" are terrified of being subsumed and destroyed by female reproductive parts. For Quentin, the womb conjures up images of "liquid putrefaction like drowned things floating like pale rubber flabbily filled," ever waiting to be unleashed and overcome by "some man" (*Sound and the Fury* 128). In *Light in August*, Joe Christmas retches at the sight of womb-like urns after he realizes his girlfriend, Joanna, is menstruating: "not one was perfect. Each one was cracked and from each crack issued something liquid, deathcolored, and foul" (177–78). For Joe, as for Quentin, women and women's bodies become contaminating, poisoning, and overwhelming.[15] As we will see later, Harry Wilbourne and the Tall Convict of *The Wild Palms* are also terrified by the destructive potential of the "inert monstrous sentient womb" (163). Thus, beyond feminization and sexual transgression, envisaging "the feminine within" initiates tremendous anxieties about self-annihilation that prevent Quentin from experiencing and surviving a sublime apotheosis of the imagination, of becoming literally "philoprogenitive" (*Sound and the Fury* 122); instead, Quentin throws himself into the river to avoid "drowning" in a womb within. Joe kills Joanna when she uses her "pregnant" womb to threaten him. Harry Wilbourne destroys Charlotte's womb before it can overwhelm him, and, like the Tall Convict, he eventually cloisters himself in the safe, male haven of the prison.

This anxiety about the female body and female procreativity translates into a concern about the viability of the androgyne imagination model. For if, as was suggested in *Mosquitoes*, all creation is essentially a kind of "reproduction from within," and the "dominating impulse in the world is feminine" (320), then sustaining a balance between the sexes in the psyche is a difficult proposition. Rather than a site of generative union, the image of the hermaphrodite is one of warring factions, each fighting to the death to avoid becoming subsumed by the other: "The phenomenon of war is its hermaphroditism: principles of victory and defeat inhabit the same body and the necessary opponent, enemy, is merely the bed they self-exhaust each other on" (*A Fable* 291). As figuratively the "bed they self-exhaust each other on," the male artist's mind has turned into a war zone. More often than not, as we have seen, it is the female opponent that threatens to "flood" the battlefield. Faulkner's male artists increasingly cannot survive the sublime confrontation between "male" and "female" elements within their imaginations; instead of being empowered, they more often remain engulfed by the battle.

Ironically, while Faulkner's conception of a destructive "female principle" (*Wild Palms* 57) threatens to overwhelm the male artist, it often proves hazardous to the female artist as well by making her prisoner of her body. For instance, one could argue that it is Caddy—the androgynous, independent, imaginative sister, the creator of her brothers' worlds and destinies (Gwin)—who is the only one who even comes close to being a successful artist in *The Sound and the Fury*. Yet her body seals her doom; pregnancy becomes the disease—"I'm sick" (112)—that at least figuratively kills Caddy by forcing her into a marriage that will end with her disgrace. In *Sanctuary*, although she is not an artist, Temple Drake fantasizes about erasing her female sexual organs and magically turning into a boy immediately before she is brutally raped; but, ultimately, her violated womb ends up tainting both her body and mind with its profuse bleeding. In *Absalom, Absalom!*, Rosa Coldfield is an artist—indeed the "poetess laureate" (8) of her community—yet, despite her powerful voice, she is haunted by the barrenness of her "thwarted old female flesh" (13). While claiming to be "love's androgynous advocate" (182), Rosa feels shriveled and unnatural, a "hollow woman" (181) rather than "the man which [she] perhaps should have been" (179).

Although Faulkner would appear to have exhausted any and all possibilities for engaging an androgyne imagination, it is significant that in his final novel about art and artists—a novel in which almost everyone "is depicted in androgynous terms" (McHaney, *Faulkner's* 141)—he returns to it with an even greater emphasis than before. Many of the same tensions and problems remain unresolved; nevertheless, in *The Wild Palms* Faulkner finally creates an artist who comes closest to achieving his imaginative ideal—and it turns out to be a woman. Although she—like Caddy, Rosa, and Temple—is ultimately done in by the same womb that is the figurative source for so much of her creative energy, Charlotte manages more than any other artist in Faulkner's oeuvre to balance her creative and sexual drives. At first glance, Charlotte Rittenmeyer bears a striking resemblance to Helen Baird; her physical characteristics, artistic medium (figurines), and connection with the Gulf Coast recall the enigmatic and elusive lover from Faulkner's past. Yet like Eva Wiseman in *Mosquitoes*, Charlotte maintains ideas about art and creativity that are definitely Faulkner's own (see endnote 17). In her self-conscious abandonment of traditional gender distinctions, Charlotte has been called by one critic "a man in disguise" (Blotner 391). Charlotte's deep intellectual affinities with Faulkner suggest that this "masculine" woman is in important ways the novelist in disguise.

Why would Faulkner want to "become" female? As we saw with Eva Wiseman, disguising himself as a woman is one strategy by which Faulkner can safely explore the possibilities of an androgyne imagination and venture his transgressive ideas about art and love, without the risk of appearing the effeminate or emasculated male. Charlotte, like Eva, becomes Faulkner's "fall guy"; indeed, while critics have consistently faulted her for her bohemian depravity, condemning the "essential sterility of Charlotte's ideal" (Millgate 171), they have left Faulkner unscathed. Yet even this subversive strategy does not take away the author's fear and ambivalence. If a part of Faulkner is Charlotte, a part him remains the tormented male, attracted to but terrified by Charlotte's transgressive fecundity, threatened by the combined effect of her intellectual and reproductive powers. Splitting himself in two, Faulkner finally lets his "male" half—Harry Wilbourne—kill off the "woman."

Although Charlotte Rittenmeyer is ultimately not allowed to get away with it, for a while, she masterfully transcends the blockage that dooms Faulkner's male artist-heroes. While they often let their fears of being feminized and marginalized prevent them from achieving their artistic potential, she is willing to sacrifice everything to her aesthetic ambitions, insisting, "I had rather drown in the ocean than be urped up onto a strip of dead beach and be dried away by the sun into a little foul smear with no name on it" (83). Unlike Quentin and the young Elmer, who in their ambivalence about the feminine aspect of their imaginations displace it onto their sisters, Charlotte refuses the pitfalls of psychic and physical incest, by marrying because "you can't sleep with your brother" (40), and she fully accepts herself as "that always androgynous creature, the artist" (Blotner 391). Another of Faulkner's epicene women, Charlotte has no problem incorporating a "masculine" side to her consciousness, and she is most at home in men's pants and overalls. By being a woman, Charlotte escapes the fear of "feminization" that haunts Quentin and the rest. Yet interestingly, Faulkner allows Charlotte to escape the withering masculinization that turns his other androgynous women artists—Rosa and Eva—into sexless freaks of nature. While the doctor's wife, whose voice is "a good deal more masculine" than her husband's, is described as a "gray-faced Medusa-headed" woman with a mind as cold and sterile as her barren womb (288, 289), Charlotte is fertile (she has borne two children) and sexually attractive, with a face "gentler than not, assured, courteous and successful" (40), and she wears "pants that was just exactly too little for her in just exactly the right places" (7).

What kind of art does this lively, powerful, androgynous artist produce? Like Faulkner, whose ambition was "to create flesh-and-blood, living, suffering, anguishing human beings" (*University* 47), Charlotte strives in her sculpture to invent something solid, substantial, "something with weight in your hand that you can look at the behind side of. . . . Not something to tickle your taste buds for a second" (41). With "deft untiring hands," she makes "deer and wolfhounds and men and women, lean epicene sophisticated and bizarre," "effigies elegant . . . fantastic and perverse" (89, 87, 89). Provocative and transgressively modern, Charlotte's work—like Faulkner's —disrupts categories such as male and female, high and low, and it draws its inspiration precisely from the blurring of these culturally imposed divisions.[16] Asked to produce some representations of Chicago's past, Charlotte stuns her audience with sculptures of "Mrs. O'Leary with Nero's face and the cow with a ukelele, Kit Carson with legs like Nijinsky and no face, just two eyes and a shelf of forehead to shade them with, buffalo cows with the heads and flanks of Arabian mares" (87). Her wildly impressionistic, yet lifelike, puppets are also "fragile perverse and disturbing" (91); interestingly, they are of literary characters—Quixote, Falstaff, Cyrano, Roxanne—whom Faulkner liked the most (see *Lion* 251; Brooks 139). Seeing a buck run off into the woods, Charlotte says of her own creations, "that's what I was trying to make. . . . Not the animals, the dogs and deer and horses: the motion, the speed" (99–100). In a similar vein, Faulkner would later argue that "the aim of every artist is to arrest motion, which is life, by artificial means" (*Lion* 253).[17]

Despite the parallels to Faulkner's aesthetic ambitions—which most critics have ignored—many readers of *The Wild Palms* have questioned Charlotte's legitimacy as an artist. Calling her work "a sham, only satire and caricature" (McHaney, *Faulkner's* 86), they view her figurines as "perverse . . . exclusive, warped, and life-negating" (Harrington 71). Charlotte's "effigies" do fail at capturing the "motion, the speed" of life, yet I would argue that her failure would make her all the more a "success" in Faulkner's opinion. Throughout his published interviews, he insisted that "failure to me is the best. To try something you can't do, because it's too much [to hope for], but still to try it and fail, then try it again. That to me is success" (*Lion* 88). Indeed, "failure" became Faulkner's primary criterion for evaluating his contemporaries. For example, Faulkner consistently downplayed Hemingway's artistic merit because of his opinion that Hemingway did not reach high enough to fall short of his goal. Of himself, Faulkner would proudly boast that he failed more splendidly than any other artist, excepting Thomas Wolfe (*Lion* 81).

Charlotte would also earn Faulknerian artistic legitimacy through her singular dedication to her work. Watching her with a kind of fear and awe, Harry comments: "there was a part of her which neither he nor Rittenmeyer had ever touched; which did not even love love . . . he returned and found her at the bench again, in a profound excitement which he had never seen before—an excitement without exultation but with a grim and deadly quality of irresistible driving as she told him about it" (90). Neither dabbler nor dilettante, Charlotte works with "tense and concentrated fury" (90). Like Faulkner, who said he felt constantly "demon-run, under compulsion, always being driven" by his writing (*Lion* 220), Charlotte has that insatiable appetite which is not from the belly but from the soul; when showing Harry its location, "she touched his breast" (86). Brilliant, fiery, and irrepressible, her drive to create is "like a skyrocket or a roman candle or at least one of those sparkler sticks for little children that sparkle away into a live red coal that's not afraid to die" (95).

Burning with inspiration and creative drive, Charlotte would appear to be unstoppable. But she is stopped, and it is neither her fierce romantic idealism nor her rejection of traditional female roles that finally kills her. She has proven herself capable of earning enough money to live on, and the husband she has abandoned has left her alone. What destroys Charlotte is the other artist in the novel, the failed male artist who is most threatened by the (pro)creative powers with which he cannot compete. It is more than coincidence that Charlotte's lover Harry Wilbourne ends up literally (and symbolically) destroying both sources of Charlotte's creativity—her physical womb as well as the womb of her imagination when he botches her abortion. For Harry has failed miserably in all the areas in which Charlotte triumphs—as lover, provider, and, most important, as artist; Harry muses throughout the novel, "*She is not only a better man and a better gentleman than I am, she is a better everything than I will ever be*" (207). Harry, the self-described "sparrow," is ultimately unable to "be the consort of a falcon" (141). Not coincidentally, just when Charlotte is closest to achieving Faulkner's imaginative ideal, he "aborts" the project, although with ambivalence and regret.

In contrast to Charlotte's undimming creative energy, Harry's artistic efforts can only be described as themselves "abortive." While Charlotte and Harry are at the cabin on the coast, he demands that she give him half her pad and paints, but he discovers he is color blind and makes a calendar instead. Much later in the story, after Charlotte is suffering from the infection resulting from the botched abortion, Harry responds to the doctor's inquiry into his profession by saying "I paint pictures. . . . At least I think I do" (18), but we never see any evidence of his new "vocation." Harry does work harder at being a writer, but after a "sustained frenzied agonizing rush" of effort, he succeeds only in "birthing" a "batch of moron's pap" (121, 122). In contrast to his lover's "sophisticated and bizarre" creations, Harry's stories are cliched and "moronic," with first lines such as "I had the body and desires of a woman yet in knowledge and experience of the world I was but a child," or "at sixteen I was an unwed mother" (123, 121, 123). This kind of forced androgyny, unlike Charlotte's, produces nothing but trite "sexual gumdrop[s]" and an awareness of "the depths of depravity of which the human invention is capable" (123, 132–33). While his lover hungers for the skyrockets of inspiration, Harry settles for "the anesthesia of his monotonous inventing," which, however bland, at least provides some material rewards (122, 132).

If art empowers Charlotte, it feminizes Harry. Although claiming to have abandoned his writing career because he had become too "respectable" and "had turned into a husband" (132), what really scares him is that he fears he has turned into a wife. Working at home, Harry's routine threatens to turn him into "the Complete Householder": "each morning, so that my wife could leave for her job, I would wash the coffee pot and the sink twice a week. . . . I would buy from the same butcher the groceries we needed" (133, 134). While the arrangement does not seem to bother Charlotte, Harry makes the couple resettle where he can use his medical training to provide for them, ironically pointing out to the officials at the mining company to which they "escape" that "none of us are androgynous" (129). The statement is, of course, untrue; nevertheless, it suggests that Harry has a significant amount of anxiety about transgressing his "male" role.

Yet what is even more frightening to Harry than Charlotte's superior "manliness" and artistic success is the unfathomable power of her body. At one point, he tries measuring time by her menstrual periods, but he is thrown off when one cycle lasts six weeks, and he finds himself behind on all his calculations. Lamenting that, "*I have been seduced to an imbecile's paradise by an old whore; I have been throttled and sapped of strength and volition by the old weary Lilith of the year*" (114–15), Harry repeatedly fights feelings of engulfment and impotence.[18] While, on the one hand, Harry revels in Charlotte's all-encompassing love, "existing in a drowsy and foetuslike state, passive and almost unsentient in the womb of solitude and peace" (110), on the other hand, he fears that he will ultimately be destroyed by her passion.

These anxieties are nowhere better expressed than in a conversation Harry has with the newspaper reporter McCord, who befriends the couple. Describing his experience of losing his virginity, Harry explains:

> you herd the beast you have ridden all your life, the old familiar well-broken nag, up to the precipice. . . . Maybe you thought all the time that when the moment came you could rein back, save something, maybe not, the instant comes and you know you can-

> not . . . you are the one single abnegant affirmation, one single fluxive Yes out of the terror in which you surrender volition, hope, all—the darkness the falling, the thunder of solitude, the shock, the death, the moment when, stopped physically by the ponderable clay, you yet feel all your life rush out of you into the pervading immemorial blind receptive matrix, the hot fluid blind foundation—grave-womb or womb-grave, it's all one. (138)

In this bizarre passage, Harry essentially associates sexual intercourse with a sublime confrontation that suddenly stops playing by the rules. As Edmund Burke suggests: "The passions which belong to self-preservation, turn on pain and danger; they are simply painful when their causes immediately affect us; they are delightful when we have an idea of pain and danger, without being actually in such circumstances. . . . Whatever excites this delight, I call *sublime*" (47). Riding up to the precipice—suggestive of height, danger, and magnitude of the depth of the vagina—Harry expects to be able to rein back and thereby save something. He counts on feeling the pleasurable terror, the thrill of sensing the nearness of death without actually experiencing it. But instead of being entertained by surviving what is in essence a fictional sensation of annihilation, Harry suffers a complete loss of autonomy and control, and he ends up figuratively smashed to pieces in Charlotte's "hot fluid blind . . . grave-womb." Utterly engulfed and devastated, Harry finds himself basically "embattled and doomed and lost before the entire female principle" (57).

The violence of this image suggests that for Harry the female body is powerful, terrifying, and threatening. Although in the context of the passage Harry is describing the experience of sexual intercourse, one could safely assume that for him—and I would argue for a part of Faulkner as well—any attempt at merging with the female is a risky endeavor. How does one reconcile the womb as both fertile half of the male imagination and as devouring, flooding force of female power? Harry cannot. Performing the abortion with a knife, he cuts into that threatening womb until it ends up subsuming itself and poisoning Charlotte at her core.

Harry is not the only man in the novel that wishes to destroy, or at least escape from, the devouring womb. As Janet Carey Eldred points out, there are several other male characters in the novel who "see themselves as victims of a powerful female force" (152). Most dramatic is the example of the Tall Convict, hero of the interweaving narrative entitled "The Old Man," which serves as "counterpoint" to the story of Harry and Charlotte (*Lion* 247). The nameless pregnant woman that the Tall Convict must rescue from the flood becomes symbolic of that female principle. Taking on a life of its own, her swollen belly is described as "a separate demanding inert yet living mass of which both he and she were equally victims" (154). Terrified by her "inert monstrous sentient womb" (163), the Convict, nevertheless, cannot destroy it as Harry does; instead, he finds himself prisoner to the flood of her birth waters—a power far greater and more terrifying than that of the authorities. Wishing he could turn his back "on all pregnant and female life forever and return to that monastic existence of shotguns and shackles where he would be secure from it" (153), the Convict turns himself in to the authorities as soon as he possibly can.

Like Harry, the Convict is ultimately afraid of women, sex, and even androgyny. After the woman has her child on a muddy riverbank, they are all picked up by a steamer. When the Tall Convict has a bad reaction to liquor, one of the crew suggests the Convict is hemophiliac; during the now incarcerated Convict's frame narrative, however, his audience gets it wrong, thinking he means hermaphrodite. One convict suggests: "That's a calf that's a bull and a cow at the same time." Another one says: "it's a calf or a colt that ain't neither one" (242). Is the first convict, the narrator, positive hermaphrodite or castrated eunuch? Is constructing a hermaphroditic imagination an image of fecundity or irreversible sterility? Whichever the case, in the novel "all agree that it is an insult" (Duvall 55).

Driven by "images of fertility and sterility, of birth and death" (McHaney, *Faulkner's* 114), *The Wild Palms*—and especially Harry and Charlotte's narrative—dramatizes Faulkner's convictions about the potentially unlimited power of the androgynous artist as well as the tension his characters experience between the male artist and the "female principle." Although the woman becomes the more successful creator, she (like Caddy, Rosa, Lena, Joanna, and Temple) is "betrayed" by her anatomy—precisely the symbol of her creativity—and that is what sets her apart from the dissatisfied artistic man.

Destroyed by an infection from within the womb, she becomes an ironic victim of the symbolic source of her greatest artistic potential. What are we to make of this? Are we, as one critic suggests, ultimately "to realize that this female creative power, this 'dominating feminine impulse' is a threat to the race" (Eldred 156)? Faulkner never answers this question, although the provocative last line of the novel, "Women ——t!" (339), indicates an ironic and troubled confusion, not an unequivocal misogynist condemnation.

For it is important to note that, despite her punishment, Charlotte is presented more sympathetically than either Harry or the Tall Convict. Although critics have valorized the characters' dedication to their women, their choice of life over death, they ignore the fact that in many ways Faulkner shows them as extremely limited human beings. Harry has none of Charlotte's self-assuredness or initiative or talent. The Tall Convict is ignorant even to the point of being stupid; he robs a train to impress a young woman because it sounded glamorous in the dime-store novels that he read, and then he blames her when she leaves him.

Moreover, Faulkner's conception of an androgyne imagination does posit some aspect of the female as necessary for literary authorization and creative empowerment. To put it another way, if the power of the female is feared, it is also admired. Critics such as Sandra Gilbert and Susan Gubar point to the huge number of sexually wounded men in the literature of male modernists and attribute it to the sex war (*War of the Words* 36). Faulkner certainly does create many impotent male figures—Benjy, Popeye, Quentin, the Convict—but, at the same time, he creates powerful and attractive women characters such as Caddy, Rosa, and Charlotte, whom he (unlike some of his male characters) seems genuinely to respect, not blame.

It is in trying to incorporate that energizing, creative "female principle" into his psyche, to somehow identify with it, however, that Faulkner's model fails. Attempting a perilous mental confrontation with and introjection of that female principle, his male artist-characters soon find themselves overcome and overpowered by their efforts. Expecting the frightening but finally empowering experience of the sublime, they more often find themselves consumed and annihilated when their heightened fears about the feminine turn that experience into a literally life-threatening one. Thus, while its rewards are gestured toward, Faulkner's model of the imagination never works in practice; perhaps Charlotte and Elmer come closest to achieving it, even though, as we have seen, the former is killed off and the latter's story remains unfinished. Such a strategy for artistic empowerment was finally too threatening for Faulkner to carry through.

Yet despite his characters' failures, and the problems with his imaginative model, Faulkner managed to produce poems, short stories, a play, and over twenty novels. Has Faulkner, then, managed to survive the confrontation with the powerful feminine principle? Has he, unlike his artist-heroes and artist-heroines, succeeded in constructing that androgyne imagination? At one point, Faulkner did boast, "I'm convinced I can improve on the Lord," and, later, he mysteriously commented that "I think that a writer is a perfect case of split personality. That he is one thing when he is a writer and he is something else while he is a denizen of the world" (*University* 123, 268).

In the final analysis, however, whether or not Faulkner was able to utilize the model of imagination toward which he gestures in *The Wild Palms* may not be so important after all. As Faulkner never tired of saying:

> All of us failed to match our dream of perfection. So I rate us on the basis of our splendid failure to do the impossible. In my opinion, if I could write all my work again, I am convinced that I would do it better, which is the healthiest condition of an artist. That's why he keeps on working, trying again; he believes each time and this time he will do it, bring it off. Of course he won't, which is why this condition is healthy. Once he did it, once he matched the work to the image, the dream, nothing would remain but to cut his throat, jump off the other side of that pinnacle of cut perfection into suicide. (*Lion* 238)

For Faulkner, perhaps inspiration finally is drawn from the struggle itself. And even if he never quite achieved it, the possibility of an androgyne imagination never ceased to inspire him.

5

"A Toy Boat on the Serpentine, It's Ecstasy—Ecstasy"

Woolf's Sublimating Sublime

> But the sight of the two people getting into the taxi and the satisfaction it gave me made me also ask whether there are two sexes in the mind corresponding to the two sexes in the body, and whether they also require to be united in order to get complete satisfaction and happiness. And I went on amateurishly to sketch a plan of the soul so that in each of us two powers preside, one male, one female. . . . Coleridge perhaps meant this when he said that a great mind is androgynous. It is when this fusion takes place that the mind is fully fertilized and uses all its faculties. Perhaps a mind that is purely masculine cannot create, any more than a mind that is purely feminine, I thought.
>
> —*A Room of One's Own*, Virginia Woolf

Among literary critics—especially feminists—"androgyny" has become virtually synonymous with "Virginia Woolf." Unquestionably the most debated and discussed passage in her vast oeuvre, this brief excerpt has been singled out by many scholars over the past twenty years as the definitive litmus test for Woolf's success or failure as an artist and, more important, as a woman.[1] In the 1970s, for example, Carolyn Heilbrun pronounced Woolf the prophet of sexual liberation, the messenger of an enlightened androgynous vision (115). Writing at approximately the same time, Nancy Topping Bazin and Elaine Showalter used the androgyny passage to advance a more critical view of their author. For Bazin, the taxicab image was the work of a manic-depressive woman writer, alternately swinging between the effusive *jouissance* of femininity and the paralysis of patriarchy; for Showalter, the passage reveals a halfhearted rebel constructing a "myth that helped her evade confrontation with her own painful femaleness and enabled her to choke and repress her anger and ambition" (Showalter 264).[2] More than a decade later, the few Woolf critics who still talk about androgyny (now considered a passé debate) use more theoretically complex terms but have returned to Heilbrun's familiar venerative mode. No longer the powerful and enlightened prophet or the confused and reluctant rebel, Woolf has now been labeled the subversive, even deconstructive, feminist. While Frances C. Restuccia reads the androgyny passage as "a curtain draped over the more subversive defense of female difference" (Restuccia, "'Untying'" 262), Toril Moi goes so far as to say that it uncovers Woolf's attempt at "a non-essentialist form of writing" as well as "a deeply sceptical attitude to the male-humanist concept of an essential human identity" (9). More recently, Kari Elise Lokke and Karen R. Lawrence have found in Woolf's ambiguously sexed characters what Jane Marcus once called a kind of "collective sublime" (10).[3]

All these scholars allow us to read and understand Woolf in profound and exciting new ways. However, their contradictory portraits of the artist—briefly recounted here—turn on a late-twentieth-century definition of androgyny, as a mixture of so-called masculine and feminine personality characteristics such as strength and compassion, rather than on an historically grounded one. Yet I would like to change lenses and consider Woolf's attraction to androgyny from the perspective of her cultural moment. Specifically, I will demonstrate how her androgyne trope not only is tied to the same socio-scientific antecedents as the other modernist writers in this study but that it functions as a means by which she too attempts to authorize and stabilize her identity as both a woman and a writer. Threatened most immediately by explosive revelations of patriarchal repression and its inhibiting effect upon herself as a woman writer, Woolf responds by forging a sublime union between herself and her vision of an androgyne imagination in order to generate authority and inspiration. Like those of the other modernists in this study, however, her solution is most often problematic and troubling; for Woolf, as with H. D., experiencing the empowering transport of the sublime ironically necessitates the repression of nothing less than her own body.

The particular mechanics of that repression, and of the sublime energy it is designed to promote, are evident in a large number of Woolf's texts but are most lucidly presented in "A Sketch of the Past," an autobiographical essay written near the end of her life and published in a posthumous collection entitled *Moments of Being*. A close look at this document will provide us with the missing piece to the androgynous puzzle of the sixth chapter of *A Room of One's Own*, a text to which we will then return. It is only after developing a clearer picture of Woolf's androgynous aesthetics that we can move on to those novels in which issues of sexual indeterminacy figure most prominently: *To the Lighthouse*, *Orlando*, and *The Waves*. In those texts, we will see how and why Woolf's androgynous sublime ultimately falls apart.

Although written at the end of her career, "A Sketch of the Past" reveals Woolf's most personal and provocative comments about her artistic method. Yet while many critics are quick to wrap her famous *Moments of Being* in the triumphant mantle of epiphany, a closer look at Woolf's experience of inspiration discloses its excruciating underside.[4] The "Sketch of the Past" section begins as she recalls three childhood examples of revelatory moments: getting into a fight with her brother Thoby and realizing the violence of which humans are capable, seeing a flower and comprehending its relation to the whole of the world, and associating a tree in her yard with a former guest's suicide. What is striking about the list is that only one of these experiences was nonthreatening; moreover, the fact that she cites the negative ones both first and last is indicative of their preponderance. The hoped-for sensation (which she did receive in the second example) is of an uplifting, even transportive, sense of oceanic unity with all Being; seeing the flower, Woolf-as-girl exclaims, "That is the whole" (*Moments* 71). Rather than a blissful and empowering unity, however, what she experiences most often is "a feeling of hopeless sadness . . . as if I became aware of something terrible; and of my own powerlessness" (*Moments* 71). Beyond Woolf's awareness of the violence and brutality of which humanity is capable is a recognition of her vulnerability. What horrifies Woolf most about Thoby's blows and the suicide's choice is the revelation not of evil but of the precariousness of her own identity, most particularly (as we shall see more clearly later) of her female identity. Woolf explains: "I seemed to be dragged down, hopelessly, into some pit of absolute despair from which I could not escape. My body seemed paralysed" (*Moments* 71). Rather than an empowering experience, poetic revelation becomes for Woolf a terrifying one in which all boundaries disappear and the self collapses.

She goes on to explain these moments in greater detail. The following passage crystallizes Woolf's sense of the creative process:

> I only know that many of these exceptional moments brought with them a peculiar horror and a physical collapse; they seemed dominant; myself passive. This suggests that as one gets older one has a greater power through reason to provide an explanation; and that this explanation blunts the sledge-hammer force of the blow. I think this is true, because though I still have the peculiarity that I receive those sudden shocks, they are now always welcome; after the first surprise, I always feel instantly that they are particularly valuable. And so I go on to suppose that the shock-receiving capacity is what makes me a writer. I hazard the explanation that a shock is at once in my case followed by a desire to explain it. . . . It is only by putting it into words that I make it whole; this wholeness means that it has lost its power to hurt me; it gives me, perhaps because by doing so I take away the pain, a great delight to put the severed parts together. Perhaps this is the strongest pleasure known to me. It is the rapture I get when in writing. (*Moments* 72)

Rather than a quasi-religious experience of ecstasy, the moment of inspiration is for Woolf a shock comparable to being beaten with a sledgehammer. That she has to work so hard to transform these painful revelations into rapturous and delightful ones demands attention. What is it about creative vision that is so caustic, so threatening, so dangerous? First of all, it implies a loss of power and agency through a kind of victimization from which she is (at least at first) helpless to protect herself. Inspiration is figured as something that happens to her, a visitation to which she must passively submit. Yet unlike Milton, who treasures his nightly directives from Urania, Woolf represents herself as an unwilling recipient of what becomes a kind of psychic violence over which she has no control. It is important to point out that such experiences are not limited to her childhood. Even at the end of her life Woolf admits, "I still have the peculiarity that I receive these sudden shocks" (*Moments* 72). Rather than a privilege, such moments present themselves—at least initially—as a kind of curse.

However, the particular agony of this curse is not merely the experience of assault, disempowerment, and surprise but, more important and basic, a sense of psychic collapse. What gets beaten by the sledgehammer is her ego. Exploding her previous understanding of the world, and I would argue of herself, into "severed parts" (*Moments* 72), the blows of vision leave Woolf's psyche in fragments. For "the pain of discovering that people hurt each other" (*Moments* 72)—and that they hurt themselves—reminds her of the precarious stability of her own personhood as well as of her authority as an artist. Promoting sensations of mutilation, decomposition, and unraveling, creative inspiration presents itself as a violent, destructive, and explosive force. Although this World War II text bears the influence of Woolf's growing fears of a German invasion, such violent depictions of the creative process appear—as we will soon see—in many of her earlier works as well. This is not exactly a comforting picture of artistic enlightenment.

What is the ultimate source of these painful shocks? Why would inspiration begin as a terrifying experience? Although the answers to such questions are left vague in this passage, they are suggested clearly enough by the rest of the "Sketch of the Past" narrative. Most specifically, the explanations are traceable to the direct assault (both literal and figurative) of repressive late-Victorian patriarchal assumptions about women and women's bodies upon Woolf's identity, authority, and self-presence. Particularly striking is the degree to which her descriptions of those shocking and agonizing moments of being are similar to her depictions of patriarchal violence—throughout "A Sketch of the Past" as well as her letters and diaries. Describing the deaths of her mother and her half-sister, Stella, as "mutilating" (*Moments* 137) to her ego, Woolf explains how it "tortured and fretted and made [her] numb" (136) by exposing both Virginia and Vanessa to the full brunt of their father's "brutality" (145): "Very soon after Stella's death we realized that we must make some standing place for ourselves in this baffling, frustrating whirlpool. Every day we did battle for that which was always being snatched from us, or distorted. The most imminent obstacle, the most oppressive stone laid upon our vitality and its struggle to live was of course father" (143–44). Central to this passage is an agonizing sense of disintegration, mutilation, and dispersal of the self. Woolf's pain consists in the terrifying realization that her identity and authority are being snatched away while she remains powerless to stop it. As with the sledgehammer moments, she remains ever in "horror and the terror," ever conscious of "the anticipation of torture" by her father's rage (146, 144). Like the beginning of those previously described moments of being, what is especially frightening about this agony is Woolf's awareness of her impotence. The real torture is that she must remain passive: "Never have I felt such rage and such frustration. For not a word of what I felt—that unbounded contempt for him and of pity for Nessa—could be expressed" (*Moments* 144). The sledgehammer assault of patriarchy renders her mute and deprives her of identity. It is for this that she "thought him brutal" (146).

The Law of the Father snatches her voice in other ways as well. While allowed to read and write in private, Woolf is expected to feign ignorance in public: "we could and indeed must, sit passive and applaud the Victorian males when they went through the intellectual hoops" (*Moments* 154). Her first example of womanhood—her mother—"was taught . . . to put out tea; to hand them their strawberries and cream; to listen devoutly, reverently, to their wisdom," and to unabashedly prefer her son to her daughters (*Moments* 88, 83). Yet when Virginia attempts to conform to these expectations, she finds herself beaten once again. Desperately trying to make herself presentable to the expectations of her social audience, she submits to her half-brother

George Duckworth's painful evaluations and inspections. Yet trying on a new dress was like being auctioned at a market: "he looked me up and down for a moment as if I were a horse brought in to the show ring" (*Moments* 151). Such humiliating objectification brings on the pain: "I was conscious of fear; of shame; of something like anguish" (*Moments* 151). Here again—as with her father—Woolf finds herself unable to respond. Lamenting that she "knuckled under to his authority," she explains that she felt she "must obey because he had force—age, wealth, tradition—behind him" (*Moments* 152, 154).

Woolf's agonizing negotiations with her social audience prefigure those with her literary one. Her most precious early memories are of her mother's few moments of interest in her work: "how excited I used to be when the 'Hyde Park Gate News' was laid on her plate on Monday morning, and she liked something I had written! Never shall I forget my extremity of pleasure—it was like being a violin and being played upon" (MB 95). Yet how different was the response of the cultural community in which she lived: "Society in those days was a perfectly competent, perfectly complacent, ruthless machine. A girl had no chance against its fangs. No other desires—say to paint, or to write—could be taken seriously" (*Moments* 157). Constantly fretting about her husband's reaction to her novels, Woolf became severely agitated when one of her male literary contemporaries disliked one of her works and flung herself into ecstasies when she was praised by another (*Diary* 4: 35, 43–44). As Woolf admitted, "What I want is to be told that this is solid & means something" (*Diary* 4: 45)—particularly from that skeptical male audience whose recognition meant the possibility of being acknowledged as a central writer of her day. This is made especially clear by her comments to her diary after the success of *Orlando:* "I felt . . . I had no longer anything to envy him [James Strachey] for . . . how for the first time I think, he thought of me, as a writer, with some envy" (3: 234). However, despite these rare moments in which she believes herself accepted, Woolf for the most part remains fearful that she "will not be taken seriously" (*Diary* 3: 262).

This paralyzing assault of patriarchal oppression was not limited to her creative mind but forced itself on her body as well, with devastating consequences. It is no coincidence that Woolf recalls her experience of sexual abuse at age six or seven by her half-brother Gerald Duckworth merely a couple of pages before her pronouncements about those sledgehammer moments in which "something happened so violently that I have remembered it all my life" (*Moments* 71). What is striking about her descriptions of those revelatory shocks is their similarity to the experience of sexual assault (DeSalvo, *Virginia* 106). Although I agree with recent Woolf biographer Hermione Lee that one must guard against over-hypothesizing (124) the significance of Woolf's memories of sexual abuse, one cannot ignore Woolf's words. When, for example, she recalls one such moment that was triggered by her inability to step over a puddle, she describes a sensation of "hopeless sadness; that collapse I have described before; as if I were passive under some sledge-hammer blow; exposed to a whole avalanche of meaning that had heaped itself up and discharged itself upon me, unprotected, with nothing to ward it off, so that I huddled up in my end of the bath, motionless" (*Moments* 78). Woolf's language is strikingly and unabashedly sexual. That merciless sledgehammer is transformed into a phallic presence violently "heaping" and "discharging" its pent up store of "meaning" upon her unprotected body. In this sense, Woolf's moments of being can be compared, initially, to a kind of rape of the consciousness in which her mind is penetrated savagely, exploded into fragments. Why would Woolf experience inspiration in terms of a rape? Precisely, I would argue, because the meaning such moments generate is, among other things, the realization of the awesome power of a male-dominated cultural and literary establishment (symbolized at the beginning of her life by her father and half brothers) that works to thwart her desire for self-expression at every turn.

Yet if for Woolf the experience of artistic inspiration starts out feeling like the experience of sexual assault, it does not remain that way for long. In a troubled but defiant response, Woolf does manage to transform a moment of terrifying victimization into one of delightful "rapture" through the mechanics of sublimation. In Freudian psychoanalysis, sublimation refers to an often unconscious psychic defense mechanism in which an individual transforms a painful or problematic impulse or feeling into a positive, or at least nonthreatening, one essentially by recontextualizing it. Instead of allowing herself to succumb to or be incorporated by the threat of patriarchal repression that these sledgehammer assaults announce, Woolf—in her *Moments of Being* passage—redefines the moment of injury as instead "a revelation . . . some real thing behind appearances" that she can "make . . . real by putting it into words." In contrast to the terrifying realization of psychic instability, her efforts—through writing—to identify it, to respond to it, result in nothing less than "rapture" (*Moments* 72). By making her art—the enunciation of such repression—the repository of meaning, she experiences the "great delight" of an utter expansion of identity. Ever searching for the wholeness of "the thing itself," for the "pattern hid behind the cotton wool" (*Moments* 73) of modern life, Woolf uses her writing as a kind of "rod" or "scaffolding" (73) that can support her disintegrating universe, protect her from those shocking moments of dissolution, take away the pain of the void. And yet one can sense the desperation behind her need to write, the sense that "by writing I am doing what is far more necessary than anything else" (*Moments* 73). From the ruins of exploded consciousness, Woolf recovers the lost oceanic feeling. The problem with this strategy, however, is that in doing so she represses the real causes of the trouble: those anxieties about the vulnerability of both her artistic authority and her female body that the sledgehammer blows—those memories of male violence and cultural oppression—revive.

As those anxieties continue to resurface, the only way to protect herself is to repeat the act of sublimation over and over again. Instead of remaining overwhelmed by recurring revelations of patriarchal power, she rereads those terrifying experiences as positive ones (in the sense that they challenge and inspire her to call them into question), and, in so doing, she transforms blockage into inspiration and turns what could potentially be a violent, incorporating principle into an emblem of empowerment. This sublimating strategy bears a remarkable resemblance to the dynamics of the sublime. Traditionally, those dynamics consist in the individual's confrontation and attempted union with a threatening, awesome, omnipotent object or entity and the resulting sensation of transport that such a union would promote. By incorporating the destructive and powerful element—in her case the threat of modern patriarchal norms—within her own aesthetic framework, Woolf is thus able to imagine a level of higher reality that she can attain through her writing, a reality in which she has the power to restore lost being, feel the rapture in "making a scene come right; making a character come together" (*Moments* 72). As with H. D.'s overmind model, these sublime moments create a space in which Woolf can transcend the insecurity she feels as a woman writer. However, while H. D. cannot reconcile her female body with her creativity, Woolf cannot reconcile herself to her female body at all. Admitting her capacity for "feeling ecstasies and raptures spontaneously and intensely and without any shame or the least sense of guilt, so long as they were disconnected with my own body" (*Moments* 68), Woolf reveals another motivation behind her hunger for the sublime: the sublimation not only of her patriarchally induced anxieties but of her vulnerable, corporeal self. However, as we shall soon see, despite Woolf's attempts to transcend it, the painful realm of the physical and the sexual body will continue to resurface.

Now we can begin to understand why, despite her earlier insistence that "it would be a thousand pities if women wrote like men, or lived like men, or looked like men" (*Room* 88), Woolf argues at the end of *A Room of One's Own* for an "androgynous" imagination. Woolf is emphasizing not that women writers ought to attempt to conform to universal stylistic standards or patriarchal practices but rather that they must find a way to deal with a current social and political reality in which Victorian sexual hierarchies, while beginning to dim, are far from being extinguished. Such a reality demands that the artist—particularly the female artist—must find a way to transcend the potentially annihilating force of a system that closes the gates of Oxbridge to women, that has driven Shakespeare's sister to suicide.

If we return to a passage near the end of *A Room of One's Own* in which Woolf describes the androgynous process of poetic production, we can see the striking resemblance it bears to the sledgehammer shocks of "A Sketch of the Past":

> It is fatal for any one who writes to think of their sex. It is fatal to be a man or woman pure and simple; one must be woman-manly and man-womanly. . . . Some collaboration has to take place in the mind between the woman and the man before the act of creation can be accomplished. Some marriage of opposites has

> to be consummated. The whole of his mind must lie wide open if we are to get the sense that the writer is communicating his experience with perfect fullness. There must be freedom and there must be peace. Not a wheel must grate, not a light glimmer. The curtains must be close drawn. The writer, I thought, once his experience is over, must lie back and let his mind celebrate its nuptials in darkness. He must not look or question what is being done. Rather, he must pluck the petals from a rose or watch the swans float calmly down the river. (104)

What Woolf gestures toward in this passage is precisely the troubled sublime experience she refers to later in "A Sketch." Although at first the passage seems less violent, the scene less threatening, the dynamic taking place here is initially the same: that of sexual assault. Forced to lay her mind "wide open" in order to become inspired, the writer "must not look or question what is being done." Instead, she must divert her attention from the sexual consummation occurring within her consciousness by plucking at a flower or gazing at a river. Yet as in the *Moments of Being* passage, Woolf recasts this devastating moment in a positive light. Turning blockage into inspiration, powerlessness into strength, she insists that this moment of violation "has" to occur in order to be able to write. Rather than fighting it, or trying to resist it, the writer must remain prostrate, allow her mind to stay open to the explicitly sexual designs of the male presence. Rape turns into marriage ("nuptials") as Woolf contends that such a union between female consciousness and a male presence (even if it might cause pain) will nevertheless spark creativity. Even despite such efforts, however, there is still the sense that desiring or accepting what she later will describe as a sledgehammer assault is a strategy with which she already feels uneasy. That Woolf admonishes the writer that she must divert herself with peaceful visions of rose petals and swans instead of trying to resist the psychosexual experience within her mind points to the real degree of her pain and desperation at having to engage this troubled creative model. While throughout the passage Woolf uses the masculine pronoun "he" to refer to the writer, the unequivocal similarity between this experience and those that she describes herself as encountering in "A Sketch" suggests that it is primarily to the woman artist that she is referring.

In her biography of Virginia Woolf, Louise DeSalvo argues for a reading of Woolf's novels from the perspective of her experience of childhood sexual abuse. Noting the ways in which writing became, for this author, a transgressive but remarkable kind of therapy, DeSalvo insists that it allowed Woolf to recover her autonomy (236, 251) and self-respect. Yet DeSalvo overlooks many of the complex aesthetic strategies that make such recovery possible, as well as the fact that Woolf's aesthetics are not merely the result of her experience of sexual abuse. Neither simply a courageous response to her victimization nor a regressive capitulation to patriarchal demands, Woolf's androgynous sublime represents a creative attempt to restore her female sensibility and authority in the face of the paralyzing assault of patriarchal strictures, both physical and psychic. Yet if my reading of Woolf's aesthetics offers a broader, and in that sense more empowering reading of Woolf's work, it does not go as far as that of Jane Marcus. Arguing that Woolf promotes a "democratic feminist 'collective sublime'" that begins with the female artist's "liberation from the ego" (10, 9), Marcus provides a vision of Woolf's motives that seems overly optimistic to me. Rather than liberation *from* identity, Woolf, in my reading, is striving *for* a woman to possess an identity. However, as we shall soon see, even this goal is agonizingly difficult for Woolf to achieve.

A brief glance at Woolf's first novel, *The Voyage Out*, will help us understand how her interest in androgyny and the experience of the sublime developed. Like Joyce, Woolf attempts to work out the problematics of her aesthetics through her artist characters. Yet it is significant that after the death of Rachel Vinrace, it would be twelve years before Woolf would attempt to center another novel around a female artist. Why? To begin, let us take a closer look at what happens to Rachel. A budding musician, she begins and ends her sojourn to South America resisting patriarchal demands upon her destiny. Proclaiming, "I won't have eleven children. . . . I won't have the eyes of an old woman" (327), Rachel condemns her cloistered upbringing and demands to know "why should one be shut up all by oneself in a room?" (335). Daring to tell her fiancé, Terence Hewett, that "she wanted many more things than the love of one human being—the sea, the sky" (336), Rachel for a short time in the novel seems to be carving out a place for herself that would allow for autonomy, artistic fulfillment, and independence from patriarchal laws.

Throughout her journey, however, Rachel is constantly reminded of the power she is up against. Instead of experiencing creative growth she has had to endure "an agony, living, wanting—" (292) of unfulfilled desire. Her fiancé (also an artist) ignores her commitment to her work, convinced that "women . . . don't think" (323); while he contemplates his novel on silence, he "allows" Rachel to indulge in her music as long as what she plays is "helpful to [his] literary composition" (324). Even then, however, it must take second place to her other wifely duties (such as responding to their letters); Rachel protests: "here am I, the best musician in South America, not to speak of Europe and Asia, and I can't play a note because of you in the room interrupting me every other second" (324). Yet "the horrors" (335) of patriarchal marriage are not limited to the repression of her artistic ambitions. They include everything that would destroy her desire for self-expression: motherhood, "stability," the constraints of London society. As Claire Kahane argues, *The Voyage Out* foregrounds a "universe . . . that does not allow the articulation of a female subject" at all (122). In her depiction of this tragedy, Woolf portrays Hewett as just as much a prisoner of these suffocating social norms as is Rachel. Even he recognizes that he does not "satisfy" (336) his beloved; although, distressingly, neither one believes "they could . . . love each other sufficiently to overcome all these barriers" (336). So impotent are they in the face of patriarchal norms that they can challenge them neither through rejecting those assumptions nor by leaving one other.

So what is Rachel to do? How can she escape? It is not coincidental that right before Rachel becomes ill, Terence reads aloud some lines by Milton about a water nymph that prompt her mind to follow "curious trains of thought suggested by words such as 'curb' and 'Locrine' and 'Brute'" (363). Rachel here clearly meditates on the association between repression (suggested by 'curb') and the father (Locrine and Brute are the nymph's father and grandfather, respectively); that this state of mind directly precedes her illness suggests at least an implied causal connection, an unconscious suicidal drive. Daniel Albright offers the assessment that Rachel's fever is an unconscious suicide, but one precipitated by her wish to escape the confines of the material, bodily universe. Arguing that Rachel considers the physical as an impediment to the access of spiritual vision, Albright goes on to posit that for Woolf, "corporality is, more simply, evil; it is a principle in the universe that is hostile to the eye, that hinders the development and expansion of the self, that tricks us into doubting the power of the imagination . . . [that] manage[s] to quash any sort of visionary or oceanic feeling" (129). Interpreting Rachel's death, then, as self-inflicted, Albright demonstrates her attempt to disengage herself from the confines of the flesh by "imagin[ing] her body growing until her knees are mountains, her toes wholly separated from her body, her mind flitting discarnate around the corners of her sickroom" (133).

The problem with Albright's reading is that he ignores the degree to which, for Rachel, the specifically *female* body inhibits the acquisition of the oceanic feeling because of its vulnerability to patriarchal assault. From the beginning of the novel, we share Helen's speculation that Rachel has already been sexually abused by her father; by the time they reach South America, she has been assaulted by Richard Dalloway as well. What is perhaps even more traumatizing for Rachel, however, is that she herself—or, more properly, her body—is blamed for the attack. After kissing Rachel, Richard says to her ominously and accusingly, "you tempt me" (77), as if she should feel grateful he did not go further. Yet when Rachel finally tells Helen, she advises her to "think no more about it" (82). Thus not only is Rachel physically unable to ward off these degrading and devastating advances, she is psychically impotent as well. Not even permitted to conceive of herself as "victim," Rachel remains a permanently passive prisoner to male desire: "She dreamt that she was walking down a long tunnel, which grew so narrow by degrees that she could touch the damp bricks on either side. At length the tunnel opened and became a vault; she found herself trapped in it, bricks meeting her wherever she turned, alone with a little deformed man who squatted on the floor gibbering, with long nails" (78). A veiled image of the vaginal canal and uterus, the tunnel and vault of Rachel's dream show the degree to which she feels absolutely trapped by her own body. Able to violate her at will, to pin her to the slime of her own flesh, the lust of patriarchy—represented by the grotesque and obscene man with sharp phallic claws—will forever hold her prisoner. For Rachel, death is the only way she can escape this ultimate vulnerability of the body. Louise DeSalvo and Christine Froula point out how "the ideal of virginity murders women" in the sense that women are taught that their "nature as a woman is so inherently vile and dangerous that she must be kept behind locked doors" (DeSalvo, "Virginia" 181). The only place Rachel can be whole, safe, inviolate is when she can escape her body; the only way she can resist patriarchal power is through death. It is no wonder, then, that her lifelong desire "to be flung into the sea . . . was incoherently delightful" (331).

Such is the fate of Woolf's first female artist. Although Woolf clearly has those shocks of vision that reveal to her, among other things, the stark reality of the repressiveness of Victorian gender roles, she nevertheless remains passive, unable to respond to them or prevent them from utterly incorporating her. It is not until the late 1920s that Woolf writes a female artist character out of this impasse through the paradigm we have already seen. Like Rachel, Lily Briscoe is paralyzed by an artistic blockage that is in part due to her realization of the extent of her social marginalization and her vulnerability to patriarchal dismissal. As we see in *To the Lighthouse*, "It was in that moment's flight between the picture and her canvas that the demons set on her who often brought her to the verge of tears and made this passage from conception to work as dreadful as any down a dark passage for a child. Such she often felt herself—struggling against terrific odds to maintain her courage; to say: 'But this is what I see; this is what I see,' and so clasp some miserable remnant of her vision to her breast, which a thousand forces did their best to pluck from her" (19). Specifically, these demons consist in Lily's feelings of "her own inadequacy, her insignificance" (19), feelings prompted by her marginal status as spinster, as well as by men such as Mr. Tansley (or Mr. Ramsay) who nearly convinces her that "women can't paint, women can't write" (48). Of all these demons, however, it is perhaps Mrs. Ramsay who is the most difficult for Lily to resist. The figure of the patriarchal woman, Mrs. Ramsay can only appreciate Lily through her marriage potential or lack of one, asserting that "one could not take her painting very seriously" (17).

The fact that the mother remains Woolf's ultimate object of desire is exactly what makes her so dangerous, for, in effect, merging with her means merging with the patriarchal ideology her mother was forced to adopt.[5] Having been taught "to take such part as girls did then in the lives of distinguished men" (*Moments* 88), Woolf's mother had little time or sympathy for her daughter's intellectual talents. Nevertheless, her maternal influence literally "obsessed" Virginia until the completion of *To the Lighthouse*, a novel she later admitted contains descriptions of "my feeling for her" (*Moments* 81). Woolf's ambivalence is reflected in Lily's troubled negotiations with Mrs. Ramsay; "about to say something criticizing" (47) her, Lily is taken aback in awe at Mr. Bankes's reverence of the maternal woman. Yet when Lily tries to do the same thing—to make Mrs. Ramsay her maternal muse—"Nothing happened. Nothing! Nothing!" (51). Instead of empowerment, Lily experiences a renewed sense of despair. Despite her desire for connection, Lily realizes that "no woman could worship another woman in the way he worshipped" (48); while men such as Bankes can gaze at Mrs. Ramsay from the detached position of power, for Lily such a project involves cementing her self-image to a conception of womanhood that would subject and, ultimately, destroy her. It is no wonder that Woolf, in a January 21, 1931 speech before the National Society for Women's Service in London, revealed that "the villain of my story was a woman, and I propose to call her, after a figure in a well known poem, the Angel in the house" (*Pargiters* xxix).

Even after Mrs. Ramsay's death, her image—replete with all its patriarchal resonances—continues to haunt Lily every time she picks up her brush: "this form, were it only the shape of a white lampshade looming on a wicker table, roused one to perpetual combat, challenged one to a fight in which one was bound to be worsted. Always (it was in her nature, or in her sex, she did not know which) before she exchanged the fluidity of life for the concentration of painting she had a few moments of nakedness when she seemed like an unborn soul, a soul reft of body, hesitating on some windy pinnacle and exposed without protection to all the blasts of doubt" (158). Once again, Woolf figures inspiration as a kind of sledgehammer attack; what makes this one so dangerous is that the patriarchal enemy appears in its seductively maternal guise. Convinced of her own failure,

Lily nevertheless attempts to confront it. For in order to be able to paint at all, she finds she needs to expose herself, passive and naked, "to all the blasts of doubt." In other words, Lily must allow herself to surrender to the "voice saying she couldn't paint, saying she couldn't create" (159); she must permit that voice—seemingly insurmountable, paralyzing, omnipotent—to penetrate her.

That Lily, unlike Rachel, manages to survive this terrifying confrontation is due to her recourse in the dynamics of the sublime: "Can't paint, can't write, she murmured monotonously, anxiously considering what her plan of attack should be. For the mass loomed before her; it protruded; she felt it pressing on her eyeballs. Then, as if some juice necessary for the lubrication of her faculties were spontaneously squirted, she began precariously dipping among the blues and umbers . . . fallen in with some rhythm which was dictated to her" (159). Ironically, it is the fact that she has immersed herself in the destructive element that allows Lily to create. Transforming blockage into inspiration, paralyzing doubt into angry determination, she manages to push through the impasse and allow for a kind of creative release. The blockage—that giant, threatening "mass" signifying the repressive influence of her subject, Mrs. Ramsay—is significantly described as a "looming," "protrud[ing]," even phallic, incarnation of patriarchal power that presses on her eyeballs, demands to be recognized. Yet allowing that phallic presence to release itself upon her—to show her its vision—results in the "lubrication" of Lily's creative mind. In other words, the painful revelation of patriarchal power becomes the inspiration by which she gains her creative energy. Like Woolf, who claimed that "whenever I felt the shadow of her wings or the radiance of her halo upon the paper I took up the inkpot and flung it at her" (*Pargiters* xxxii), Lily transforms the repressive influence of the traditional "mother" figure into a motivation to overpower her through her writing.

With her mind now "lubricated," Lily has appropriated that once daunting phallic power, that sublime and terrifying presence: "she lost consciousness of outer things, and her name and her personality and her appearance, and whether Mr. Carmichael was there or not, her mind kept throwing up from its depths, scenes, and names, and sayings, and memories and ideas, like a fountain spurting over that glaring, hideously difficult white space, while she modelled it with greens and blues" (159). Lily now represents her mind as a phallus, her creativity as an ejaculative, lubricating fountain. Having identified with the threatening power, incorporated it, and essentially used it against itself, Lily here experiences the transportive empowerment of the sublime. However while this strategy is to a certain degree subversive, it nevertheless involves the repression of her body, her femaleness, her sexual identity. Of all these, she "loses consciousness" to be able to participate in the act of creation. Yet, as we shall see (especially in *Orlando* and Woolf's later novels), this repression cannot be sustained for long.

Nevertheless, the reality that this dynamic is an important one for Woolf—at least at this stage of her career—is implied by the fact that she shows Lily going through it several more times in the novel. Each time Lily wants to paint, she must open herself up to Mrs. Ramsay, experience the despair resulting from her realization that truly merging with this woman will result in creative and spiritual death. As if to emphasize the agony this realization precipitates, Woolf interjects the following bracketed image after one of Lily's crises of confidence: "Macalister's boy took one of the fish and cut a square out of its side to bait his hook with. The mutilated body (it was alive still) was thrown back into the sea" (180). Suggestive as a figure for Lily's psyche, this image of the mutilated fish recalls the agonizing pain of what Woolf would later label those moments of being. Suffering, like Rachel, from "the pain of the want" (181)—from the agony of unfulfilled desire—Lily finally immerses herself in the realization that to society she is incomplete, that "she remain[s] a skimpy old maid, holding a paint brush" (181). Interestingly, once again, it is only after this seeming submission that Lily retrieves the ability to create, and the pain begins to ease. This cycle repeats itself once more near the end of the novel, where we find Lily confronting the image of Mrs. Ramsay, the patriarchal mother, once again "feeling the old horror come back—to want and want and not to have. Could she inflict that still?" (202).

Lily cannot complete her vision by having to engage in these unlimited confrontations with the paternalistic maternalism of Mrs. Ramsay, however. What finally enables Lily to master her creative blockage is a strange communion with the other artist in the novel, Augustus Carmichael. An inscrutable, enigmatic figure, Mr. Carmichael is even more bodiless than Lily. Although we know he is male, a poet, is somewhat unkempt and likes to smoke opium, we are provided with few other details related to his person. Not only do we have almost no idea what he looks like we have no idea what he sounds like since he says almost nothing during the entire novel. Yet what we do know is that unlike Lily, Augustus is almost maddeningly content; "whether people laughed at him or were angry with him he was the same" (96). Untroubled by the outside world, he lives in an internal one of his own, lying in the sun, "brooding . . . over his poetry," "basking like a creature gorged with existence" (96, 178). Seemingly conscious of none of the anxieties that trouble Lily, Augustus manages to become a successful, even famous, poet by the end of the novel.

What do we make of this character? What accounts for Carmichael's rather unexpected success? Why does Augustus appear to be the final key to the completion of Lily's vision? Surprisingly, almost no one has attempted to make sense of this profound aspect of the novel. In perhaps the most sustained treatment of Carmichael's function, J. Hillis Miller suggests that this inscrutable, ambiguous character is most similar to the narrator; both are "anonymous, impersonal, ubiquitous, subtle, penetrative, insidious, sympathetic, and indifferent all at once" (173). In the conclusion of his article, Miller goes on to speculate as to whether the combination of Woolf/Carmichael anticipates the writing of *A Room;* does it "fulfill Woolf's desire to write like a woman whose mind is fertilized by the presence of a man in it? In somewhat covertly granting Augustus Carmichael creative power too, along with Lily Briscoe, does Woolf not already express that desire for an equivocal androgynous rhythm of style, beyond of combining the contradictory penchants of sexual difference?" (189). I agree with Miller that Carmichael plays a significant role in the enactment of a kind of androgynous model of creativity; however, the problem with Miller's description is that—like all other scholars who write about Woolf's interest in androgyny—he assumes it involves the idealistic union of abstractly benign masculine and feminine components, and he thus ignores the desperate cultural motivation behind the desire for and the image of the androgyne.

What is crucial about the character of Mr. Carmichael is that he offers an alternative to the oppressive Law of the Father, an alternative that Woolf would explore in greater detail in her next novel, *Orlando*. In particular, Augustus suggests for Lily the possibility of identifying with a third sex that exists beyond patriarchal norms. It is of distinctive importance, I would suggest, that Mr. Carmichael is homosexual (a fact that the narrator suggests when Mrs. Ramsay tells us of his especial fondness for her eldest son, Andrew, and of his penchant for inviting him to his room to "show him things" [96]). We must remember that homosexuality was theorized in the late nineteenth and early twentieth centuries as a form of gender *inversion*, or a third sex exhibiting both masculine and feminine characteristics. Writers such as Edward Carpenter argued that this specifically androgynous makeup freed homosexual unions from the oppressiveness of patriarchal norms; we have already seen that virtually all the scientists agreed that homosexuals commonly possess heightened creative abilities.[6] As Barbara Fassler reminds us, by 1918, the Bloomsbury group had read Ellis and Carpenter and much of the other scientific literature on homosexuality. Indeed, most of their group were homosexual or bisexual (Strachey, E. M. Forster, Clive Bell, even Virginia and Vanessa), and they all shared the "common belief [propounded by Ellis, Carpenter, Krafft-Ebing, and many others] that to be artistic one must have the unique combination of masculine and feminine elements found in hermaphrodites and homosexuals" (Fassler 250). For Woolf, then, the attraction of the androgyne was no mere whim or passing fancy; as with the other modernist writers we have studied, it was based on a culturally specific association of this once mythic figure with real and transgressive sexual and artistic characteristics that offered Woolf a possible solution to her painful crisis of authority.

We see evidence of such desirable attributes in the character of Mr. Carmichael. One of the most striking things about this androgynous individual is not only that he is an artist but that he is seemingly unaffected by the often stifling demands of patriarchal society. Barely concealing his distaste for Mrs. Ramsay, he manages to alienate Mr. Ramsay as well by refusing to acknowledge his primacy (Carmichael enrages Ramsay by insisting on having another serving of soup and thus postponing the next course at dinner). Unburdened and unbothered by the anxieties of heterosexual/patriarchal relations, Carmichael is described as "sailing serenely through a world which satisfied all his wants" (179). To Lily, "he remained benignant, calm—if one chose to think it, sublime" (180). Unthreatening and even inspiring to her, Carmichael sanctions her as an artist—or, more properly, he allows Lily to sanction herself by offering her the alternative of a third sex—and through it an alternative mode of creativity, one that remains uncompromised by the travails of the sexual norm.

In the last pages of the novel, Lily actively engages in an inner dialogue with Augustus, or at least with that which he represents to her since he does not "speak" to her out loud. This inner "conversation" amounts to a kind of meditation on the possibility of inhabiting a different subject position and of thereby attaining a protective and empowering creative perspective. Lily muses, "so much depends . . . upon distance: whether people are near us or far from us; for her feeling for Mr. Ramsay changed as he sailed further and further across the bay" (191). The realization of Carmichael's detachment and impersonality makes Lily think that "as a traveller," as a social outsider, "life was most vivid then. One could be at one's ease. . . . One need not speak at all" (194, 192). One need not respond even to patriarchal demands. This impersonality, this distance, allows Lily to feel sorry for the Ramsays—for the parents, for Prue—to recognize that their world "was no monotony of bliss" (199). When the familiar agony associated with Lily's old longing for Mrs. Ramsay resurfaces, it no longer assaults her, it no longer leads to despair: "quietly, as if she refrained, that became a part of ordinary experience, was on the level with the chair, with the table" (302). Part of everyday objective reality, it is separate from Lily, and she can leave it behind, even doubt its existence. If Mr. Ramsay can make a chair or table disappear by thinking about it "when you're not there" (23), Lily can now accomplish something similar with his and Mrs. Ramsay's image.

It is at this moment—the moment in which Lily is finally able to free herself from her attraction to and desire for Mrs. Ramsay, from the pain of her recognition of patriarchal repression—that she notices that the boat carrying Mr. Ramsay, Cam, and James has disappeared from view. It is as if they reach the Lighthouse only when Lily can free herself from them. What has really happened, however, is that she has merely transferred her desire onto something/someone else:

> Then, surging up, puffing slightly, old Mr. Carmichael stood beside her, looking like an old pagan god, shaggy, with weeds in his hair and the trident (it was only a French novel) in his hand. He stood by her on the edge of the lawn, swaying a little in his bulk and said, shading his eyes with his hand: "They will have landed," and she felt that she had been right. They had not needed to speak. They had been thinking the same things and he had answered her without her asking him anything. He stood there as if he were spreading his hands over all the weakness and suffering of mankind; she thought he was surveying, tolerantly and compassionately, their final destiny. Now he has crowned the occasion, she thought, when his hand slowly fell, as if she had seen him let fall from his great height a wreath of violets and asphodels which, fluttering slowly, lay at length upon the earth. (208)

Not coincidentally, this scene occurs at the moment that Mrs. Ramsay no longer radiates with the glow of the madonna that Carmichael changes into an authorizing androgynous divinity. The laurels are literally transferred; Mrs. Ramsay's flower basket metamorphoses into Carmichael's wreath. Part Neptune, part Christ, part divine Emperor, part "male," and part "female" (in the sense of the social constructions of the terms), Mr. Carmichael becomes Lily's new muse. Unlike merging or uniting with Mrs. Ramsay—which for Lily would mean certain strangulation in her patriarchal nets—identification with Augustus affords a kind of freedom and release which enables Lily to complete her "vision." Thus Lily manages to escape Rachel's fate, and she becomes an artist by painfully transforming patriarchal blockage into artistic inspiration and, ultimately, by identifying with a culturally specific third sex whose authority transcends the paralyzing imminence of the male poet–female muse dyad and the patriarchal politics on which it is based.

Would identification with the image of Augustus Carmichael—essentially as androgyne—render the sublime dynamics of Lily Briscoe's creative process less painful by putting an end to the recurrent blockage of patriarchal censure? It is interesting that Woolf makes some fun of Lily's new "religion"; emphasizing that Carmichael's trident is really only a French novel and pointing to the "shaggy" and unkempt appearance of this new "god," the narrator of *To the Lighthouse* undercuts the transcendent quality of Lily's vision and indicates that she may be merely exchanging one form of tyranny for another. Enthralled by the idea of objective impersonality and transcendence—strategies which afford her an escape from her sexuality and her female body—Lily has ironically located inspiration in a practice that involves the repression of her identity. The novel's subtly equivocal ending suggests that Woolf is ambivalent about the androgyne figure. In *Orlando*, Woolf allows herself to explore the ecstasies as well as the agonies of such a stance.

Despite the fact that *Orlando*, more than any of Woolf's other novels, is centrally preoccupied with the issues of politics, gender, and creativity, critics have virtually erased it from the canon. From the 1970s, when Nancy Topping Bazin omitted the novel from *Virginia Woolf and the Androgynous Vision*, to the 1990s, when Louise DeSalvo left it out of her acutely sex-conscious biography, *Virginia Woolf: The Impact of Childhood Sexual Abuse on Her Life and Writing*, critics have on the whole tended to ignore this pivotal work. Their dismissal is probably, in part, because of Woolf's deprecatory comments about the novel. Despite her initial rush of enthusiasm for *Orlando*, when she was finished she consistently referred to it in her diaries and letters as "a joke," "a freak," "frivolous," "not . . . 'important'" (*Diary* 3: 177, 180, 177, 184), and "untrue" (*Letters* 661), even though it became one of her most popular and successful works in her day. Seemingly deferring to Woolf's discomfort and/or embarrassment, scholars have typically limited their reading of this fascinatingly troubled text to the contexts of its lesbian undertones (in particular, Woolf's relation to Vita Sackville-West) or of its critique of the genre of biography.[7] Those who have written about its motif of androgyny echo each other in viewing the novel as Woolf's unmitigated celebration of sexual indeterminacy.[8] Insisting that "unlike [Eliot's] Tiresias, upon whom the worst of both sexes has been inflicted, Orlando has the best of both sexes in a happy multiform that she herself has chosen" (Gilbert and Gubar, *Sexchanges* 345), virtually all the scholarship on *Orlando* has interpreted its use of androgyny using anachronistic, character-centered, 1970s definitions of the term.[9]

The price we have paid for our disregard and/or misreadings of *Orlando* has been the perpetuation of an incomplete understanding of Woolf's aesthetics. What Woolf's dismissive comments reveal is not so much a failure in the novel as an uncomfortable realization of the conclusions it reaches and the implications of these conclusions for the success of her artistic method. More specifically, Woolf's deprecations of the novel gesture toward the painful and insistent struggle in the text between art and the body and the more subliminal crisis over how to enable the former without disabling or repressing the latter. Like Woolf's equivocal comments about it, *Orlando* presents a portrait of the artist that is ultimately unfinished and unresolved—sexually, artistically, and historically. Rather than a novel about identity, it is a novel about identity crisis, gender trouble, and cultural change that ultimately presents not "Orlando" or "Virginia Woolf" but rather the struggle behind both artists' attempt at "being."

Before proceeding to an extended analysis of *Orlando*'s troubled conclusion, I would like to point out that this novel is as much a narrative of artistic development as it is a biography. Despite its predominantly pre-twentieth-century setting, *Orlando* is essentially yet another version of *A Portrait of the Artist*, one that foregrounds the disillusionment of its aesthetically minded hero in regard to romantic and social ambitions and his/her attempted escape into the "purer" and "higher" realm of art. For Woolf's artist hero/ine (as with H. D.'s), the attraction of this aesthetic realm is connected with a wish for an empowering alternative to the limiting horizons of traditional sex roles. From the beginning of the novel, we are quick to apprehend that both of Orlando's parents offer little for him in the way of a fulfilling destiny. An absent yet fearsome imperialist, Orlando's father "had struck many heads of many colours off many shoulders, and brought them back to hang from the rafters" (13). Although, on the one hand, the sensitive and romantic Orlando finds the energy and excitement of such a life appealing, "a landscape of pine and snow, habits of lust and slaughter, did not entice him" (50). On the other hand, Orlando's mother, "a very beautiful lady in green walking out to feed the peacocks with Twitchett, her maid, behind her" (15–16), comes closer to mirroring his aesthetic sensibility; however, the sight of her "disturbed him" (15) as well, most likely because she is so distant and emotionless. Unable to identify with either man or woman, Orlando—like Lily Briscoe (with Augustus Carmichael)—finds an alternative in the androgyne.

Foreign and transgressive, Sasha represents for Orlando not so much a lover as an androgynous muse. Replete with the "speed and vigour" and the "legs, hands, carriage" (38) of a man and the mouth, breasts, and eyes of a woman, Sasha epitomizes the third alternative—a third sex uniting the virtues of both power and beauty—that Orlando has been seeking.[10] Her "extraordinary seductiveness" (37) thus consists not in her sexual body but in her transcendence of conventional categories of identity that stimulate his imagination to new heights of creative expression: "Images, metaphors of the most extreme and extravagant twined and twisted in his mind" (37). The fact of her very unrepresentability in conventional modes of discourse drives Orlando mad with an insatiable desire to possess her in language: "Orlando ran wild in his transports and swept her over the ice, faster, faster, vowing that he would chase the flame, dive for the gem, and so on and so on, the words coming on the pants of his breath with the passion of a poet whose poetry is half pressed out of him by pain" (47). The extremely sexual imagery of this passage refers primarily to Sasha's power to excite his imagination; indeed, he describes being with her as a kind of aesthetic masturbation resulting in "the words coming on the pants of his breath." Yet while Orlando seems convinced that his attraction to her is primarily aesthetic, the abundance of thinly veiled sexual imagery makes it clear that there is more to the story.

The aestheticization of Orlando's affair with Sasha points to the hidden cost of Woolf's adoption of an androgynous, or third-sexed, imagination: the need to repress the telltale features of the writer-narrator's sexual body. It is not insignificant that of all Orlando's physical attributes, the only ones that the narrator describes are his/her face and legs, and nothing in between. Instead, throughout the novel we are presented with an elaborate series of veils that serve to distract and deflect our attention from Orlando's biological sex in order to preserve his/her androgynous subject-position from the imposition of patriarchal norms. Even from the first page of the novel, Orlando appears draped in clothes which "did something to disguise" (13) the definitiveness of his sexual body.

The most dramatic examples of this sexual repression are the mysterious trances, or seven-day sleeps, that overtake Orlando as soon as the body and its desires threaten to make themselves visible. The first of these occurs soon after Sasha's betrayal. As the aestheticized "frozen" landscape of the London carnival is replaced by the tempestuous, apocalyptic upsurge of the flood, Orlando seems about to confront the seething mass of his frustrated sensual desires. Spectator to this horrific event, Orlando watches as icebergs float by which contain representations primarily of sex and food: "Among other strange sights was to be seen a cat suckling its young; a table laid sumptuously for a supper of twenty; a couple in bed; together with an extraordinary number of cooking utensils" (63). Symbolic of sensual desire—the physical appetites—these objects wash into Orlando's consciousness as he watches helplessly. Immediately afterward, he falls into a supernatural sleep that lasts for seven days and seven nights and leaves him with "an imperfect recollection of his past life" (66). Speculating on the function of the trances, the narrator identifies them as modes of repression that function by aestheticizing experience: "Are they remedial measures—trances in which the most galling memories, events that seem likely to cripple life for ever, are brushed with a dark wing which rubs their harshness off and gilds them, even the ugliest, and basest, with a lustre, an incandescence?" (67). Once he awakens, Orlando is able to sublimate the dangerously powerful passions, the avowal of physicality that nearly drowned him, into his art, and he finds that "for the first time since the night of the great flood he was happy" (83).

Just as the first trance follows from the disavowed frustration of sexual desire, so does the second ultimately emerge from the repression and denial of sensual appetites and of the sexual body. Although connected to the sex change, this next bout of extended unconsciousness can be traced to Orlando's flight from the Archduchess Harriet and her grotesque physique, which he describes as reminding him of a six-foot hare. Yet despite Orlando's insistence on his disgust, what makes Harriet so threatening is that she causes him to be sexually aroused and thus sexually "exposed." As the Archduchess bends over to fasten his buckle, "Orlando heard, suddenly and unaccountably, far off the beating of Love's wings" (116). To his dismay, however, he soon discovers that "it was Lust the vulture, not Love, the Bird of Paradise that flopped, foully and disgustingly, upon his shoulders" (117–18). What disturbs Orlando the most about this event is that the "baseness" of the body and its lusts is capable of penetrating the sacred androgynous realm, of contaminating the purity of the body's aesthetic space: "Vainly, it seemed, had he furnished his house with silver and hung the walls with arras, when at any moment a dung-bedraggled fowl could settle upon his writing table" (118). Wanting to preserve the infinite distance between art and the body, between poetry and excrement, Orlando flees to Constantinople, followed close at heel by "a certain great lady . . . from England" (125)—Harriet. Shunning human attachments, Orlando attempts to live a solitary existence, culminating in his apotheosis into Dukedom.

Escaping the body, however, is not so easy, even if one runs halfway across the world to be rid of it. Immediately after Orlando crowns himself, a riot erupts in the crowds of Constantinople similar to the mass hysteria subsequent to the advent of the great flood. As a result of the uproar, the common folk break into the banqueting rooms and ceremonial halls, smashing things and shrieking. Chief among these marauders is "a certain lady, who was said to be dying for love for Orlando"—may we suggest the Archduchess once again—who "seized a candelabra and dashed it to the ground" (131). Unwilling to be denied, the bodily, the sexual, the "low" breaks in upon Orlando with a vengeance and culminates with his offstage affair with Rosina Pepita. Not surprisingly, it is after this "regression" that our hero attempts his most drastic strategy of all: transforming his body, changing his sex in order to escape it. What is particularly noticeable about the trance–sex change scene is its de-emphasis on the physical body and emphasis on mystical veils and supernatural resistance. The spirits Purity, Chastity, and Modesty, while ultimately banished, are permitted to postpone the moment of revelation for a full four pages. Even when "THE TRUTH" is made manifest, all we have is the narrator's avowal of Orlando's "ravishing" nakedness (137, 138), not a direct description of the body. As if to forestall objections that "such a change of sex is against nature," the narrator rather weakly resolves to "let other pens treat of sex and sexuality; we quit such odious subjects as soon as we can" (139). Yet the inquiry Orlando so self-consciously abstains from answering once again calls into question the struggle behind the sex change and the motivations that lead to it.

However, the mysterious trances and veils are not the primary strategies by which Orlando manages to repress his/her awareness of the sexual body in order to maintain an androgynous and aesthetic self-consciousness. The other, less drastic, methods involve actual transgression into that low realm he/she has disavowed. Repeated "safe" escapes into the sphere of the repressed provide Orlando with a means of forestalling the grand eruptions that call for more extreme measures. As the narrator informs us, Orlando "had always a liking for low company" (28), but, as we shall see, their attraction for him is but a symptom of his psychic repression. Throughout the text Orlando frequently does seek out the company of the lower classes: he is transfixed by a peek at a poor poet meditating with his beer; he—along with Sasha—escapes from the noble's enclosure to experience the London carnival among the "apprentices; tailors; fishwives; horse dealers; cony catchers; starving scholars; maid-servants in their whimples; orange girls; ostlers; sober citizens; bawdy tapsters; and a crowd of little ragamuffins" (56); he enjoys entertaining the shocking and wheezing poet Nick Greene; he disguises himself in order to be among the common people of Constantinople (123); she initiates her life as a woman by living among the gypsies; she escapes the oppressive society of the wits by conversing with prostitutes. These people fascinate Orlando, I would argue, precisely because they become symbolic of the bodily realm that she has attempted to deny.

In *The Politics and Poetics of Transgression*, Peter Stallybras and Allon White argue that "The bourgeois subject continually defined and redefined itself through the exclusion of what it marked out as 'low'—as dirty, repulsive, noisy, contaminating. Yet that very act of exclusion was constitutive of its identity . . . disgust always bears the imprint of desire. These low domains, apparently expelled as 'Other,' return as the object of nostalgia, longing, and fascination" (191). Although Orlando is clearly a member of the upper classes, he/she engages in a similar mode of repression in order to disavow his/her physical (sexual) component. Thus, we cannot view Orlando's forays into the low as liberatory or positively subversive; in the words of Stallybras and White, "it would be wrong to associate the exhilarating sense of freedom which transgression affords with any necessary or automatic political progressiveness" because it is essentially just a form of "counter-sublimation" (201). In other words, Orlando allows him/herself the opportunity to experience the body only from a distance; as we shall see, this dynamic is what eventually ends up destroying her. Alienating herself from herself—her own body—Orlando will become so bifurcated that the fragile connection between psychic and corporeal selves severs altogether. As Stallybras and White point out, the repression of the lower body—particularly the woman's lower body—ultimately leads to hysteria (188), a condition that Freud described as being traceable to "a repressed bisexual conflict" (Kahane x–xi).

What all Orlando's machinations indicate is the fact that endeavoring to employ an androgynous model of the imagination involves the painful and continuous repression of the body, that ultimate indicator of sexual difference (and, for a woman, that ultimate site of sexual violation and enslavement). Yet the attempt to dissociate the self from the prison of the body ironically threatens to dissolve that self entirely. Woolf, who in a speech before the National Society for Women's Service in London at approximately the same time she wrote *Orlando* admitted the importance of "speak[ing] the truth about her body" (*Pargiters* xxxx), cannot finally deny those consequences. In my reading, the ending of *Orlando*, rather than being euphoric, is riddled with pessimism and despair. Woolf reports her increasing frustrations with maintaining her sense of pleasure with the novel, finding that "for some reason, I am hacking rather listlessly at the last chapter of Orlando, which was to have been the best. . . . I miss the fun" (*Diary* 3: 175). When she at last does finish it, not only does she vehemently assert that she never wants to be "accused" (*Diary* 3: 185) of writing a novel again but she expresses a profound wish to escape the exercise of the imagination altogether by writing "some very closely reasoned criticism" or "something abstract poetic next time—I don't know" (*Diary* 3: 185). Conceding to herself the truth about *Orlando*—"I expect I began it as a joke, & went on with it seriously" (*Diary* 3: 185)—Woolf nevertheless seems reluctant to admit her work's conclusions; repressing the terrifying sense of madness and dislocation with which the novel ends, Woolf escapes into a fantasy of control.

Strangely, virtually all the critics who have written about *Orlando* view its end as an empowering release of imaginative *jouissance*, a celebration of androgynous fusion.[11] Yet the final chapter of this novel is anything but unperturbed. As the nineteenth century draws to a close, Orlando experiences a profound sense of relief: "she had only escaped by the skin of her teeth. She had just managed, by some dextrous deference to the spirit of the age . . . to pass its examination successfully" (265–66). Rather than a blithe and liberatory escapade, being an artist involves a constant, exhausting, and terrifying effort to assure that "the transaction between a writer and the spirit of the age" (266) can be made at all. Forced to engage in the constant politics of subterfuge lest the authorities at hand find within her consciousness "something highly contraband for which she would have to pay the full fine" (265), Orlando is anything but free from cultural expectations and demands. Although Orlando does manage to finish "The Oak Tree," it takes only one conversation with the (now) eminently respectable Nick Greene to make her "feel—it was an extremely uncomfortable feeling—one must never, never say what one thought. . . . They made one feel, she continued, that one must always, always write like somebody else (the tears formed themselves in her eyes)" (285). Despairing that she can never hope to imitate those "manly" (285) Victorian critics and novelists, can never enjoy their rituals much less satisfy their rigid demands, Orlando nearly surrenders altogether: "Damn it all! she exclaimed, launching a penny steamer so vigorously that the poor little boat almost sank in the bronze colored waves" (286).

Hovering at the brink of the abyss, Orlando nevertheless manages to ward off madness for a while by transforming this terrifying moment of being into a sublime moment of becoming. Like Lily Briscoe, Orlando turns creative blockage into ecstatic empowerment by aestheticizing the shock. Given the complexity of her methodology, I will quote the full passage:

> Now, the truth is that when one has been in a state of mind (as nurses call it)—and the tears still stood in Orlando's eyes—the thing one is looking at becomes, not itself, but another thing, which is bigger and much more important and yet remains the same thing. If one looks at the Serpentine in this state of mind, the waves soon become just as big as the waves on the Atlantic;

> the toy boats become indistinguishable from ocean liners. So Orlando mistook the toy boat for her husband's brig; and the wave she had made with her toe for a mountain of water off Cape Horn; and as she watched the toy boat climb the ripple, she thought she saw Bonthrop's ship climb up and up a glassy wall; up and up it went, and a white crest with a thousand deaths in it arched over it; and through the thousand deaths it went and disappeared—"It's sunk!" she cried out in agony—and then, behold, there it was again sailing along safe and sound among the ducks on the other side of the Atlantic.
>
> "Ecstasy!" she cried. "Ecstasy! . . . " (286–87)

Essentially, Orlando sublimates her terror over the possibility of being inundated, drowned, extinguished by the condemnation of critics such as Greene into an imaginative fantasy over which she maintains total control. Transforming the toy boat into a complex and layered image—first of her lover-husband, Shelmerdine, and his brig but ultimately of herself and her precarious condition as a(n androgynous) woman writer—Orlando is thus able literally to imagine herself out of danger, to convince herself that her real predicament is just a fiction, just a "toy boat" after all. Orlando's ecstasy hereby arises from the realization that rather than being inundated by the sublime force of patriarchy, she can control it by using it against itself, incorporating it aesthetically. Rather than the shocks they first appear to be, such moments of being become "a spirt; a splash; like those hyacinths (she was passing a fine bed of them); free from taint, dependence, soilure of humanity or care for one's kind; something rash, ridiculous, 'like my hyacinth, husband'" (287). They allow one to escape the terrifying prison of the body into the ecstasy of the imagination.

That such a solution is tenuous at best is made apparent by the fact that almost immediately after this revelatory moment Orlando gives birth to a child, ostensibly as a kind of homage or sacrifice to the demands of the age. Although—as with the sex change—the narrator attempts to veil and to repress this avowal of the corporeal realm for a full four pages, such natural bodily processes ultimately refuse to be silenced or denied. The failure of the imagination to repress them unleashes terrifying anxieties about self-fragmentation (here, between mind and body) that figure themselves as "dreams which splinter the whole and tear us asunder and wound us and split us apart in the night when we would sleep" (295).

Unable to veil a consciousness of her body yet unable at the same time to accept it, it is not long before Orlando's psyche becomes lost in these excruciating nightmares. Increasingly paranoid and disoriented, her mind receives the uncertainty of the present moment as a "terrifying revelation" (298). Unable to register reality, distinguish between objects, or presuppose any pure and stable singularity Orlando finds herself on the verge of hysteria: "Nothing is any longer one thing. I take up a handbag and I think of an old bumboat woman frozen in the ice. Someone lights a pink candle and I see a girl in Russian trousers. . . . I hear goat bells. I see mountains" (305). Crying, frustrated, infuriated, Orlando finds herself screaming at other motorists' words of anguish about herself: "Confound it all. . . . Don't you know your own mind?" (306). Yet when she calls out for identity, presence, "the one she needed most [the conscious self, or the united self] kept aloof" (310).

In a singular moment of lucidity, Orlando realizes that she has been "Haunted! ever since I was a child" (313) by that myth of wholeness, a myth symbolized for her by the wild goose. Like the Oak Tree, the goose represents the thing behind appearances, the transcendental original, the scaffolding holding up reality that we saw Woolf write of in "A Sketch." As Orlando points out, "it was anything indeed, so long as it was hard, for he felt the need of something which he could attach his floating heart to" (19), a solid, stable, singular identity to fall back on. Yet such a presence, like the wild goose, is ever elusive. Mourning that "always I fling after it words like nets" but have never captured "the great fish" (313), Orlando (and Woolf) begins to doubt that such a presence exists. Even the Oak Tree refuses to contain her, protect her by encapsulating her book; the roots are so shallow that she cannot even bury it there for fear the dogs will dig it up (324). As Orlando says, somewhat sadly and ironically, "no luck ever attends these symbolical celebrations" (324).

After this realization of her creative mind's instability and, particularly, its alienation from the body to which it is attached, Orlando's psyche falls apart. Feeling estranged even from the protection of her house, she interprets the "please do not touch" (318) signs on the furniture—which she had written—as a self-directed message. Increasingly convinced of her own inability to keep up with each age's mincing and threatening demands, realizing that self-preservation is completely dependent upon self-presentation, Orlando can no longer brave the passage of time: "Braced and strung up by the present moment she was also strangely afraid, as if every time the gulf of time gaped and let a second through some unknown danger might come with it. The tension was too relentless and too rigorous to be endured long without discomfort" (321). When the clock finally strikes, "she saw with disgusting vividness that the thumb on Joe's right hand was without a finger nail and there was a raised saucer of pink flesh where the nail should have been" (321). Symbolic not only of the grotesqueness of the body (and possibly the phallus) but, more important, of its precarious and unstable exterior, the gardener's absent nail serves as a symbol of the peeling away of all semblance of solid, reliable protection, of the illusion of anything "hard." In the shadow of her swoon, Orlando "composed them [these images] into something tolerable, comprehensible" (322) by once again sublimating her anxiety through aestheticization and denial. This time, however, she will be unable to re-enter the realm of the real.

By end of the novel, Orlando is so alienated from her body and all external reality that it "was not necessary to faint now in order to look deep into the darkness where things shape themselves and to see in the pool of the mind now Shakespeare, now a girl in Russian trousers, now a toy boat on the Serpentine, and then the Atlantic itself" (327). Permanently lost in a fantasy world created out of her need to sublimate her anxieties about the body, Orlando finally and completely falls prey to madness. The novel ends at the stroke of midnight as Orlando waits for the arrival of her androgynous lover-husband, Shelmerdine, paralleling that night early in the novel when she once awaited Sasha. Yet although Orlando thinks she joins her lover—essentially a projection of herself—in the ecstasy of union, I would argue that he never comes at all. The "ecstasy" Orlando experiences is finally the ecstasy of insanity in which reality—like Joe's fingernail—peels away. How do we know this, given that the novel as a whole is so infused with fantastic events? Specifically because this time memory and fantasy become one as she begins to hallucinate visions of the dead Queen that Orlando is unable to distinguish as her own: "'The house is at your service, Ma'am,' she cried, curtseying deeply. 'Nothing has been changed. The dead Lord, my father, shall lead you in'" (328). Although always fluid in the novel, the lines between reality and fantasy, desire and memory are irrevocably broken. The wild goose that accompanies Orlando's vision of her reunion with Shelmerdine is Woolf's ironic, self-mocking ending; that emblem of pure meaning, pure presence is as insubstantial as Orlando's hallucinations.

The tragedy of *Orlando* is thus twofold: not only does the novel chronicle the painful legacy of the androgynous sublime, specifically the repression of the body, it refuses to provide an alternative model of poetic production to replace it. No wonder Woolf was so eager to call it "a joke." Yet despite the fact that Woolf was unable to own *Orlando*'s implications consciously, they nevertheless become her next novel's major theme. In *The Waves*, Rhoda—essentially Orlando's incarnation—is doomed from the start.[12] Mercilessly and self-consciously replaying key scenes and moments from *Orlando* in *The Waves*, Woolf finally rejects the creative model of the third-sexed (or androgynous) imagination, recognizing the degree to which it represents a self-destructive, culturally imposed solution to the modern woman writer's crisis of authority.

It is no mere coincidence that we first catch sight of Rhoda sailing floating flower petals in a basin. As with Orlando's toy boat, the fate of Rhoda's petals comes to symbolize a displaced version of her experience: "The waves rise; their crests curl; look at the lights on the mastheads. They have scattered, they have foundered, all except my ship which mounts the wave and sweeps before the gale and reaches the islands where the parrots chatter" (19). Sublimating her fear of being marginalized, of having "no face" (43), into a sublime fantasy of transcendence, Rhoda essentially creates an imaginative world in which she can triumph. "Afraid of the shock of sensation that leaps upon" her (130), Rhoda aestheticizes it—like Lily and Orlando—into an image she can control, into an ecstasy she can experience. Yet unlike her precursors, Rhoda realizes that the empowerment such a model would provide is minimal at best: "Alone, I rock my basins; I am mistress of my fleet of ships. But here, twisting the tassels of this brocaded curtain in my hostess's window, I am broken into separate pieces; I am no longer one" (106). By repressing the vulnerable corporeal realm—which for her seems so painfully exposed—Rhoda initially thinks she can avoid the ever-immanent "disaster" of self-dissolution (43). Ironically, however, Rhoda's solution precipitates the feelings of fragmentation and bifurcation that she has been trying to avoid by splitting herself in two.

Longing to feel empowered, Rhoda thus imaginatively re-creates herself as a ship that has sailed through the storm or a fearsome Russian empress whose "attitude is one of defiance" (56). Ultimately, such reverie "gives [Rhoda] no satisfaction" and nothing to hold on to; rather than an Oak, she can only conjure "a papery tree . . . [that] is not solid" (56). Desperately needing to "stretch and touch something hard" (159), to merge with something powerful, Rhoda is plagued by the realization that the sublime moment is painfully brief and, in the end, insubstantial; whatever strength it affords her is not even enough to help her cross "the puddle" (64). Unable to sustain her creative energies, she can only survive by mimicking the initiatives of others; Rhoda explains, "since I wish above all things to have lodgment, I pretend . . . to have an end in view" (131). In order to prevent herself from falling to pieces, she forces herself into the degrading and humiliating position of pretense.

Despite her underlying suspicion of her sublime strategies for empowerment—personal and poetic—Rhoda is finally unable to free herself from them or even imagine alternatives. Seeking "to replenish [her] emptiness, to stretch [her] nights and fill them fuller and fuller with dreams" in a mystical space above people's heads and "beyond our reach" (139), Rhoda persists in her faith in a transcendental solution. Rereading her failure as personal rather than ontological, she insists connection, empowerment, and sublimity are still possible, "'if we could mount together, if we could perceive from a sufficient height . . . if we could remain untouched without any support'" (231). As Rhoda's hopes continue to be dashed, however, these "if only's" contribute to an increasingly virulent self-hatred.

Rhoda's inability to surrender an imaginative model she knows to be flawed corresponds to her inability to surrender her artistic ambitions. Hungering for the ability to know, to represent the real—"the thing that lies beneath the semblance of the thing" (163)—she attempts throughout the novel to express the essence of experience in poetic language. "'Peaked clouds,' said Rhoda, 'voyage over a sky dark like polished whalebone'" (146). Compared by Neville to a wild goose who "flies with her neck outstretched and blind fanatic eyes, past us" (198), Rhoda remains fixated on an ever-elusive truth. Yet like Orlando, Rhoda fails to survive this journey (or even to become an accomplished artist in the first place) because she fails to transcend the paralyzing assault of the patriarchal demands and expectations of the Nick Greenes of the world: "I am rocked from side to side by the violence of my emotion. I imagine these nameless, these immaculate people, watching me from behind bushes. I leap high to excite their admiration. . . . Therefore I hate looking-glasses which show me my real face. Alone, I often fall down into nothingness. I must push my foot stealthily lest I should fall off the edge of the world into nothingness. I have to bang my hand against some hard door to call myself back to the body" (43–44). Here Woolf suggests that it is precisely the gaze of the "immaculate" people—the critics, the evaluators, the patriarchal public—that forces Rhoda to adopt an aesthetic grounded in the repression of her femaleness. Ever trying to reflect back the pure and unthreatening image that society wishes to see, consents to accept, Rhoda—like Orlando—becomes so alienated from her physical self that she can only be made aware of it by literally slamming herself against a door—or a tree. By thus proposing that this self-alienation is the source of Rhoda's (and Orlando's) madness and suicide, Woolf exposes their androgyny as a kind of female castration, a forced lack, a requisite sublimation that precipitates a terrifying void of sexless absence. For although Rhoda does not advertise her androgyny, she does emphasize her fear of her female body and of the male gaze, as well as her attempts to transcend them. Thus, ironically, while Rachel Vinrace dies because she lacks a model of empowerment, Orlando and Rhoda die because they have one—figured as an androgynous sublime—and it kills them.

Yet what about the novelist Bernard, who, on the surface at least, appears to have succeeded? Indeed, quite a few critics have argued that it is in fact he—not Rhoda—whom Woolf posits as her self-modeled androgynous hero.[13] It is true that Bernard identifies himself with the androgyne: "but 'joined to the sensibility of a woman' (I am here quoting my own biographer) 'Bernard possessed the logical sobriety of a man'" (76). However, the quality that looks at first to be a kind of enlightened sexual indeterminacy is soon unveiled as little more than a patriarchal act of appropriative violence. Bernard's proudly stated maxim, "I do not believe in separation" (67), essentially amounts to a kind of psychic imperialism in which he seeks to appropriate the experience of both sexes for his own use. Like a vampire, he "need[s] the stimulus of other people" (80) in order to suck their life energy into his insatiable mind. Unable to recognize the autonomy of others, Bernard "sees everyone with blurred edges" (51) and thus makes "foolish comparisons" (38) that demean the quality of real experience. Indeed, Bernard seems to revel in appropriating actual pain—such as Neville's grief over Percival's death (88)—into "a 'story'" (37) of his own, and he cannot even write a love letter that does not refer to himself (78).[14]

Ironically, however, Bernard's patriarchal, appropriative form of androgyny ends up subverting itself. By defining himself in terms of the subjectivities he incorporates, he soon loses control over his psyche and ultimately "cannot be entirely sure what is my self" (116). Like Rhoda, Bernard hungers for the "true story, the one story to which all these phrases refer," yet as the boundaries between self and Other, reality and fiction, begin to dissolve, he admits "sometimes I begin to doubt if there are stories" after all (187, 144). As his artistic method collapses, Bernard is forced to question it—"why impose my arbitrary design?"—and to sense its limitations; instead of leading to something new, "making phrases, had recorded merely changes" (188, 285).

For a time, then, Bernard abandons his egotistical sublime for Rhoda's androgynous sublime. For the first time, he admits he does not "know if I am man or woman" (281). Forswearing control, mastery, essentially the realm of the beautiful—"how tired I am of phrases that come down beautifully with all their feet on the ground" (238)—Bernard places his hopes on a transcendent language "such as lovers use, broken words, inarticulate words" (238). Rejecting his imperialistic aesthetics, he thus looks for inspiration in uncertain moments of struggle: "I begin to seek some design more in accordance with those moments of humiliation and triumph that come now and then undeniably. . . . What delights me then is the confusion, the height, the indifference and the fury" (238–39). This hunger for sublimity, however, is a dangerous craving. As with Rhoda, it precipitates a terrifying loss of boundaries until Bernard, "weightless and visionless" "begin[s] to doubt the fixity of tables, the reality of here and now" (285, 288). Although Bernard persists in positing Rhoda as his unstable opposite, and imagines talking her out of suicide, he must finally admit that "in persuading her I was also persuading my own soul" (281). For in the sublime moment reality and fiction blend so completely that soon he too loses control over reality, does "not altogether know who I am" (276); the only thing he is sure of is that the old Bernard "is dead" (291). Possessed by the ethereal, he becomes increasingly alienated from the realm of the body: "how unutterably disgusting life is! . . . Disorder, sordidity and corruption surround us" (292). Visibly relieved when his lunch guest departs and "the pressure is removed" (294), Bernard seems precariously close to madness and suicide: "I have done with phrases. [paragraph break] How much better is silence" (295).

In the face of the sublime abyss, Rhoda commits suicide. Bernard manages to survive, however, because he finds refuge in the patriarchal legacy of the "I": "However beat and done with it all I am, I must haul myself up, and find the particular coat that belongs to me; must push my arms into the sleeves; must muffle myself up against the night air and be off. I, I, I, tired as I am, spent as I am, and almost worn out with all the rubbing of my nose along the surfaces of things, even I, an elderly man who is getting rather heavy and dislikes exertion must take myself off and catch some last train" (296). In *A Room of One's Own*, Woolf remarks that the overabundance of the personal pronoun is distinctive of (modern) men's writing. Although she admires this literature, it nevertheless disturbs her "partly because of the dominance of the letter 'I' and the aridity, which like the giant beech tree, it casts within its shade" (*Room* 100). According to Woolf, the male writer's escape into the "I" stems from his anxiety about his artistic authority in the face of the emergent success of women artists as such. Ironically, however, "protesting against the quality of the other sex by asserting his own superiority"—a strategy he selects to authorize his work—ultimately "block[s] the fountain of creative energy" by limiting it within the confines of culturally constructed "masculine" norms (101).

What does this mean in the context of *The Waves*? Faced with the collapse of his egocentric, appropriative form of androgyny as well as the exposure of this creative method as limiting and finally useless, Bernard first flirts with an alternative, the androgynous sublime. Soon, however, terrified by the possibility of being feminized, he escapes back even more vehemently into the more familiar realm of "perpetual warfare" (269). Desperately attempting to persuade himself that, like Percival, "I too can be heroic" (156), Bernard races out of the pages of the novel "with my spear couched and my hair flying back like a young man's" (297), defiant against feminization, which for him means nothing less than death.

Is there no alternative to the ultimate self-destructiveness, the self-alienating effect of the androgynous sublime? Although barely visible, the "lady writing" refuses to be imprisoned by Bernard's devouring pen; she has a "fixity" (241) that both he and Rhoda do not possess. Bernard recalls his encounter with her:

> Down below, through the depths of the leaves, the gardeners swept the lawns with great brooms. The lady sat writing. Transfixed, stopped dead, I thought, "I cannot interfere with a single stroke of these brooms. They sweep and they sweep. Nor with the fixity of that woman writing." It is strange that one cannot stop gardeners sweeping nor dislodge a woman. There they have remained all my life. It is as if one had woken in Stonehenge surrounded by a circle of great stones, these enemies, these presences. Then a wood-pigeon flew out of the trees. And being in love for the first time I made a phrase—a poem about a wood-pigeon—a single phrase, for a hole had been knocked in my mind, one of those sudden transparences through which one sees everything. (240–41)

What is immediately striking about this passage is that Bernard describes his encounter with the lady writing much as Woolf describes her moments of being. Rather than a muse, this woman writer gives

Bernard a shock; she becomes a kind of supernatural presence that violently opens his psyche to creative vision. Sublimating her threat by aestheticizing it into the artistic image of the bird in flight, Bernard manages to transcend the danger. Nevertheless this woman remains within his psyche, refusing to be appropriated or completely silenced. Terrifying in her excessive impersonality, she possesses a power that both Rhoda and Bernard lack.

The lady writing prefigures not so much a new as a reconstituted direction for Woolf's aesthetics. Replacing the position of "androgyne" with that of the outsider, she attempts to avoid the painful consequences of her former model while preserving and even augmenting the degree of its empowering potential. Although first envisioned in *The Waves*, Woolf more fully realizes this outsider position in *Three Guineas*. For after her agonizing efforts at writing *The Years*, a novel which Woolf referred to (in its early drafts as *The Pargiters*) as both "first cousin to *Orlando*" (*Diary* 4: 133) and companion piece to *Three Guineas* (*Diary* 5: 148), she found herself overwhelmed once again by a historical and cultural reality in which women's "sexuality and by implication their creativity—their potential as 'artists' of their own destiny—has been to all intents and purposes erased" (Roe 127). Determined but terrified, Woolf set out to write *Three Guineas* convinced "I'm going to be beaten, I'm going to be laughed at, I'm going to be held up to scorn & ridicule" (*Diary* 5: 64). As expected, her scathing critique of patriarchal culture, full of derisively confrontational references to the the male-centered "your world" (*Three Guineas* 18) alienated her from many of her friends and rendered her literary reputation more equivocal than it had been in years (see *Diary* 5: 170).

Yet, once again, Woolf rereads the shock of censure as an opportunity for triumph: "I am an outsider. I can take my way: experiment with my own imagination in my own way. The pack may howl, but it shall never catch me. And even if the pack—reviewers, friends, enemies—pays me no attention or sneers, still I'm free" (*Diary* 5: 141). This time, instead of sublimating her anxiety about her body by aestheticizing the shock—here figured as the howl of the reading public: the "pack"—she accepts and even embraces alienation. As Woolf explains, "my position is ambiguous. . . . In a way it is a relief" (*Diary*

5: 189). If she accepts marginalization, she can thus no longer be affected by the threat of it. And she would no longer need to deny her femaleness. For Woolf finds that it is possible to be the lady writing when one realizes one does not have to stand alone, that there is a female "our" to oppose the patriarchal "your"; as Woolf writes in *Three Guineas*, "it would seem to follow then as an indisputable fact that 'we'—meaning by 'we' a whole made up body, brain and spirit influenced by memory and tradition—must still differ in some essential respects from 'you'"(18). Having found strength in opposition and a kind of solidarity in a new class of "daughters of educated men" (13) who, by 1938, possessed the franchise as well as "the right to earn [their] living" (17), a right that Woolf argued would free them from the need to "acquiesce" (17) to patriarchal demands, Woolf eschews any mention of androgynous accommodation in *Three Guineas*. Instead, she claims membership in a powerful, "anonymous and secret Society of Outsiders" (109)—whom she defines as comprised of women who "have only had a positive existence for twenty years—that is since the professions were opened to the daughters of educated men" (115). It is thus the conclusion of *Three Guineas* that a woman can find her greatest position of political and social power "not by joining your [patriarchal] society but by remaining outside your society but in co-operation with its aim . . . of Justice, Equality, and Liberty" for all (143).

Speculating about what was to be her final novel, *Between the Acts*, Woolf decides it will include "anything that comes into my head; but 'I' rejected: 'We' substituted" (*Diary* 5: 135). The importance of this seemingly simple move cannot be underscored enough. For here she seems to find a way to protect the vulnerable female subject by replacing it—or perhaps just really bolstering it—with the impersonal collective voice of the marginalized and, specifically, of women. Rejecting the ephemeral and sublimating sublime, essentially the hunger for transcendence, Woolf comes at the end of her career (and of her life) to an aesthetic rooted in a far more earthly solidarity. Yet the fact that shortly before her suicide, in her 1940 *Moments of Being*, Woolf was still ambivalent about her "shocks" of inspiration and remained troubled about her artistic role suggests that her crisis of imagination and authority was never finally resolved.

6

Another Look at the Androgyne

Modernism and the End of "The Author"

In the preceding pages, I have considered modern writers' attraction to the androgyne primarily in the context of turn-of-the-century sex theory and its implications for artistic models of creativity. In my discussions of Joyce, H. D., Faulkner, and Woolf, I have endeavored to show the connection between cultural change, most particularly turn-of-the-century scientific reconstructions of the body and various depictions of a multiple-sexed imagination. More specifically, I have attempted to demonstrate the ways in which the modern sexual landscape precipitated an acute crisis of artistic authority for both male and female writers by destabilizing and, ultimately, invalidating old imaginative models based on the male poet–female muse dynamic. In showing the degree to which new ideas about the "third sex" inspired modernist representations of an "androgynous" imagination, I have illustrated how the imagination can be considered a cultural artifact rather than an invariant psychic reality.

Despite the androgyne's attraction for so many modernists, however, we have observed how enough "negative" associations surrounded the figure in the early twentieth century to render it a risky persona to adopt. While Joyce and Faulkner agonized over its feminizing potential, H. D. and Woolf remained troubled by the threat of ego-incorporation that an androgynous model of the imagination could portend; in each case, the artist admitted such fears virtually from the start, ironically recognizing the unlikely success of his or her sublime scenarios while at the same time pursuing them with an ever-increasing sense of desperation mingled with self-mockery. We have seen evidence for this simultaneous sense of optimism and defeat in Joyce's link between sublimity and masochism, Faulkner's obsession with his "most perfect failures," H. D.'s painful interactions with Ray Bart, and Woolf's continually agonizing moments of being. It remains for us now to address this paradox more fully. Why did these writers persist for so long in an enterprise that showed no signs of offering them the comforting and stable sense of authority they desired? Might there have been another, more implicit motivation for their efforts to make the androgyne part of their artistic self-definition besides a culturally induced sense of gender trouble?

One important clue to this mystery lies in the inescapable doubleness of the androgynous figure. Kari Weil argues that this age-old image embodies two different ideologies about the nature of subjectivity, ideologies that she labels "androgyne" and "hermaphrodite." While the former claims for itself the ideal status of a Derridean "transcendental signified" by positing a unified being or mind that exists beyond the body, the latter contradicts the notion of a stable subject altogether, embracing "the notion of an original confusion or chaos of sexes and desires" (Weil 10, 11). Taking Plato and Ovid as her exemplars, Weil demonstrates the ways in which Aristophanes' myth of the primal androgyne (in *Symposium*) privileges a unitarian denial of difference while Ovid's Hermaphroditus (in *Metamorphoses*) "blurs the distinction between male and female" in order to represent a "being *in* difference" (18, 30). In other words, the figure of the androgyne is always "A figure of antithesis . . . [that] depends upon a stable opposition between male and female, and on knowing the difference. But the irony of irony, or the irony of androgyny, reveals the hermaphrodite within the androgyne—the constantly shifting lines of difference that rhetoric alone maintains—and hence, the impossibility of knowing the difference" (Weil 47). Since sex and gender boundaries are always fluid and not fixed, the androgyne remains a body continually at war with itself. Constantly poised between self-enunciation and self-erasure, this figure thus never attains the ideal state of harmony toward which it gestures.

As Weil points out, the irony inherent in androgyny became of increasing interest to writers and artists of the mid- to late nineteenth century, such as Honoré de Balzac and Théophile Gautier, whom we have already seen were tremendously influential for moderns such as H. D. and Faulkner.[1] Her description of the growing ambivalence with which these nineteenth-century precursors regarded the trope is thus particularly important for our study of modernism. Calling their troubled fascination with the figure of the androgyne "symptomatic of a more profound and pervasive skepticism toward the very possibility of universal ideals" (84), Weil suggests another way for us to interpret twentieth-century writers' attraction to the double-sexed figure. As the incarnation of the debate over the possibility of transcendental categories, the androgynous body becomes the perfect symbol of ever-increasing modern ontological uncertainty. I believe that we can extrapolate from Weil's argument to suggest that for Joyce, H. D., Faulkner, and Woolf, the androgyne incarnates a heightening suspicion not only of the validity of universal ideals but even of the idea of a self-contained mind or imagination that would be capable of producing them.

One important legacy of decadent writers for our modernists is thus an increasing realization that the human subject exists not in "androgynous totality but hermaphroditic fragmentation, and the endless play of (sexual) 'différ*a*nce'" (Weil 141). The androgyne in the early twentieth century becomes, in part, a symbol of that ideal vision of the self that can never quite be realized, that is always under erasure, that is simultaneously both present and absent. As a figure for the modern imagination, it ultimately fails not only because it threatens the artists' security in their sexual identities but because it affirms the existence of a transhistorical, transcultural, indeed, transcendental subject while simultaneously denying it. Put differently, it both posits and erases itself in the same gesture. We need to remember that common to all historical myths of the androgyne is the presupposition of primal unity, a unity that "was divided or broken in order that the world or humanity could be born" (Eliade 114).[2] As

Alan W. Watts points out, nostalgia for this sense of wholeness contributes to the heightened valuation of "the hermaphroditic or androgynous sage or 'divine man,' whose consciousness transcends the divisiveness of earthly opposites and who, therefore, knows himself to be one with the cosmos" (46). Invoking the metaphor of the androgyne in the twentieth century is thus, to a certain extent, to invoke a spiritual icon of mystical union. It is to identify with a Being. To use Lionel Trilling's phrase, this Being exists "beyond culture," indeed beyond the human.[3] It is to express a fantasy of wholeness, a wish for an inviolate substantiveness beyond the corporeal that is at once utopian and nostalgic. It is not difficult to see the appeal of such an image for modernist artists confronted with the fragmentation of traditional notions of the sexual body and, even, of consciousness by, among other things, the First World War, modern science, and the increasing encroachment of a burgeoning mass culture upon formerly privileged aesthetic domains. Yet at the same time, as Weil indicates, the figure of the androgyne is always on the verge of destroying itself, as the various components of its unstable body increasingly refuse to be contained.

Realizing that the "center cannot hold,"[4] many modernist artists nevertheless seem to want to avoid admitting that there may never have been a center at all. Determined to cling to what they have already realized are "heroic illusions" (Huyssen 218) about the uniqueness of their imaginative visions, many modern writers attempt to preserve their faith in an unassailable experience of subjectivity and, essentially, their faith in their imaginations as vehicles for social change. This gesture is anything but naive; each of these authors understands that once subjectivity is no longer a privileged, transhistorical construct, any notion of individual artistic identity or authority must certainly fall apart. For most of the writers in this study, such a realization is even more threatening and terrifying than the sublime confrontation with the androgyne.

In the previous chapters, we have witnessed these modern authors' investment in the preservation of a powerful Other-self that would compensate for their lived experiences of vulnerability and insignificance. Unlike his hero, Stephen Dedalus, Joyce comes closest of all the artists we have studied in realizing the futility of the attempt to transcend cultural inheritances and influences. As the ghost of Virag reminds us, "from the sublime to the ridiculous is but a step." For H. D., however, such a realization was one she remained reluctant to accept. Prompted by the painful impact of the First World War and her ambivalent sexuality to "fasten our old selves and our new selves together, like the Jason with a separate head and a body, yet who makes a perfect whole" (*Paint* 65), H. D. longs to capture the transcendental unity of the androgyne. Yet despite her agonizing recognition in later texts such as *Narthex* and "Murex" that her construction of an androgyne imagination was smothering her female identity, she continues to repress the reality of culture and the body by ending her writing career with an epic showcasing "myself, Helen out of the body, in another world" (*Compassionate* 17). Faulkner, too, seems to prefer the glory of a "most splendid failure" to the ignominy of abandoning his privileged status as artist. Yet if we recall the poem "Hermaphroditus" in *Mosquitoes*—his own poem presented under the authorship of the character Eva Wiseman—we remember that this author clearly knew that the figure of transcendent androgyny was ever accompanied by the figure of agonized, unsatisfied, solipsistic, incestuous desire. While Woolf seeks the safety of a third-sexed position beyond and outside of culture and the assaults of patriarchy, she cannot escape the reality of her own body. Terrified by the implications of an individual identity porous to the often violent and always threatening encroachments of the dominant patriarchal culture, Woolf attempts to find refuge in the impersonality of the collective female "we" by the end of her career.

Simply to talk about writers such as Joyce, H. D., Faulkner, and Woolf in these terms is, of course, to ignore not only their literary output but their individual realization of the paradoxes latent in their aesthetic models. Although each addresses the problems within their aesthetic with varying degrees of success, all experimented toward the end of their careers with ways of thinking about their art that would leave out the idea or concept of an imagination. Joyce's last novel, *Finnegans Wake*, and, to some degree, *Ulysses* most directly challenge the convention or idea of authorship by replacing a recognizably constructed narrative with constantly shifting modes of discourse that make it extremely difficult to identify or to trace any single subjective impression. Similarly, during her investigations into the occult during the 1940s and 1950s, H. D. experimented with the idea of automatic writing. Although she never formally adopted this mode of inspiration as an aesthetic stance, her interest in the idea of narrative as transcription rather than invention shows her attempting to bypass the painful, unstable arena of the self. After writing *The Wild Palms*, his last work centering on the androgynous artist, Faulkner went on to explore less "artistic" genres such as the mystery novel (in *Sanctuary* and *Requiem for a Nun*) and the historical novel (in his Snopes trilogy). Common to all these works is a marked lessening of Faulkner's trademark florid prose style and an emphasis on the narrative's objective pose. Much in the same way, Woolf, in *The Years*, writes a novel without an imaginative center in character, theme, or narrative. As if making a kind of collage, she pieces and pastes together the thoughts of each figure in the novel to make a whole narrative; even the last scene escapes any kind of central ordering principle or subjectivity, as Peggy's thoughts are continually interrupted by incoherent children and rambling adults.

For postmodern writers as different as Thomas Pynchon, Julian Barnes, Margaret Drabble, and Bobbie Ann Mason in works as diverse as *Crying of Lot 49*, *History of the World in 10 1/2 Chapters*, *The Waterfall*, and *In Country*, the exposure of the imagination as a cultural product of a constantly shifting collective unconscious has become a central theme. Always deflating our romantic narrative expectations, each of these authors (and their contemporaries) remind us of the futility of postulating any inviolable divisions or distinctions between high and mass culture, fiction and reality, meaning and meaninglessness. Creativity for contemporary avant-garde writers and critics, rather than as the product of a private imaginative space, is now considered in terms of various configurations of desire (sexual, economic, political).[5] If the modernists pronounced the end (or "Death," to use the term that Barthes would later supply) of the Author-Subject as a transcendental category, postmodernists have more fully replaced him/her with a being-in-history circumscribed by variables such as race, gender, class, and nationality; although for the latter "it does matter who is speaking or writing" (Huyssen 213), it matters for different, less psychospiritual reasons.

Taking a second look at modernist aesthetics can help us learn to identify the cultural sources of our own ideas about art. Even more important, however, the analysis of creative origins—the places or spaces from which we represent texts as issuing—can tell us a great deal about a historical era as a whole, particularly its cultural values. Like any discourse about origins, discussion of the imagination in its various guises has formed—particularly in the post-Renaissance era—a constantly evolving sacred text in which the work of creation is attributed to different sorts of "makers." From the romantic muse to the modernist androgyne to newer incarnations such as the postmodern cyborg (a trope appearing in the works of contemporary writers such as Donna Haraway and William Gibson), the iconography of creativity mirrors and reflects the perceived loci of power within culture. We are witnessing its transfer from (male/female) mind to the vast networks of increasingly human machines. One can only speculate about what future gospels remain to be written.

Notes

1. Modernism, Androgyny, and the Sublime

1. For these perspectives on the theory of the subject, see Butler (Judith) 5, Achebe 1193, Derrida 66.

2. See, for instance, Foucault's *History of Sexuality*, Laqueur's *Making Sex*, and Haraway's *Simians, Cyborgs, and Women*, as well as her first book, *Primate Visions*.

3. In other texts Plato describes poetic composition as a kind of possession. See *The Republic* (Book X) and *Phaedrus* (48,70).

4. Of course, Plato has other reasons for banishing the poets (most notably, their inferior imitations of what was already a shadowy reality as well as their lamentable representations of the uninspiring emotional outbursts of warrior-heroes). However, the inherent danger of being possessed by the Muse was noted by poets well before he. One recalls Homer's description of the plight of men who fell victim to the seductive voices of the sirens as well as Hesiod's report that the muses claim to "know to tell many lies that sound like truth" (Hesiod 3).

5. While Aristotle spends the majority of *Poetics* detailing the precise aesthetics of his craft, he does allow for the possibility of a more mysterious artistic experience: "the composition of poetry is an affair of either the well-endowed or the manic individual; for of these two types the ones are impressionable while the others are liable to be 'possessed' from time to time" (Aristotle 48).

6. See, in particular, Horace, Ovid, and Virgil in their poetic invocations.

7. The concept of Mother Nature has been commonplace since the beginning of the seventeenth century and has roots in classical mythology in which Earth is figured as a female and maternal entity. Recently, several feminist critics, including Frances Ferguson and Anne K. Mellor, have noted the ways in which Burke,

in the mid-eighteenth century, conflates the aesthetic category of the beautiful with both the female body and the less massive and rugged forms in nature. Most important, Alexander Pope—even as he uses the term "Nature" to refer to a more universal human reality—nevertheless uses the female pronoun when referring to "her just standard" (l. 69). Moreover, later in his "Essay on Criticism," Pope conflates Nature and the female Muse. He starts a verse paragraph describing "how learn'd Greece her useful rules indites" (l. 92)—and here "her" refers to Nature in the previous verse paragraph—and he finishes his meditation substituting for "Nature" the word "Muse," explaining how she leads the ancients "upward to their spring." He continues to gender Nature as female throughout the remainder of the poem, often using the term "Muse" in the same context.

8. For a detailed discussion of Burke's gendering of the sublime and the beautiful, see Frances Ferguson's *Solitude and the Sublime* as well as Anne K. Mellor's *Romanticism and Gender.*

9. Other female romantics—including Ann Radcliffe and Mary Tighe—challenge the male literary tradition with a cooperative and domestic aesthetic. For further discussion, see Mellor's *Romanticism and Feminism* and *Romanticism and Gender*. We must note as well Mary Shelley's criticism of masculine romanticism and its egotistical sublime in her portrait of monstrous creation, *Frankenstein.*

10. Diane Hoeveler, in *Romantic Androgyny*, makes a convincing case for the male romantics' interest in these specific female types and explores in detail the ways in which these poets go about appropriating their feminine energies while erasing their identities.

11. See Hoeveler, Alan Richardson, Ross, Mellor, and Ellison.

12. Ross, Hoeveler, Alan Richardson, and Mellor all agree on this point as well.

13. Even if Keats rejects the Wordsworthian "egotistical sublime," he nevertheless—as we have just seen—insists on his own artistic autonomy.

14. Anthropological work by Swiss historian J. J. Bachofen and British theorist J. F. McLennan, in *Patriarchal Theory* (1885), on the existence of primitive matriarchy spur a huge debate over the role of women in society. For a sampling of the anthropological controversy their theories of primitive matriarchy initiate, see Eliza Burt Gamble's *The Sexes in Science and History* (1916); Jane Harrison's *Prolegomena to the Study of Greek Religion* (1903) and *Themis* (1912); C. Gasquoine Hartley's *The Position of Women in Primitive Society* (1914); Andrew Lang and J. J. Atkinson's *Social Origins and Primal Law* (1903); Bronislaw Malinowski's *The Sexual Life of Savages* (1929); Lewis Morgan's *Ancient Society* (1877); Mathilde Vaerting and Mathias Vaerting's *The Dominant Sex* (1922). For a theoretical discussion of primitive matriarchy, see Lisa Rado.

15. In *Gender on the Divide*, Jessica R. Feldman describes the late-nineteenth-century phenomenon of the dandy as a major challenge to "the rigid separations of the two-sex system" (11), which, I would argue, precedes the even more radical experiments of the moderns.

16. For a sample of the 1970s androgyny debates, see the *Women's Studies: An Interdisciplinary Journal* 2.2 (1974) special issue on the topic. For examples of the treatment of modernism and androgyny from an ahistorical perspective, see Lisa Appignanesi's *Femininity and the Creative Imagination* (1973); Nancy Topping Bazin's *Virginia Woolf and the Androgynous Vision* (1973); Declan Kiberd's *Men and Feminism in Modern Literature* (1985); Carolyn Heilbrun's *Toward a Recognition of Androgyny (1973);* and Elaine Showalter's section on Virginia Woolf in *A Literature of Their Own* (1977). While these scholars do note the degree to which the new constructions of sexuality presented a liberating opportunity for female modernists, even Gilbert and Gubar (in *Sexchanges*, the second volume of *No Man's Land*, 1989) neglect to point out the ambivalence with which these same women approach androgyny. In addition, they refuse to allow androgyny to be a positive imaginative option for literary men, claiming that while men "occasionally had kind words for female precursors and contemporaries," they ultimately were so threatened by women that any association with androgyny became an emasculating horror.

17. For further discussion of social and cultural circumstances leading to the development of modern sexual science, see Weeks (1977 and 1981), Bland and Doan (1998 and 1998), and Porter and Hall (1995).

18. Scottish biologists Patrick Geddes and J. Arthur Thomson, in their book, *The Evolution of Sex* (1889)—a book which Havelock Ellis published as the first volume of his influential and widely available Contemporary Science Series—discuss the affective characteristics of ovum and sperm as evidence of human gender characteristics. Otto Weininger's *Sex and Character* (1906), as we shall see, goes further to postulate the existence of both male and female gendered cells in the human body.

19. Feminist historians Sheila Jeffreys, in "Women and Sexuality" (1995); Margaret Jackson, in *The Real Facts of Life* (1994); and Lillian Faderman, in *Odd Girls and Twilight Lovers* (1991), all argue that the sexologists used the mantle of science to corrupt early constructions of lesbianism and more widely to punish women in response to their efforts toward economic and political emancipation.

20. Ironically, both the political right and left use publicly the science of sexology, as demonstrated by its contrary use as evidence in both the Oscar Wilde and Radclyffe Hall trials (see Eve Sedgwick's *Between Men* [1985] and *Epistemology of the Closet* [1990] for more on the association of these trials with discourses of sexual "inversion"). Overall, however, most scholars—including, among others, Judy Greenway, Lesley A. Hall, Suzanne Raitt, Laura Doan, and Lucy Bland—agree that numerous intellectual "women as well as men were drawing on sexology as part of the process of formulating an identity" (Greenway 39).

21. Among the sex theorists following Richard von Krafft-Ebing's degenerative views of homosexuality are Jean Martin Charcot, Ambroise Tardieu, Paul Moreau, Cesaire Lombroso, Paolo Mantegazza, and Carl von Westphal. See, in particular,

Lombroso's *Criminal Anthropology* (1891); Cesaire Lombroso and Guglielmo Ferrero's *The Female Offender* (1895); Mantegazza's *Anthropologisch Kulturhistorische über die Geschlechtsverhältnisse des Menschen* (1885); and Albert Moll's *Perversions of the Sex Instinct: A Study of Sexual Inversion* (1891). Somewhat more middle-of-the-road stances include those of Auguste Forel, in *The Sexual Question* (1906), and Otto Weininger, in *Sex and Character* (1906).

22. See Weeks (1981), p. 149.

23. For a sampling of J. G. Kiernan's work, see Murray Lewellyn Barr's *The Human Nervous System: An Anatomical Viewpoint* (1983).

24. Weininger's theory of sex plasms is heavily influenced by the Spanish scientist G. DeLatamendi's theory of male and female human germ cells.

25. Beyond the numerous editions of the works of Krafft-Ebing, Ellis, Carpenter, and Weininger that persisted in print in English throughout the early part of the twentieth century, feminist journals such as *The Freewoman* and the privately circulated *Urania* published serious debates about the sexologists' writings and claims (see Greenway and Oram). Author Ford Maddox Ford writes, in *Women and Men* (1923), that Weininger's theories in particular "had an immense international vogue" (Ford 30), and while he is then referring primarily to Weininger's misogyny, Judy Greenway suggests that "the combination of Weininger's universalism with Carpenter's high valuation of intermediacy produced a self-affirming context" (Greenway 36) in which many modern intellectuals begin to understand themselves, as she shows in her analysis of numerous private letters and diaries. Moreover, we know that many modernist intellectuals owned copies of one or more of these works in their personal libraries; Vita Sackville-West, close friend of Virginia Woolf, for example, owned a copy of Ellis's *Sexual Inversion*, Carpenter's *The Intermediate Sex*, and Weininger's *Sex and Character* (see Raitt 152). Additional evidence consists in the fact that the sexologists' writings appear implicitly or by name in popular works of literature. For instance, as Merl Storr proposes, the book that Radclyffe Hall's lesbian protagonist of *The Well of Loneliness* (1928) is reading early in the novel is considered by scholars "almost certainly" (Storr 11) to be a copy of Krafft-Ebing's *Psychopathia Sexualis;* moreover, the opening of the novel features a "Commentary" written by none other than Havelock Ellis, who endorses the "notable psychological and sociological significance" of the book's presentation of "one particular aspect of sexual life." In his second novel, *Mosquitoes* (1927), author William Faulkner goes even further than Hall in making direct reference to "Dr. Ellis and your Germans" (251), and we shall see more evidence of literary borrowings by Joyce, H. D., Woolf, and others in the remainder of this study.

26. See, again, Sedgwick's discussion of the effects of these high-profile trials in *Between Men* and *Epistemology of the Closet.*

27. D. H. Lawrence's vehemence is particularly ironic given his own experiments with androgynous characterizations in *The Rainbow.*

28. Suzanne Guerlac, in her study on the French modern sublime, asserts the opposite; in her reading, the modern sublime "challenges both representation and subjectivity" and is characterized by its "impersonality" rather than by its search for selfhood. I would argue that while the presentation of modernist subjectivity is in fact quite different from, say, romantic models, it is nevertheless completely invested in the idea of unique and unassailable identity; we can see evidence of this most clearly in the stream-of-consciousness novels by Faulkner, Woolf, Joyce, H. D., Marcel Proust, Dorothy Richardson, etc.

29. In *H.D. and the Victorian Fin de Siècle*, Cassandra Laity writes extensively on the attraction of several male modernist poets not included in my study (Yeats, Eliot, Pound) to figurations of androgyny. As she explains, "the hypermasculine slogans of male modernist anti-Romanticism often bore no relation to male modernist poetic practice, which was frequently steeped in the 'female' and androgynous poetics they outwardly deplored" (6). She also traces a similar, if less conflicted, attraction to the figure of the androgyne in the works of Oscar Wilde, A. C. Swinburne, and Walter Pater.

2. "From the Sublime to the Ridiculous Is But a Step"

1. Margot Norris, in her book *Joyce's Web*, argues for a culturally grounded feminist reading of Joyce's works.

2. See, in particular, Brivic, Byrnes, Ellmann, Reizbaum, Sultan, and Walkley.

3. Critics who have noted Joyce's interest in androgyny include Beja, Boone, Boyle, Brown, Burgan, Byrnes, French, Froula, Gose, Henke, Heilbrun, Jeri Johnson, Shechner, Sultan, and Unkeless.

4. Joyce makes it clear that Stephen's "muse-ing" leads not only to sexual sublimation (and the painful realization of it) but also to social alienation. Substituting "phantasmal comrades" for real ones, Stephen has never experienced the "pleasure of companionship with others" (84, 96). As Joyce's narrator comments, "By his monstrous way of life he seemed to have put himself beyond the limits of reality. Nothing moved or spoke to him from the real world unless he heard it in an echo of the infuriated cries within him" (92). Throughout *A Portrait of the Artist as a Young Man*, Joyce makes constant references to Percy Bysshe Shelley, especially the fragment, "Art thou pale for weariness / Of climbing heaven and gazing on the earth, / Wandering companionless" (96, 103, 164). Suggestive of "Alastor," the verses recall the narcissism and alienation of the romantic artist. Although professing "joy of his loneliness," Stephen can only temporarily repress the reality of "his own futile isolation" and the "loneliness which he feared" (68, 98, 247). Throughout the text, other characters disparage him for his behavior: "Dedalus, you're an antisocial being, wrapped up in yourself," and "You're a terrible man, Stevie, said Davin. . . . Always alone" (177, 201). Terrified of sex, of connection, when Stephen is able to admit some affection for Emma, he seems to lose all his

moorings, sense of direction, artistic and otherwise: "Then, in that case, all the rest, all that I thought I thought and all that I felt I felt, all the rest before now, in fact . . . O, give it up, old chap! Sleep it off!" (252). See also Beja on Joyce and the "artist manque."

5. Henke (*James Joyce* 56) argues that Stephen's incestuous longings are part of his narcissism; Lillienfield sees "incest in *A Portrait* appears as a gap, an absence, an unmentionable arena of longing" and traces Stephen's desires to his wish for his mother's "purity, her religious conviction, her piety" (170).

6. Those in support of the poem as "art" include Gose and Scholes. Those against it include Benstock, Bowers, Day, Henke, Kenner, and Rossman.

7. On swallows as symbols of death, see Don Gifford's *Joyce Annotated*, 268.

8. Terry Castle, in her interesting article on the use of the male birth metaphor, asserts that different literary periods have responded to it differently. In the eighteenth century, for instance, artists who used the trope were denigrated for needing to use/depend upon physical (and debased) methods of artistic production, while the nineteenth-century romantics embraced the trope, as it reflected their idea that the male poet's mind is fertilized by a female nature, that poetic production is thus natural and spontaneous. Castle notes that modern writers use the birth metaphor all the time (207); she does not deal with their particular reasons for being interested in it, however.

9. Christine Froula, in *Modernism's Body*, also argues forcefully the ways in which Stephen mourns "his early self merged with the mother, a self 'buried' . . . upon his initiation into masculine culture" (46). In Froula's reading, Stephen is able to recapture his feminine side—lost to the ruthless Law of the Father—by figuring himself as an artist whose creativity is "both modeled on and exalted over female procreativity" (60). My reading of Stephen's attraction to his mother differs from Froula's in subtle but important ways. I argue that Stephen seeks to embody an androgyne imagination as a response to a specifically *artistic* crisis of authority and that his "solution" of identification with the Daedalian artist-figure who creates out of the womb of his imagination is uncomfortable and ultimately unsatisfying to him. I agree with Froula that Joyce laments in *A Portrait* a culture that forces its men to renounce any vestige of the feminine within their personas; however, in Stephen's case, I would claim that Joyce is also attempting to work through an urgent dilemma regarding artistic authority that he shares with his protagonist. The fact that the culturally available model—the androgyne—is also culturally problematic makes this aesthetic crisis all the more troublesome for this modernist author.

10. See, in particular, the *James Joyce Quarterly* special issue on Joyce and homosexuality (31, no. 3 [1994]), and especially articles by Lamos, Mahaffey, Valente, and Weir.

11. Boone maintains that Bloom's acceptance of androgyny is threatened by

his "internalization of [Dublin's] values" (68), but he focuses neither on Joyce's connection between androgyny and creativity nor his complex critique of the sublime.

12. While some scholars note the influence of Sacher-Masoch's text on "Circe" (Ellmann 369; Restuccia; Shechner; Siegel), they concentrate on Joyce's use of specific masochistic rituals (being whipped; trod underfoot by a large, powerful woman) and fetishes (feet, large breasts, furs) for details in Bloom's fantasies. These critics also assert that Joyce engages the vocabulary of the masochist to represent Bloom's fear of feminization (castration anxiety) and troubled attitude toward his latent homoerotic impulses.

13. Both Gilles Deleuze (1967) and Bernard Michel (1989) argue for Sacher-Masoch's progressive outlook on gender relations, his interest in androgyny, and his attraction to Swiss historian J. J. Bachofen's theories of primitive matriarchy.

14. Here I agree with Boone, Brown, and others who contest Gilbert and Gubar's position.

15. Sandra Gilbert also supports this position—see her 1980 article in *Critical Inquiry*.

16. In writing *Ulysses*, and especially "Penelope," Joyce takes on the thesis of Samuel Butler's *The Authoress of the Odyssey*, which is that the poet of the *Odyssey* could not possibly have been male because of the narrative's feminine sympathies.

3. "The Perfection of the Fiery Moment"

1. More recently, as Susan Edmunds has described, feminist critics have emphasized in H. D.'s oeuvre "the symptomatic or self-diagnostic status of its crises, slippages, and failures" (Edmunds 3). However, while they acknowledge the dilemmas, both personal and historical, that attend her writing, virtually all accept as "commonplace" (see Laity, *H.D.* 204 n. 5) that by the latter end of her career, H. D. had found a way to transcend her early anxieties about gender and authorship by developing "a theory of poetic inspiration that recognized and critiqued the centrality of the mother-child dyad in the inner life of all artists" (Hollenberg 5; see also Kloepfer); even as she reads H. D.'s career somewhat more ambivalently, Cassandra Laity also insists that this modernist author ultimately succeeds in invoking the mother-muse through the agency of the femme fatale.

2. Among these male artists and analysts were Ezra Pound, Richard Aldington, John Cournos, D. H. Lawrence, Kenneth McPherson, Walter Schmidberg, and Sigmund Freud.

3. Sandra Gilbert and Susan Gubar have recently argued that modernist women were actually more empowered than their male counterparts. In the second volume of *No Man's Land*, they postulate that the First World War was a lib-

erating event for women writers of that generation: "not only their society but also their art had been subtly strengthened, or at least strangely inspired, by the deaths and defeats of male contemporaries" (307). Claiming that "the war was [H. D.'s] . . . muse," Gilbert and Gubar insist that the fighting brought her and other female modernist writers "a dream of global regeneration, a vision of patriarchy defied and denied" (308, 304). Yet rather than being inspired, H. D.'s poetic voice is constantly in danger of being paralyzed, repressed, and regimented by her war experience. The heroine of *Paint It To-Day* (1921), for example, "wanted the songs that cut like a swallow wing the high, untainted ether, not the tragic legions of set lines that fell like black armies with terrific force and mechanical set action, paralyzing (11). Instead of empowering her, the war underscores her vulnerability and insignificance as a woman and as a writer; not uncoincidentally, the heroine of this novel is alternately called "Midget" and "a nebulous personality . . . [who] shall have no name" (25). At one point, Midget identifies with a statue of a hermaphrodite that she sees in a Rome museum: "This was a gentle breathing image, modeled in a strange, soft, honey-colored stone. The small head lay on the perfect child-like arm. It was a child, here in Rome, no monster. . . . This was a spray of honey-flower caught in the shadow of a dark wall" (65). That the dark wall in which the hermaphroditic figure—and by extension, Midget—are caught is later identified as symbolic of the war (66) suggests the effect of the conflict was not to empower the androgyne but to overshadow, imprison, and blot it out.

4. Nevertheless, as we saw in chapter 1, Weininger does insist that the female component of consciousness is comparatively weak and degraded.

5. See, in particular, Friedman, Hollenberg, and Laity, who read the jellyfish metaphor as "the uterine center from which female eros and creativity proceed" (Laity, *H.D.* 81). Hollenberg speaks in the vein of all these critics when she argues that modernist women writers "by deliberately confounding the literal (childbirth) with the figurative (creativity) . . . blurred the distinction between life and art, suggesting the philosophical basis for a new pattern of social organization" (11); while H. D. certainly does elevate the womb to a level of consciousness, she stops short of reversing the masculine brain–feminine body hierarchy, as I shall argue momentarily.

6. Susan Stanford Friedman, in her groundbreaking work on H. D.—particularly *Psyche Reborn* and *Penelope's Web*—was first to argue extensively that H. D. linked her creativity to her androgyny. However, Friedman (and DuPlessis as well) ultimately maintain that this androgynous model was only an early stage of this author's artistic development, that it coincided with and was ultimately replaced by a gynocentric model of creativity. While I find much of their work enormously useful in approaching H. D.'s vast oeuvre, I believe that they underestimate and elide the degree to which H. D. remained prisoner to her authorial

anxieties, and, more specifically, to her desire for the validation and acceptance by her male cohorts and colleagues. More recently, Cassandra Laity and Eileen Gregory have linked H. D.'s attraction to the artist-androgyne to her interest in decadent writers—especially Swinburne, Wilde, and Pater—as well as the Pre-Raphaelites, whose interest in the figure of the androgyne and hermaphrodite body they trace to late-Victorian Hellenism and occultism. Laity, in particular, has connected H. D.'s appropriation of what she calls the decadent figure of the "white aesthete androgyne" (Laity xvi) to the sexual aftermath of both the 1890s Wilde trials and, more sketchily, to sexology's classification of the homosexual; specifically, Laity contrasts the struggle of early-twentieth-century male British and American authors to evade what they experienced as a feminizing association between gender and the artist with H. D.'s desire to actively employ the "mask" of the androgyne to liberate herself from the inhibiting "object position in the discourse of male desire" (Laity 37). However, as I have argued throughout this study and as Laity admits in her book, images of "androgynous men . . . ran wild throughout male modernist prose and poetry" (Laity 26); moreover, I add to Laity's argument about H. D.'s employment of the trope the strong evidence of sexology's further influence in attracting H. D. to the androgyne as well as of H. D.'s unwillingness, even at the end of her career, to abandon this metaphor for her creativity.

7. See also Arensberg, especially Diehl's article.

8. Although Laity does not discuss the influence of the turn-of-the-century debates about a third sex, and thus construes H. D.'s employment of the androgyne metaphor as a more essentially male mask, her description of the *cost* of H. D.'s incorporation of an androgynous artistic self-image seems undeniable to me; what H. D. sacrifices, in Laity's words, is "the empowering difference of her female body" (Laity, *H.D.* xvi).

9. See, in particular, Friedman, *Penelope's Web*; DuPlessis, *Writing Beyond* and *H.D.*; Laity, *H.D.*

10. Laity also discusses H. D.'s interest in and textual references to two other poems by Swinburne, "Hermaphroditus" and "Fragoletta," both of which present contrasting images of the androgyne (*H.D.)*.

11. Borrowing from the work of Richard Jenkyns, who, in *The Victorians and Ancient Greece*, asserts that the color white, reflective of nude Greek statues, was a code for male homoerotic desire, Laity, in particular, argues that the imagery of snow, frost, and stars in *HERmione* evokes her attraction to the figure of the androgyne, or the "white, marble boy/girl" (Laity, *H.D.* 39) that Fayne at times seems to embody. Eileen Gregory also associates these images in H. D.'s writing with the "Dorian model of male homoeroticism" (99) and concomitant androgyny that Pater and other decadent writers celebrated.

12. Laity maintains that the images of the femme fatale pervading H. D.'s fic-

tion and poetry serve to "force the maternal feminine body/text into representation" (*H.D.* xvi). While I agree that H. D. seems unable to let herself forget the female sexual self she has repressed in order to sustain her androgyne aesthetic, I do not, as Laity and others such as Friedman and DuPlessis do, believe that she ultimately transcends this struggle to embrace a more expressly feminine aesthetic.

13. The ambivalence about her sexuality revealed in *HERmione* is expressed equally vividly in *Hedylus*, H. D.'s other significant *Künstlerroman*. In this novel, H. D. actually splits herself into two characters: mother (Hedyle) and poet-son (Hedylus). Susan Stanford Friedman suggests that she does so in order to authorize herself as a writer. Ultimately, however, this strategy does not help this "daughter in drag" (Friedman, *Penelope's Web* 256) rid himself/herself of the ambivalences about the mother/muse that plague him/her. Hedylus, who has a huge scar on his forehead from a childhood injury, has "always been striving self with self, the two distinct halves, reft" (100). His head wound, "the direct manifestation of his spiritual cleavage" (100), reflects H. D.'s own psyche, torn between maternal and paternal inheritances, and it directly affects his success as an artist; even his mother exclaims at the beginning that had he not sustained the symbolic splitting head injury he could have been "another Sophocles" (19). The relationship between poet and muse is thus a troubled one, intimately infused with sublimated oedipal desires; both terrified by and attracted to the mother-figure, Hedylus is plagued by half-repressed incestuous longings that are intimately bound up with his ability to write. This ambivalent dependence toward the mother who both represents the source of creativity and its repression suffuses the rest of the novel. Hedylus finally abandons his mother for his spiritual father, Demion, and his sexless muse, Irene.

14. In "Narthex" (1928), this suppression of H. D.'s female side is also apparent. Once again we are presented with a split self in the image of two interconnecting love triangles—that of Ray Bart–Gareth (Bryher)–Daniel (McPherson) and Raymonde–Katherine (Frances Gregg)–Mordant (the man Katherine "selects" for Raymonde)—at which Raymonde is at the center. On the one hand this would seem a transcendent and mystical connection: "They were superimposed like two mystic triangles, the two triangles that make a star, a seal of Solomon. Triangle pointing up, triangle pointing down . . . the seal of utter wisdom" (249–50). Yet on the other hand, "keep[ing] up her double role, base and tip of the pyramid at the same moment" (250) becomes about as difficult as trying to be two places at the same time. For one triangle contains Raymonde and one Ray Bart, and increasingly one "self" is shown to be so much more powerful than the other. Raymonde is part of a "smouldered burnt out triangle" (263), while once again Ray Bart is connected to "a sort of platinum white self-luminous white thing . . . [that] you couldn't dissipate" (263)—note here the repetition of

the "white" androgyne code; this hierarchy constantly threatens to overshadow and overcome the repressed female self. How to establish, even momentarily, a balance between the two plagues Raymonde throughout this novel until the doubleness within herself becomes stifling and suffocating rather than liberating or fulfilling. Lamenting that "the intellect grows sterile being bi-sexual . . . or asexual" (233), Raymonde comes close to rejecting herself, her sexuality, and her artistic ambitions.

15. Like "Murex," "Narthex" also concludes somewhat more hopefully. In order to evade the paralyzing influences of sex and consciousness, Raymonde escapes to Saint Mark's "temple" (27) in Venice. The vast cathedral becomes "a fine carved and exquisite tomb for the body of a spirit" (282). It also becomes a kind of womb in which Raymonde hopes "to crawl in and forget everything" (283); as H. D. later wrote in *Compassionate Friendship*, it is "the mother who is sub-consciously and consciously invoked" (86a). Entering this "pre-natal" (283) paradise allows her to reconcile her two sides, at least for a moment. Symbolically returning to her own embryonic state—those "first germs of a child"—she lets go of her sexual and artistic liasons and anxieties and becomes the "slim intellectual wand-bearer, herself narthekophoros" (283). A wand carried by mystical initiates, as well as the stalk by which Prometheus carried fire, the "narthex" is a symbol of transcendence and defiance. Appropriating its "phallic" power, Raymonde at least temporarily unites masculine and feminine aspects of consciousness and in doing so experiences a resurgence of confidence and creative energy. Significantly, while the (re)union with the mother has initiated this psychic apotheosis, H. D. still is unable to envision her empowerment without some connection with the masculine. This is not "penis envy" but rather a wish or desire for the intellectual and artistic authority granted to the male sex.

16. After reading this "acute book," Marianne Moore writes H. D. that "the idea of the ka—so exactly a part of your attitude—make[s] one feel gross and impermissible" (October 15, 1934); her discomfort with this version of the androgyne imagination, like H. D.'s, is mitigated by a sense of guilt at her own engagement with it.

17. Friedman points out that "Freud's value-laden perspective did not legitimate such transcendence of traditional gender identities and sex roles" (1982, 129); nevertheless, she insists that he "gave her permission to be 'different'" (1990, 311). Freud certainly privileged the heterosexual orientation, insisting that H. D. would never be "biologically" happy with Frances Gregg; moreover, while he was fond of Bryher, he found her homosexuality limiting: "She is only a boy" ("Advent" 152, 171).

18. Friedman and DuPlessis show that in doing so, H. D. "transforms Freud's image of powerlessness into one of power" (424). As we shall soon see, however, she cannot sustain her few moments of confidence any longer than she can sus-

tain her sublime moments of overmind. Moreover, while Laity argues that overall, Freud's efforts "enabled H. D. to imagine a marginalized male culture of sympathetic fathers and brothers outside the punitive Law of the Father" (Laity, *H.D.* 150), I argue that H. D.'s writing suggests she had difficulty adapting such a perspective in practice.

19. Friedman, for instance, reasons that in this novel H. D. is finally able to embrace an androgynous identity that is "anchored in, not transcendent of, her womanhood" (Friedman, *Penelope's Web* 161); Laity finds the text filled with imagery of "realization and rebirth" (*H.D.* 81); and Hollenberg proclaims it the "lyrical finale" in which H. D. establishes once and for all a "woman centered theory of the emotional source of creativity with which to counter the restrictive phallocentrism of her male contemporaries" (173).

20. In her extended discussion of *Trilogy* and *Helen in Egypt*, Cassandra Laity agrees with the majority of H. D. scholars (including, among others, Friedman, Kloepfer, DuPlessis, Hollenberg, and Susan Edmunds) that both poems depict H. D.'s "movement away from the male mask and attendant myth of androgyny toward a more immediate female-female connection with the mother muse" (Laity, *H.D.* 118).

21. Laity (argues that H. D.'s renewed interest in Pound toward the end of her career is evidence that she has succeeded in accomplishing a "refiguration of the father/brother as the feminine, romantic, 'instigator' of a New Age" (Laity, *H.D.* 159). As I will explain, to me Pound's legacy for H. D. remains more ambivalent.

4. "A Perversion That Builds Chartres and Invents Lear Is a Pretty Good Thing"

1. For a discussion of the effects of World War I on constructions of gender, see Jones, Fussell, and Gilbert and Gubar.

2. Karl argues that Donald Mahon represents part of Faulkner's self-image, but only in his pose as wounded warrior.

3. See McHaney ("Elmer Papers" 291) and Karl (151).

4. Surprisingly, *Mosquitoes* has remained virtually untouched by critics. There does exist a special issue of *Faulkner Studies* 1.1 (1991), on the novel; however, this new journal is rather inaccessible as it is published in Japan. Judith Bryant Wittenberg, a well-known Faulkner scholar, contributed an essay to that issue, "Configurations of the Female and Textual Politics in *Mosquitoes*"; unlike my argument, however, Wittenberg's essay focuses on a Lacanian as opposed to an historical reading of Faulkner's experiments with sexual difference. Frann Michel has written an excellent article on the novel, "William Faulkner as a Lesbian Author," to which I refer in this chapter.

5. Initially, androgyny (both psychic and physical) was explained by German sex theorists such as Krafft-Ebing as symptomatic of the effects of genetic degen-

eracy and homosexuality (considered degenerate as well). Krafft-Ebing later abandoned this hypothesis; the association between androgyny and sexual deviancy remained and competed with more attractive theories about the intermediate sex(es). See chapter 1 for more details.

6. Frann Michel argues that Faulkner uses the lesbian character Eva as a means of "splitting the feminized male writer from the feminized male invert by presenting same-sex sexual activity as something that occurs between women" (16). I agree that Eva becomes one of a number of strategies by which Faulkner attempts to allay potential suspicions about his sexuality; however, what Michel leaves out is that the artistic identity that Faulkner privileges and indeed embraces in this text is not feminine but androgynous, and Gordon represents Faulkner's attempt safely to incarnate this model into a male figure.

7. Karen Ramsay Johnson notes the androgyny of Eva Wiseman's name (5).

8. For an introduction to the work of Bachofen, see *Myth, Religion, and Mother-Right.* The work of Bachofen and his contemporary J. F. McLennan (who independently arrived at Bachofen's thesis) was recuperated and debated by late-nineteenth- and early-twentieth-century historians and anthropologists, including (among others) Ernest Crawley (*The Mystic Rose);* C. Gasquoine Hartley (*The Position of Woman in Primitive Society: A Study of the Matriarchy);* Eliza Burt Gamble (*The Sexes in Science and History);* Andrew Lang and J. J. Atkinson (*Social Origins and Primal Law);* Lewis Morgan (*Ancient Society);* E. B. Tylor, (*Primitive Culture);* Mathilde Vaerting and Mathias Vaerting (*The Dominant Sex);* Edward A. Westermarck (*The History of Human Marriage).* In general, women anthropologists tended to read the phenomenon of matriarchy as proof of women's equality (or even superiority) to men and as impetus for the success of the burgeoning woman's movement; male anthropologists, if they accepted Bachofen's thesis, tended to de-emphasize the role of primitive matriarchy in the overall development of humans. Nevertheless, the issue was hotly debated by both sexes.

9. See Benson 150; Backman; Vickery; Brylowski 65, 72–85; Cowan 10; Waggoner 49; Howe 110; Karl 343.

10. There are precedents for reading Quentin's attraction to Caddy as an attraction to a "feminine" part of himself. Snead argues that "Quentin at times wishes to unite with his antithetical counterparts" (26), and Steve Carter reads Caddy in part as a projection of Quentin's "neurotically-conceived anima" (130).

11. Faulkner read Plato in the early 1920s at the home of his friend and mentor Phil Stone.

12. Snead points out, "Caddy is more like a man than he is" (25).

13. The phrase "going to Boston the same night" recalls Caddy's marriage to Herbert, as does the passage immediately following, which consists of his memory of the house after Caddy and Herbert have departed for their honeymoon; both suggest the parallel between the two types of male/female connections—psychic and sexual.

14. Karl argues that a major theme in Faulkner's oeuvre is the unachievability of paradise, or Eden, although he does not relate this to an "ideal" androgyne imagination (334).

15. Doreen Fowler remarks on Joe's terror of androgyny (147); and John N. Duvall indicates that he has been unable to escape it (53).

16. Karl suggests that Faulkner uses the image of the flooding river in the other half of the novel purposefully "to blur all distinctions of boundaries" (605).

17. Eldred points to the "art as arresting motion" example but to none of the others that I cite (149).

18. Karl also notes that Harry fears being subsumed by Charlotte's body through sex: "caught in the Venus's-flytrap, the man becomes impotent" (602).

5. "A Toy Boat on the Serpentine, It's Ecstasy—Ecstasy"

1. As one of the first female writers to be rediscovered by feminist critics—who led her work out of obscurity and into high modernist centrality—Virginia Woolf has remained an icon for the feminist movement in academe. Held up as the symbol of the suppressed feminist of the past, her image inspired many scholars over the past twenty years to continue efforts toward the reconstruction of the canon. Not surprisingly, then, challenges of Woolf's political engagement with the feminist cause of her time have met with substantial criticism from some and frustrated disillusionment from others. This controversy has precipitated a seemingly never-ending debate over the "real" extent of her social conscience, as I will argue in a moment.

2. A victim of sexual abuse by her half-brothers (see DeSalvo), Woolf also complained often of not being accepted professionally by many of her social peers and much of the reading public. In "Sketch of the Past," an autobiographical essay in *Moments of Being*, she writes: "Society in those days was a perfectly competent, perfectly complacent, ruthless machine. A girl had no chance against its fangs. No other desires—say to paint, or to write—could be taken seriously" (157).

3. Lokke argues that through the androgyny of *Orlando*, Woolf "celebrates a mystical union of human sexuality and spirit and radically rewrites the Romantic sublime of Kant and Wordsworth" (236). Karen R. Lawrence adds that by incorporating a kind of Eastern androgyny into an English setting, Woolf critiques imperialist values, and "end[s] on a note of the domestic sublime" (274).

4. Critics who write about Woolf's moments of being—see, for instance, Gilbert and Gubar, and Carolyn Heilbrun—tend to equate them with Joycean epiphanies and read both these experiences as unequivocally positive. Although Louise DeSalvo has noticed the connection between some of Woolf's "moments" and her experiences of sexual abuse, she has not discussed the implication of this connection for the artist's aesthetics.

5. See, in particular, articles by Kushen, Lillienfield, and Rosenman for more singular perspectives on Woolf's relation with her mother/mother-figure. Elizabeth Abel has written at length about Lily's relationship to Mrs. Ramsay and has suggested that by the end of the novel "Mrs. Ramsay has evolved in Lily's eyes into a mirror image" (80). I agree that Lily transcends her inhibiting attachment to this patriarchal mother-figure; however, I would argue that she does so not by recreating her in her own image but rather (as I explain below) by first transforming her paralyzing influence into artistic inspiration and then by adopting a third-sexed subject position that escapes the mother-daughter dyad.

6. Carpenter went so far as to argue that Uranians, or homosexual androgynes, were "destined to form the advance guard of that great movement which will one day transform the common life by substituting the bond of personal affection and compassion for the monetary, legal, and other external ties which now control and confine society" (*Intermediate Sex* 196). Although less utopian in their predictions, other scientists (such as Krafft-Ebing, Ellis, and Freud) agreed with Carpenter that "Uranian temperament (probably from the very fact of its dual nature and the swift and constant interaction between its masculine and feminine elements)" (*Intermediate Sex* 192) predisposed an individual to artistic talent. By the early twentieth century, most sex theorists and biologists believed that "each sex . . . is latently hermaphrodite" (Ellis 79), and thus the association between homosexuals and artistic ability was broadened to include a wider variety of "intermediate" types.

7. On the lesbian resonances in the novel, see the important articles by Sherron E. Knopp and Jean O. Love.

8. For such "positive" readings of *Orlando*, see works by DuPlessis, Gilbert and Gubar, Marcus, Marder, Squier, and Zwerdling.

9. I take the contemporary definition of androgyny (1970s to the present) as referring to the mixture of so-called masculine and feminine character traits or physical traits in the same individual. This account leaves out the biological component (the mixture of male- and female-sexed cells in the body or brain) that was thought to predispose androgynes to artistic ability and to separate them from the "pure" male and female sexes and the male/female sexual dyad.

10. Like Augustus Carmichael, Sasha is portrayed as a figure outside the conventional boundaries between the sexes, a member of the "third sex" whose transportive empowerment Orlando (and, for a time, Woolf) wishes to experience.

11. Critics who view the ending of *Orlando* as particularly triumphant include Kushen, Hawkes, and Roe.

12. Patricia Onek Lawrence argues for a much more positive reading of Rhoda's narrative. Yet Lawrence's idea that Rhoda's character functions as "an aspect of psychological investigation of the unconscious" (147) not only ignores the validity of Rhoda's historical situation as a creative, unmarried woman in a

man's world, it functions to disembody her even before her cultural situation succeeds in doing so. To relegate Rhoda to "an aspect of mind" (148) seems thus to ignore the anguish Woolf is trying to relate.

13. A number of critics have considered Bernard as Woolf's own persona; see, for instance, Rosenman, Shanahan, Marcus.

14. Richard Pearce also notes Bernard's drive for mastery.

6. Another Look at the Androgyne

1. See Laity *H.D.* and Feldman for more lengthy discussions of the influence of decadent writers on modernist ones.

2. See, in particular, Campbell (152); Eliade (110); O'Flaherty (285–89). For a more psychoanalytic reading of androgyny, see Pacteau 78–79.

3. Quotation taken from Trilling's *Beyond Culture.*

4. This phrase is from Yeats's poem "The Second Coming."

5. Recent theories of creativity tend to represent the imagination as some construction of desire. For Edward Said, the creation of Western art can always be traced to the colonizing impulse; Monique Wittig, Karla Jay, Eve Sedgwick, and other critics within lesbian/gay studies argue that art draws its inspiration from various configurations of sexual desire; Marxist theorists such as Terry Eagleton and Fredric Jameson observe the influence of capitalism upon the creation of certain Western artistic movements—Georg Lukacs, in particular, associated modernist art with an especially insular and apolitical perspective.

Works Cited

Abel, Elizabeth. *Virginia Woolf and the Fictions of Psychoanalysis.* Chicago: U of Chicago P, 1989.

Abrams, M. H. *The Mirror and the Lamp: Romantic Theory and the Critical Tradition.* New York: Oxford UP, 1953.

Achebe, Chinua. "Colonialist Criticism." Adams 1191–98.

Adams, Hazard, ed. *Critical Theory since Plato.* New York: Harcourt, Brace, Jovanovich, 1992.

Addison, Joseph. "On the Pleasures of the Imagination." *The Spectator* 418 (30 June 1712). Adams 286–88.

Albright, Daniel. *Personality and Impersonality: Lawrence, Woolf, and Mann.* Chicago: U of Chicago P, 1978.

Anderson, Sherwood. *Winesburg, Ohio.* 1919. New York: Penguin, 1976.

Appignanesi, Lisa. *Femininity and the Creative Imagination: A Study of Henry James, Robert Musil, and Marcel Proust.* New York: Barnes and Noble, 1973.

Arensberg, Mary, ed. *The American Sublime.* Albany: SUNY P, 1986.

———. "White Mythology and the American Sublime: Stevens' Auroral Fantasy." Arensberg 153–72.

Aristotle. *Poetics.* Trans. Gerald F. Else. Ann Arbor: U of Michigan P, 1970.

Bachofen, J. J. *Myth, Religion, and Mother-Right: Selected Writings of J.J. Bachofen.* Trans. Ralph Manheim. Preface George Boas. Introduction Joseph Campbell. Princeton: Princeton UP, 1967.

Backman, Melvin. *Faulkner: The Major Years.* Bloomington: Indiana UP, 1966.

———. "Faulkner's Sick Heroes: Bayard, Sartoris, and Quentin Compson." *Modern Fiction Studies* 2 (autumn 1957).

Balzac, Honoré de. *Seraphita.* 1834. London: Dedalus Ltd., 1989.

Barbauld, Anna. "Washing Day." *Women Romantic Poets 1785–1832: An Anthology.* Ed. Jennifer Breen. London: J. M. Dent Ltd., 1992. 81–83.

Barnes, Djuna. *Nightwood.* New York: New Directions, 1937.

Barr, Murray Lewellyn. *The Human Nervous System: An Anatomical Viewpoint.* Philadelphia: Harper and Row, 1983.

Barthes, Roland. "The Death of the Author." Adams 1130–33.

Bazin, Nancy Topping. *Virginia Woolf and the Androgynous Vision.* New Bruswick, NJ: Rutgers UP, 1973.

Beja, Morris. "The Joyce of Sex: Sexual Relationships in *Ulysses.*" Ehrlich 112–25.

———. "A Poor Trait of the Artless: The Artist Manque in James Joyce." *James Joyce Quarterly* 26.1 (1988): 89–104.

Benson, Jackson. "Quentin Compson: Self-Portrait of a Young Artist's Emotions." *Twentieth-Century Literature* 17.3 (1971): 143–59.

Benstock, Bernard. "The Temptation of St. Stephen: A View of the Villanelle." *James Joyce Quarterly* 4.1 (1976): 31–9.

Bettelheim, Bruno. *Symbolic Wounds: Puberty Rites and the Envious Male.* Glencoe, IL: Free Press, 1954.

Bland, Lucy, and Laura Doan, eds. *Sexology in Culture: Labelling Bodies and Desires.* Chicago: U of Chicago P, 1998.

———. *Sexology Uncensored: The Documents of Sexual Science.* Chicago: U of Chicago P, 1998.

Bleikestan, André. *Most Splendid Failure.* Bloomington: Indiana UP, 1976.

Blotner, Joseph. *Faulkner: A Biography.* New York: Vintage, 1991.

Boone, Joseph Allen. "A New Approach to Bloom as 'Womanly Man': The Mixed Middling's Progress in *Ulysses.*" *James Joyce Quarterly* 20.1 (1982): 67–86.

Bowers, Rick. "Stephen's Practical and Artistic Development." *James Joyce Quarterly* 21.3 (1984): 231–44.

Boyle, Robert. "Joyce's Consubstantiality: Woman as Creator." Ehrlich 126–32.

Brivic, Sheldon. *Joyce between Freud and Jung.* Port Washington, NY: Kennikat, 1980.

———. *Joyce the Creator.* Madison: U of Wisconsin P, 1985.

Brooks, Cleanth. *William Faulkner: Toward Yoknapatawpha and Beyond.* New Haven: Yale UP, 1978.

Broughton, Panthea Reid. "The Economy of Desire: Faulkner's Poetics, From Eroticism to Post-Impressionism." *The Faulkner Journal* 4.1–2 (1988–89): 159–77.

Brown, Richard. *James Joyce and Sexuality.* Cambridge: Cambridge UP, 1985.

Brylowski, Walter. *Faulkner's Olympian Laugh.* Detroit: Wayne State UP, 1968.

Budgen, Frank. *James Joyce and the Making of Ulysses and Other Writings.* Oxford: Oxford UP, 1989.

Burgan, Mary. "Androgynous Fatherhood in Ulysses and Women in Love." *Modern Language Quarterly* 44.2 (1983): 178–97.

Burke, Edmund. *A Philosophical Enquiry into the Origin of Our Ideas of the Sublime and the Beautiful.* Oxford: Oxford UP, 1990.

Butler, Judith. *Gender Trouble: Feminism and the Subversion of Identity.* New York: Routledge, 1990.

Butler, Samuel. *The Authoress of the Odyssey.* London: A. C. Fifield, 1897.

Byrnes, Robert. "Bloom's Sexual Tropes: Stigmata of the Degenerate Jew." *James Joyce Quarterly* 27.2 (1990): 303–23.

Campbell, Joseph. *Hero with a Thousand Faces.* New York: Pantheon, 1949.

Carpenter, Edward. *The Intermediate Sex.* 1907. Cory 139–204.

———. *Intermediate Types among Primitive Folk: A Study in Social Evolution.* 1911. 1919. New York: Arno, 1975.

Carter, Steve. "Caddy and Quentin: Anima and Animus Orbited Nice." *Hartford Studies in Literature* 12.2 (1980): 124–42.

Castle, Terry. "Lab'ring Bards: Birth Topoi and English Poetics, 1660–1820." *Journal of English and Germanic Philology* 78.2 (1979): 193–208.

Chakovsky, Sergei. "Women in Faulkner's Novels: Author's Attitude and Artistic Function." Fowler and Abadie 58–80.

Cixous, Hélène. "The Laugh of the Medusa." *New French Feminisms.* Ed. Elaine Marks and Isabelle de Courtivron. Amherst: U of Massachusetts P, 1980. 254–64.

Coleridge, Samuel T. *Selected Poetry and Prose of Coleridge.* Ed. Donald A. Stauffer. New York: Random House, 1981. 109–428.

Cory, Donald Webster, pseud., ed. *Homosexuality: A Cross-Cultural Approach.* New York: Julian Press, 1956.

Cowan, Michael H., ed. Introduction. *Twentieth-Century Interpretations of* The Sound and the Fury*: A Collection of Critical Essays.* Englewood Cliffs, NJ: Prentice Hall, 1968.

Crawley, Ernest. *The Mystic Rose: A Study of Primitive Marriage.* New York: Macmillan and Co., 1902.

Dante Alighieri. *Paradiso.* Trans. John D. Sinclair. New York: Oxford UP, 1939.

———. *Purgatorio.* Trans. John D. Sinclair. New York: Oxford UP, 1939.

Day, Robert Adams. "The Villanelle Perplex: Reading Joyce." *James Joyce Quarterly* 25.1 (1987): 69–85.

Deleuze, Gilles. *Masochism: An Interpretation of Coldness and Cruelty.* Trans. Jean McNeil. New York: George Braziller, 1971.

———. *Presentation de Sacher-Masoch.* Paris: Les Éditions de Minuit, 1967.

DeLillo, Don. *White Noise.* New York: Viking Penguin, 1985.

Derrida, Jacques. *Of Grammatology.* Trans. Gayatri C. Spivak. Baltimore: Johns Hopkins UP, 1974.

DeSalvo, Louise. *Virginia Woolf: The Impact of Childhood Sexual Abuse on Her Life and Writing.* Boston: Beacon, 1989.

———. "Virginia, Viriginius, Virginity." *Faith of a (Woman) Writer.* Ed. Alice Kessler-Harris and William McBrien. Westport, CT: Greenwood, 1988. 179–89.

Diehl, Joanne Feit. "In the Twilight of the Gods: Women Poets and the American Sublime." Arensberg 173–214.

———. *Women Poets and the American Sublime.* Bloomington: Indiana UP, 1990.

Doolittle, Hilda (H. D.). "Advent." *Tribute to Freud.* 115–87.

———. *Asphodel.* Durham: Duke UP, 1992.

———. *Bid Me to Live (A Madrigal).* Redding Ridge, CT: Black Swann Books, 1983.

———. *Borderline—A Pool Film with Paul Robeson.* 1930. Rpt. in *Sagetrieb* 7 (fall 1987): 29–50.

———. *Compassionate Friendship.* Ts. H. D. Papers. Beinecke Library, Yale University.

———. *End to Torment: A Memoir of Ezra Pound.* Ed. Norman Holmes Pearson and Michael King. New York: New Directions, 1979.

———. "H.D. by Delia Alton." Rpt. in *Iowa Review* 16 (fall 1986): 174–221.

———. *Hedylus.* 1928. Redding Ridge, CT: Black Swann Books, 1980.

———. *HERmione.* 1936. New York: New Directions, 1981.

———. *Hirslanden Notebooks.* Ms. H. D. Papers. Beinecke Library, Yale University.

———. *Kora and Ka, with Mira-Mare.* New York: New Directions, 1996.

———. Letters to Winnifred Bryher. Beinecke Library, Yale University.

———. "Narthex." *The Second American Caravan.* Ed. Alfred Kreymborg, Lewis Mumford, and Paul Rosenfeld. New York: Macaulay, 1928. 225–84.

———. *Nights.* 1935. New York: New Directions, 1986.

———. *Notes on Thought and Vision.* San Francisco: City Lights Books, 1982.

———. *Paint It To-Day.* Ed. Cassandra Laity. New York: New York UP, 1992.

———. *Palimpsest.* Rev. ed. Carbondale: Southern Illinois UP, 1968.

———. *Selected Poems.* Ed. Louis L. Martz. New York: New Directions, 1988.

———. *Tribute to Freud: Writing on the Wall.* 1956. Boston: David R. Godine, 1974.

———. *Trilogy.* New York: New Directions, 1973.

———. *The Usual Star.* Dijon: Darantiere, 1934.

DuPlessis, Rachel Blau. "Feminist Narrative in Virginia Woolf." *Why the Novel Matters: A Postmodern Perspective.* Ed. Mark Spilka and Caroline McCracken-Flesher. Bloomington: Indiana UP, 1990. 341–48.

———. *H.D.: The Career of That Struggle.* Bloomington: Indiana UP, 1986.

———. *Writing beyond the Ending: Narrative Strategies of Twentieth-Century Women Writers.* Bloomington: Indiana UP, 1985.

Duvall, John N. *Faulkner's Marginal Couple: Invisible, Outlaw, and Unspeakable Communities.* Austin: U of Texas P, 1990.

Edmunds, Susan, ed. *Out of Line: History, Psychoanalysis, and Montage in H.D.'s Long Poems.* Stanford: Stanford UP, 1994.

Ehrlich, Heyward, ed. *Light Rays: James Joyce and Modernism.* New York: New Horizon, 1984.

Eldred, Janet Carey. "Faulkner's Still Life: Art and Abortion in *The Wild Palms.*" *Faulkner Journal* 4.1–2 (1988–89): 139–58.

Eliade, Mircea. *Mephistopheles and the Androgyne: Studies in Religious Myth and Symbol.* Trans. J. M. Cohen. New York: Sheed and Ward, 1965.

Ellis, Havelock. *Studies in the Psychology of Sex.* 3rd ed. 7 vols. Philadelphia: F. A. Davis, 1915.

Ellison, Julie. *Delicate Subjects: Romanticism, Gender, and the Ethics of Understanding.* Ithaca: Cornell UP, 1990.

Ellmann, Richard. *James Joyce.* Oxford: Oxford UP, 1982.

Eysteinsson, Estradur. *The Concept of Modernism.* Ithaca: Cornell UP, 1990.

Faderman, Lillian. *Odd Girls and Twilight Lovers: A History of Lesbian Life in Twentieth-Century America.* New York: Penguin, 1991.

Fassler, Barbara. "Theories of Homosexuality as Sources of Bloomsbury's Androgyny." *Signs* 5.2 (1979): 237–50.

Faulkner, William. *Absalom, Absalom! (The Corrected Text).* 1936. New York: Vintage, 1986.

———. *Elmer.* Ed. Joseph Blotner, Thomas McHaney, Michael Millgate, and Noel Polk. *William Faulkner Manuscripts.* Vol. 1. New York: Garland, 1987.

———. *A Fable.* 1950. New York: Vintage, 1978.

———. *Light in August.* 1932. New York: Vintage, 1972.

———. *Mayday.* Notre Dame: U of Notre Dame P, 1976.

———. *Mosquitoes.* 1927. New York: Liveright, 1997.

———. *Soldier's Pay.* 1926. New York: Liveright, 1997.

———. *The Sound and the Fury (The Corrected Text).* 1929. New York: Vintage International, 1990.

———. *The Wild Palms.* New York: Vintage, 1939.

Feldman, Jessica R. *Gender on the Divide: The Dandy in Modernist Literature.* Ithaca: Cornell UP, 1993.

Ferguson, Frances. *Solitude and the Sublime.* New York: Routledge, 1992.

Ford, Ford Maddox. *Women and Men.* Paris: Contact Editions, 1923.

Forel, Auguste. *The Sexual Question.* 1906. London: William Heinemann (Medical Books), 1908.

Foucault, Michel. *The History of Sexuality.* New York: Vintage, 1990.

Fowler, Doreen. "Joe Christmas and 'Womanshenegro.'" Fowler and Abadie 144–61.

Fowler, Doreen, and Ann J. Abadie, eds. *Faulkner and Women: Faulkner and Yoknapatawpha 1985*. Jackson: UP of Mississippi, 1986.

Freud, Sigmund. *Three Essays on the Theory of Sexuality*. Trans. James Strachey. London: Imago, 1949.

———. "The Psychology of Women." *New Introductory Lectures on Psycho-Analysis*. Trans. W. J. H. Sprott. New York: W. W. Norton, 1933. 153–85.

Friedman, Susan Stanford. "Creativity and the Childbirth Metaphor: Gender Difference in Literary Discourse." *Speaking of Gender*. Ed. Elaine Showalter. New York: Routledge, 1989. 73–100.

———. *Penelope's Web: Gender, Modernity, H.D.'s Fiction*. Cambridge: Cambridge UP, 1990.

———. *Psyche Reborn: The Emergence of H.D.* Bloomington: Indiana UP, 1981.

Friedman, Susan Stanford, and Rachel Blau DuPlessis. "'Woman is Perfect': H.D.'s Debate with Freud." *Feminist Studies* 7.3 (1981): 417–30.

French, Marilyn. *The Book as World: James Joyce's* Ulysses. London: Harvard UP, 1976.

Froula, Christine. "History's Nightmare, Fiction's Dream: Joyce and the Psychohistory of *Ulysses*." *James Joyce Quarterly* 28.4 (1991): 857–69.

———. *Modernism's Body: Sex, Culture, and Joyce*. New York: Columbia UP, 1996.

———. "Out of the Chrysallis: Female Initiation and Female Authority in Virginia Woolf's *The Voyage Out*." *Tulsa Studies* 5.1 (1986): 63–90.

Fussell, Paul. *The Great War and Modern Memory*. London: Oxford UP, 1975.

Gamble, Eliza Burt. *The Sexes in Science and History: An Enquiry into the Dogma of Woman's Inferiority to Man*. New York: G. P. Putnam's Sons, 1916.

Geddes, Patrick, and J. Arthur Thomson. *The Evolution of Sex*. London: Walter Scott, 1889.

Gelpi, Albert. Introduction. *Notes on Thought and Vision*. By H. D. San Francisco: City Lights Books, 1982.

Gifford, Don. *Joyce Annotated*. 2nd ed. Berkeley: U of California P, 1982.

Gilbert, Sandra. "Costumes of the Mind: Transvestism as Metaphor in Modern Literature." *Critical Inquiry* 7 (winter 1980): 391–417.

Gilbert, Sandra, and Susan Gubar. *The Madwoman in the Attic*. New Haven: Yale UP, 1979.

———. *No Man's Land: Sexchanges*. Vol. 2. New Haven: Yale UP, 1989.

———. *No Man's Land: The War of the Words*. Vol. 1. New Haven: Yale UP, 1988.

Gose, Elliot B., Jr. "Destruction and Creation in *A Portrait of the Artist as a Young Man*." *James Joyce Quarterly* 22.3 (1985): 259–70.

———. "Joyce's Goddess of Creation." *James Joyce: The Centennial Symposium*. Urbana: U of Illinois P, 1986. 158–69.

———. *The Transformation Process in Joyce's Ulysses*. Toronto: U of Toronto P, 1980.

Greenway, Judy. "It's What You Do With It That Counts: Interpretations of Otto Weininger." Bland and Doan 27–43.

Gregory, Eileen. *H.D. and Hellenism: Classic Lines.* Cambridge: Cambridge UP, 1997.

Guerlac, Suzanne. *The Impersonal Sublime: Hugo, Baudelaire, Lautreamont.* Stanford: Stanford UP, 1990.

Gwin, Minrose. *The Feminine and Faulkner: Reading (Beyond) Sexual Difference.* Knoxville: U of Tennessee P, 1990.

Gwynne, Frederick L., and Joseph Blotner, eds. *Faulkner in the University: Class Conferences at the University of Virginia.* Charlottesville: UP of Virginia, 1958.

Hall, Lesley A. "Feminist Reconfigurations of Heterosexuality in the 1920s." Bland and Doan 135–49.

Hall, Radclyffe. *The Well of Loneliness.* New York: Doubleday, 1928.

Haraway, Donna J. *Primate Visions: Gender, Race and Nature in the World of Modern Science.* Routledge, 1990.

———. *Simians, Cyborgs, and Women.* New York: Routledge, 1991.

Harkness, Marguerite. *The Aesthetics of Dedalus and Bloom.* London: Associated University Presses, 1984.

Harrington, Gary. *Faulkner's Fables of Creativity: The Non- Yoknapatawpha Novels.* Athens: U of Georgia P, 1990.

Harrison, Jane. *Prolegomena to the Study of Greek Religion.* Cambridge: Cambridge UP, 1903.

———. *Themis.* Cambridge: Cambridge UP, 1912.

Hart, Henry. "Robert Lowell and the Psychopathology of the Sublime." *Contemporary Literature* 32.4 (1991): 496–519.

Hartley, C. Gasquoine. *The Position of Women in Primitive Society: A Study of the Matriarchy.* London: Eveleigh Nash, 1914.

Hawkes, Ellen. "Woolf's Magical Garden of Women." Marcus 31–60.

Heilbrun, Carolyn. *Toward a Recognition of Androgyny.* New York: Knopf, 1973.

Henke, Suzette A. "Gerty MacDowell: Joyce's Sentimental Heroine." Henke and Unkeless 132–49.

———. *James Joyce and the Politics of Desire.* New York: Routledge, 1990.

———. "Stephen Dedalus and Women: A Portrait of the Artist as a Young Misogynist." Henke and Unkeless 82–107.

Henke, Suzette A., and Elaine Rapp Unkeless, eds. *Women in Joyce.* Urbana: U of Illinois P, 1982.

Hertz, Neil. *The End of the Line.* New York: Columbia UP, 1985.

Hesiod. *Theogony/Works and Days.* Trans. M. L. West. Oxford: Oxford UP, 1988.

Hoeveler, Diane. *Romantic Androgyny.* University Park: Pennsylvania State UP, 1990.

Holland, Norman. "H.D. and the 'Blameless Physician.'" *Contemporary Literature* 10.4 (1969): 478–93.

Hollenberg, Donna Krolik. *H.D.: The Poetics of Childbirth and Creativity.* Boston: Northeastern UP, 1991.

Homer. *The Odyssey.* Trans. Richard Lattimore. New York: Harper and Row, 1965.

Howe, Irving. *William Faulkner: A Critical Study.* New York: Random House, 1962.

Huyssen, Andreas. *After the Great Divide: Modernism, Mass Culture, Postmodernism.* Bloomington: Indiana UP, 1986.

Ian, Marcia. *Remembering the Phallic Mother: Psychoanalysis, Modernism, and the Fetish.* Ithaca: Cornell UP, 1993.

Irigaray, Luce. *Speculum of the Other Woman.* Trans. Gillian G. Gill. New York: Columbia UP, 1985.

Irwin, John. *Doubling and Incest/Repetition and Revenge.* Baltimore: Johns Hopkins UP, 1975.

Jackson, Margaret. *The Real Facts of Life: Feminism and the Politics of Sexuality, c. 1850–1940.* London: Taylor and Francis, 1994.

Jeffreys, Sheila. *The Spinster and Her Enemies: Feminism and Sexuality, 1880–1930.* London: Pandora, 1985.

———. "Women and Sexuality." *Women's History: Britain, 1850–1945.* Ed. June Purvis. London: UCL, 1995. 193–216.

Jenkyns, Richard. *The Victorians and Ancient Greece.* Cambridge: Harvard UP, 1980.

Johnson, Jeri. "'Beyond the Veil': Ulysses, Feminism, and the Figure of Woman." *Joyce, Modernity, and its Mediation.* Ed. Christine van Boheemen. Amsterdam: Rodopi, 1989. 201–28.

Johnson, Karen Ramsay. "Gender, Sexuality, and the Artist in Faulkner's Novels." *American Literature* 61.1 (1989): 1–15.

Johnson, Samuel. *Rambler No. 4 [On Fiction], Saturday, March 31, 1750. The Norton Anthology of English Literature.* Ed. M. H. Abrams et al. 4th ed. Vol. 1. New York: W. W. Norton, 1979. 2332–36.

Jones, Anne Goodwyn. "Gender and the Great War, the Case of Faulkner and Porter." *Women's Studies* 13.1–2 (1986): 135–48.

Joyce, James. *Critical Writings of James Joyce.* Ed. Ellsworth Mason and Richard Ellmann. New York: Viking, 1959.

———. *Letters of James Joyce.* Ed. Richard Ellmann. Vol. 2. London: Faber and Faber, 1966.

———. *A Portrait of the Artist as a Young Man.* Corrected by Chester G. Anderson and reviewed by Richard Ellmann. New York: Viking Penguin, 1964.

———. *Stephen Hero.* New York: New Directions, 1944.

———. *Ulysses.* 1922. Ed. Hans Walter Gabler. New York: Vintage, 1986.

Kahane, Claire. *Passions of the Voice: Hysteria, Narrative, and The Figure of the Speaking Woman, 1850–1915.* Baltimore: Johns Hopkins UP, 1995.

Karl, Frederick. *William Faulkner: American Writer.* New York: Ballantine Books, 1989.

Kenner, Hugh. *Dublin's Joyce.* Bloomington: Indiana UP, 1956.

———. "Homer's Sticks and Stones." *James Joyce Quarterly* 6.4 (1969): 285–98.

Kiberd, Declan. *Men and Feminism in Modern Literature.* New York: St. Martin's, 1985.

Kloepfer, Deborah Kelly. *The Unspeakable Mother: Forbidden Discourses in Jean Rhys and H.D.* Ithaca: Cornell UP, 1989.

Knopp, Sherron E. "'If I Saw You Would You Kiss Me?': Saphhism and the Subversiveness of Virginia Woolf's Orlando." *PMLA* 103.1 (1988): 24–34.

Krafft-Ebing, Richard von. *Psychopathia Sexualis.* 1892. Trans. Charles Gilbert Chaddock. 7th ed. Philadelphia: F. A. Davis, 1908.

Kristeva, Julia. *Powers of Horror: An Essay on Abjection.* Trans. Leon S. Roudiez. New York: Columbia UP, 1982.

Kushen, Betty. "Virginia Woolf: Metaphor of the Inverted Birth." *American Imago* 38.3 (1981): 279–304.

Laity, Cassandra. *H.D. and the Victorian Fin de Siècle: Gender, Modernism, Decadence.* Cambridge: Cambridge UP, 1996.

———. *H.D.:* Helen in Egypt. New York: New Directions, 1961.

———. Introduction. *Paint It To-Day.* New York: New York UP, 1992.

Lamos, Colleen. "Signatures of the Invisible: Homosexual Secrecy and Knowledge in *Ulysses.*" *James Joyce Quarterly* 31.3 (1994): 337–55.

Lang, Andrew, and J. J. Atkinson. *Social Origins and Primal Law.* London: Longmans, Green, and Co., 1903.

Laqueur, Thomas. *Making Sex: Body and Gender from the Greeks to Freud.* Cambridge: Harvard UP, 1990.

Lawrence, D. H. *Fantasia of the Unconscious and Psychoanalysis of the Unconscious.* 1921–1922. London: Penguin, 1960.

———. *The Rainbow.* 1915. London: Penguin, 1949.

———. *Women in Love.* 1920. London: Penguin, 1982.

Lawrence, Karen R. "Orlando's Voyage Out." *Modern Fiction Studies* 38.1 (1992): 253–77.

Lawrence, Patricia Onek. *The Reading of Silence: Virginia Woolf in the English Tradition.* Stanford: Stanford UP, 1991.

Lee, Hermione. *Virginia Woolf.* New York: Alfred A. Knopf, 1998.

Lillienfield, Jane. "'The Deceptiveness of Beauty': Mother Love and Mother Hate in *To the Lighthouse.*" *Twentieth-Century Literature* 23.3 (1977): 345–76.

———. "Flesh and Blood and Love and Words: Lily Briscoe, Stephen Dedalus, and the Aesthetics of Emotional Quest." Scott, *New Alliances in Joyce Studies* 165–75.

Lokke, Kari Elise. "Orlando and Incandescence: Virginia Woolf's Comic Sublime." *Modern Fiction Studies* 38.1 (1992): 235–52.

Lombroso, Cesaire. *L'Anthropologie Criminelle.* Paris: F. Alcan, 1891.

Lombroso, Cesaire, and Guglielmo Ferrero. *The Female Offender.* 1893. London: T. Fisher Unwin, 1895.

Longinus. "On the Sublime." Adams 76–98.

Love, Jean O. "*Orlando* and Its Genesis: Venturing and Experimenting in Art, Love, and Sex." *Virginia Woolf: Revaluation and Continuity.* Ed. Ralph Freedman. Berkeley: U of California P, 1980. 189–218.

Mahaffey, Vicki. "Pere-version and Im-mere-sion: Idealized Corruption in *A Portrait* and *The Picture of Dorian Gray.*" *James Joyce Quarterly* 31.3 (1994): 189–206.

Malinowski, Bronislaw. *The Sexual Life of Savages.* London: Routledge, 1929.

Mantegazza, Paolo. *Anthropologisch Kulturhistorische über die Geschlechtsverhältnisse des Menschen.* Jena: H Costenoble, 1885.

Marcus, Jane, ed. *New Feminist Essays on Virginia Woolf.* Lincoln: U of Nebraska P, 1981.

———. "Thinking Back Through Our Mothers." Marcus 1–30.

Marder, Herbert. *Feminism and Art: A Study of Virginia Woolf.* Chicago: U of Chicago P, 1968.

Mason, Bobbie Ann. *In Country.* New York: Harper and Row, 1985.

McHaney, Thomas L. "The Elmer Papers: Faulkner's Comic Portrait of the Artist." *Mississippi Quarterly* 26.3 (1973): 181–311.

———. *Faulkner's* The Wild Palms. Jackson: UP of Mississippi, 1975.

McLennan, John Ferguson. *The Patriarchal Theory.* Ed. Donald McLennan. London: MacMillan, 1885.

Mellor, Anne K., ed. *Romanticism and Feminism.* Bloomington: Indiana UP, 1988.

———. *Romanticism and Gender.* New York: Routledge, 1993.

Meriwether, James B. *The Literary Career of William Faulkner.* Princeton: Princeton University Library, 1961.

Meriwether, James B., and Michael Millgate, eds. *Lion in the Garden: Interviews with William Faulkner, 1926–1962.* New York: Random House, 1968.

Michel, Bernard. *Sacher-Masoch, 1836–1895.* Paris: Éditions Robert Laffont, 1989.

Michel, Frann. "William Faulkner as a Lesbian Author." *Faulkner Journal* 4.1–2 (1988–89): 5–20.

Miller, J. Hillis. "Mr. Carmichael and Lily Brisco: The Rhythm of Creativity in *To the Lighthouse.*" *Modernism Reconsidered.* Ed. Robert Kiely and John Hildebidle. Cambridge: Harvard UP, 1983. 167–89.

Millgate, Michael. *The Achievement of William Faulkner.* New York: Random House, 1963.

Milton, John. *Paradise Lost.* Ed. Alastair Fowler. Essex: Longman Group Ltd., 1968.

Moi, Toril. *Sexual/Textual Politics.* London: Methuen, 1985.

Moll, Albert. *Perversions of the Sex Instinct: A Study of Sexual Inversion.* 1891. Newark: Julian Press, 1931.

Monk, Samuel. *The Sublime: A Study of Critical Theories in Eighteenth-Century England.* Ann Arbor: U of Michigan P, 1960.

Moody, Elizabeth. "The Housewife: or, the Muse Learning to Ride the Great Horse Heroic." *Women Romantic Poets, 1785–1832: An Anthology.* Ed. Jennifer Breen. London: J. M. Dent Ltd., 1992. 106–110.

Morgan, Lewis. *Ancient Society.* Chicago: Charles H. Kerr and Co., 1877.

Morris, Adelaide. "The Concept of Projection: H.D.'s Visionary Powers." *H.D. Modern Critical Views.* Ed. Harold Bloom. New York: Chelsea House, 1989. 101–22.

Neverow, Vara, and Mark Hussey, eds. *Virginia Woolf: Themes and Variations.* New York: Pace UP, 1993.

Nin, Anais. *The Diary of Anais Nin.* Ed. Gunther Stuhlmann. Vol. 2, 1934–39. New York: Harcourt, Brace, Jovanovitch, 1966.

Norris, Margot. *Joyce's Web: The Social Unraveling of Modernism.* Austin: U of Texas P, 1992.

O'Flaherty, Wendy Doniger. *Women, Androgynes, and Other Mythized Beasts.* Chicago: U of Chicago P, 1980.

Oram, Alison. "'Sex Is an Accident': Feminism, Science, and the Radical Sexual Theory of *Urania*, 1915–1940." Bland and Doan 214–30.

Pacteau, Francette. "The Impossible Referent: Representations of the Androgyne." *Formations of Fantasy.* Ed. Victor Burgin, James Donald, and Cora Kaplan. London: Methuen, 1986. 62–84.

Pearce, Richard. "Virginia Woolf's Struggle with Authority." *Image and Ideology in Modern/Postmodern Discourse.* Ed. David B. Downing and Susan Bazargan. Albany: SUNY P, 1991. 69–93.

Plato. "Ion." Adams 12–17.

———. *Phaedrus and Letters 7 and 8.* Trans. Walter Hamilton. London: Penguin, 1973.

———. *The Republic.* Trans. Desmond Lee. London: Penguin, 1955.

Pope, Alexander. "An Essay on Criticism." *Alexander Pope.* Ed. Pat Rogers. Oxford: Oxford UP, 1994. 1–19.

Porter, Roy, and Lesley A. Hall. *The Facts of Life: The Creation of Sexual Knowledge in Britain, 1650–1950.* London: Yale UP, 1995.

Pound, Ezra. *Personae.* New York: New Directions, 1926.

———. *Selected Poems of Ezra Pound.* New York: New Directions, 1926.

Prosser, Jay. "Transsexuals and the Transsexologists: Inversion and the Emergence of Transsexual Subjectivity." Bland and Doan 116–31.

Rado, Lisa. "Primitivism, Modernism, and Matriarchy." *Modernism, Gender, and Culture.* Ed. Lisa Rado. New York: Garland, 1997. 283–300.

Raitt, Suzanne. "Sex, Love, and the Homosexual Body in Early Sexology." Bland and Doan 150–64.

Reizbaum, Marilyn. "The Jewish Connection, Continued." *The Seventh of Joyce.* Ed. Bernard Benstock. Bloomington: Indiana UP, 1982.

Restuccia, Frances C. *Joyce and the Law of the Father.* New Haven: Yale UP, 1989.

———. "Molly in Furs." *Novel* 18.2 (1985): 101–16.

———. "'Untying the Mother Tongue': Female Difference in Virginia Woolf's *A Room of One's Own.*" *Tulsa Studies* 4.2 (1985): 253–64.

Richardson, Alan. "Romanticism and the Colonization of the Feminine." Mellor 13–25.

Richardson, Dorothy. "Women in the Arts." Scott, *Gender of Modernism* 419–23.

Roe, Sue. *Writing and Gender: Virginia Woolf's Writing Practice.* New York: St. Martin's, 1990.

Rorty, Richard. *Philosophy and the Mirror of Nature.* Princeton: Princeton UP, 1979.

Rosenman, Ellen. "The 'Invisible Presence': Virginia Woolf and the Creative Process." *American Imago* 43.2 (1986): 133–50.

Ross, Marlon B. *The Contours of Masculine Desire: Romanticism and the Rise of Women's Poetry.* Oxford: Oxford UP, 1989.

———. "Troping Masculine Power in the Crisis of Poetic Identity." Mellor 26–38.

Rossman, Charles. "Stephen Dedalus's Villanelle." *James Joyce Quarterly* 12.3 (1975): 281–93.

Sacher-Masoch, Leopold von. *Venus in Furs.* New York: Sylvan, 1947.

Said, Edward. *Culture and Imperialism.* New York: Knopf, 1993.

Scholes, Robert. "Stephen Dedalus, Poet or Esthete?" *PMLA* 79 (1964): 484–89.

Scorn, Paul. "Hypsospadia: Linguistic Guidepost to the Themes of the 'Circe' Episode of *Ulysses.*" *Journal of Modern Literature* 4 (1974): 109–14.

Scott, Bonnie Kime, ed. *The Gender of Modernism: A Critical Anthology.* Bloomington: Indiana UP, 1990.

———. *Joyce and Feminism.* Bloomington: Indiana UP, 1984.

———, ed. *New Alliances in Joyce Studies: When It's Aped to Foul a Delfian.* Newark: U of Delaware P, 1988.

Sedgwick, Eve. *Between Men.* New York: Columbia UP, 1985.

———. *Epistemology of the Closet.* Berkeley: U of California P, 1990.

Shanahan, Mary Steussy. "The Artists and the Resolution of *The Waves.*" *Modern Language Quarterly* 36 (1975): 54–74.

Shechner, Mark. *Joyce in Nighttown: A Psychoanalytic Inquiry into* Ulysses. Berkeley: U of California P, 1974.

Showalter, Elaine. *A Literature of Their Own.* Princeton: Princeton UP, 1977.

Siegel, Carol. "'Venus Metempsychosis' and *Venus in Furs:* Masochism and Fertility in *Ulysses.*" *Twentieth-Century Literature.* 33.2 (1987): 179–95.

Slatloff, Walter J. *Quest for Failure: A Study of William Faulkner.* Ithaca: Cornell UP, 1960.

Snead, James A. *Figures of Division: William Faulkner's Major Novels.* New York: Methuen, 1986.

Spilka, Mark. *Hemingway's Quarrel with Androgyny.* Lincoln: U of Nebraska P, 1990.

Squier, Susan. "Tradition and Revision in Woolf's *Orlando:* Defoe and 'The Jessamy Brides.'" *Women's Studies* 12 (1986): 167–78.

Stallybras, Peter, and Allon White. *The Politics and Poetics of Transgression.* Ithaca: Cornell UP, 1986.

Stevens, Wallace. *The Palm at the End of the Mind: Selected Poems and a Play.* New York: Vintage, 1990.

Storr, Merl. "Transformations: Subjects, Categories, and Cures in Krafft-Ebing's Sexology." Bland and Doan 11–26.

Sultan, Stanley. *The Argument of Ulysses.* Columbus: Ohio State UP, 1964.

Symonds, John Addington. "A Problem in Modern Ethics." Cory 3–98.

Trilling, Lionel. *Beyond Culture: Essays on Literature and Learning.* New York: Viking, 1965.

Tylor, E. B. *Primitive Culture: Researches into the Development of Mythology, Philosophy, Religion, Art, and Custom.* New York: Henry Holt and Co., 1889.

Ulrichs, Karl Heinrich. *Memnon: Die Geschlechtsnatur des Mannliebenden Urnings, Eine Naturwissenschafliche Darstellung.* 1868.

Unkeless, Elaine Rapp. "Leopold Bloom as a Womanly Man." *Modernist Studies* 2.1 (1976): 35–44.

Vaerting, Mathilde, and Mathias Vaerting. *The Dominant Sex: A Study in the Sociology of Sex Differentiation.* Trans. Eden Pail and Cedar Pail. 1922. Westport, CT: Hyperion, 1981.

Valente, Joseph. "Thrilled By His Touch: Homosexual Panic and the Will to Artistry in *A Portrait of the Artist as a Young Man.*" *James Joyce Quarterly* 31.3 (1994): 167–88.

Vickery, Olga. *The Novels of William Faulkner.* Baton Rouge: Louisiana State UP, 1964.

Waggoner, Hyatt Howe. *William Faulkner: From Jefferson to the World.* Lexington: UP of Kentucky, 1959.

Walkley, R. Barrie. "The Bloom of Motherhood: Couvade as a Structural Device in *Ulysses.*" *James Joyce Quarterly* 18.1 (1980): 55–68.

Watts, Alan W. *The Two Hands of God.* New York: George Braziller, 1963.

Weeks, Jeffrey. *Coming Out: Homosexual Politics in Britain, from the Nineteenth Century to the Present.* London: Quartet Books, 1977.

———. *Sex, Politics, and Society: The Regulation of Sexuality since 1800.* London: Longman, 1981.

Weil, Kari. *Androgyny and the Denial of Difference.* Charlottesville: UP of Virginia, 1992.

Weininger, Otto. *Sex and Character.* London: William Heinemann, 1906.

Weir, David. "A Womb of His Own: Joyce's Sexual Aesthetics." *James Joyce Quarterly* 31.3 (1994): 207–31.

Weiskel, Thomas. *The Romantic Sublime.* Baltimore: Johns Hopkins UP, 1976.

Westermarck, Edward A. *The History of Human Marriage. In Three Volumes.* 1891. New York: Allenton Book Co., 1922.

———. "Homosexual Love." From *The Origin and Development of Moral Ideas.* Cory 101–36.

Wilson, Rob. *American Sublime: The Genealogy of a Poetic Genre.* Madison: U of Wisconsin P, 1991.

Wittenberg, Judith Bryant. "Configurations of the Female and Textual Politics in *Mosquitoes.*" *Faulkner Studies* 1.1 (1991): 1–19.

———. "Faulkner: A Feminist Consideration." *William Faulkner.* Ed. Harold Bloom. New York: Chelsea House, 1986. 233–45.

Wittgenstein, Ludwig. *Philosophical Investigations.* Trans. G. E. M. Anscombe. 3rd ed. New York: Macmillan, 1953.

Woolf, Virginia. *A Room of One's Own.* London: Harcourt, Brace, Jovanovitch, 1929.

———. *Diary.* Ed. Anne Olivier Bell and Andrew McNeillie. Vols. 3, 4, 5. New York: Harcourt, Brace, Jovanovitch, 1980, 1982, 1984.

———. *Letters.* Ed. Nigel Nicolson and Joanne Trautmann. Vol. 3. New York: Harcourt, Brace, Jovanovitch, 1977.

———. *Moments of Being.* Ed. Jeanne Schulkind. New York: Harcourt, Brace, Jovanovitch, 1976.

———. *Orlando.* New York: Harcourt, Brace, Jovanovitch, 1928.

———. *The Pargiters.* Ed. and Introduction Mitchell A. Leaska. New York: New York Public Library and Readers' Books, 1977.

———. *Three Guineas.* New York: Harcourt, Brace, Jovanovitch, 1938.

———. *To the Lighthouse.* 1927. New York: First Harvest, 1989.

———. *The Voyage Out.* 1915. New York: Penguin, 1991.

———. *The Waves.* New York: Harcourt, Brace, Jovanovitch, 1931.

Yaeger, Patricia. "The Maternal Sublime." *Gender and Theory.* Ed. Linda Kauffman. New York: Basil Blackwell, 1989. 191–212.

Zwerdling, Alex. *Virginia Woolf and the Real World.* Berkeley: U of California P, 1986.

Index